WRITING BLACK BEAUTY

WRITING BLACK BEAUTY

ANNA SEWELL, THE CREATION OF A NOVEL, AND THE STORY OF ANIMAL RIGHTS

CELIA BRAYFIELD

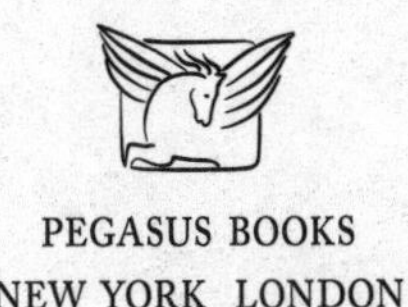

PEGASUS BOOKS
NEW YORK LONDON

This book is offered in thanks for the work
and inspiration of Mary-Joy Langdon

WRITING BLACK BEAUTY

Pegasus Books, Ltd.
148 West 37th Street, 13th Floor
New York, NY 10018

First Pegasus Books cloth edition October 2023

ISBN: 978-1-63936-499-2

10 9 8 7 6 5 4 3 2 1

Printed in the United States of America
Distributed by Simon & Schuster
www.pegasusbooks.com

It was not until thirteen years later that a crusading American activist, George Thorndike Angell, seized upon the book as the weapon that his arsenal of persuasive publishing had been waiting for. He launched a new edition of *Black Beauty* on the world and it finally seized the imagination of millions and became one of the bestselling books of all time.

Author's Note

This book explores the slow acceptance of the idea that cruelty to animals is wrong, an idea which at the time of writing is not held universally even in societies that see themselves as advanced. The story begins over 200 years ago, in England, at a time when actions which are now illegal in many countries happened every day. The attitudes that condoned and even promoted this everyday abuse seem incomprehensible to us now. In telling this story, I, like Anna Sewell, wanted to reach a wide audience, so I have not included extensive details of the cruelty that was once freely practised, particularly by vivisectionists. I judged it necessary to include some distressing material, however, because not to suggest the need for activism would have been historically inaccurate.

Content Warning

If you are sensitive to descriptions of cruelty to animals, I suggest that you do not read the descriptions of bull-baiting and the Stamford Bull Run in Chapter 2, pages 37–9, or the accounts of cruelty in the United States in Chapter 9, pages 157–8.

Some of the quotes within this book use language that would be considered inappropriate today but was commonplace at the time. They are reproduced here for historical record.

The Wright/Sewell/Stickney Family Tree

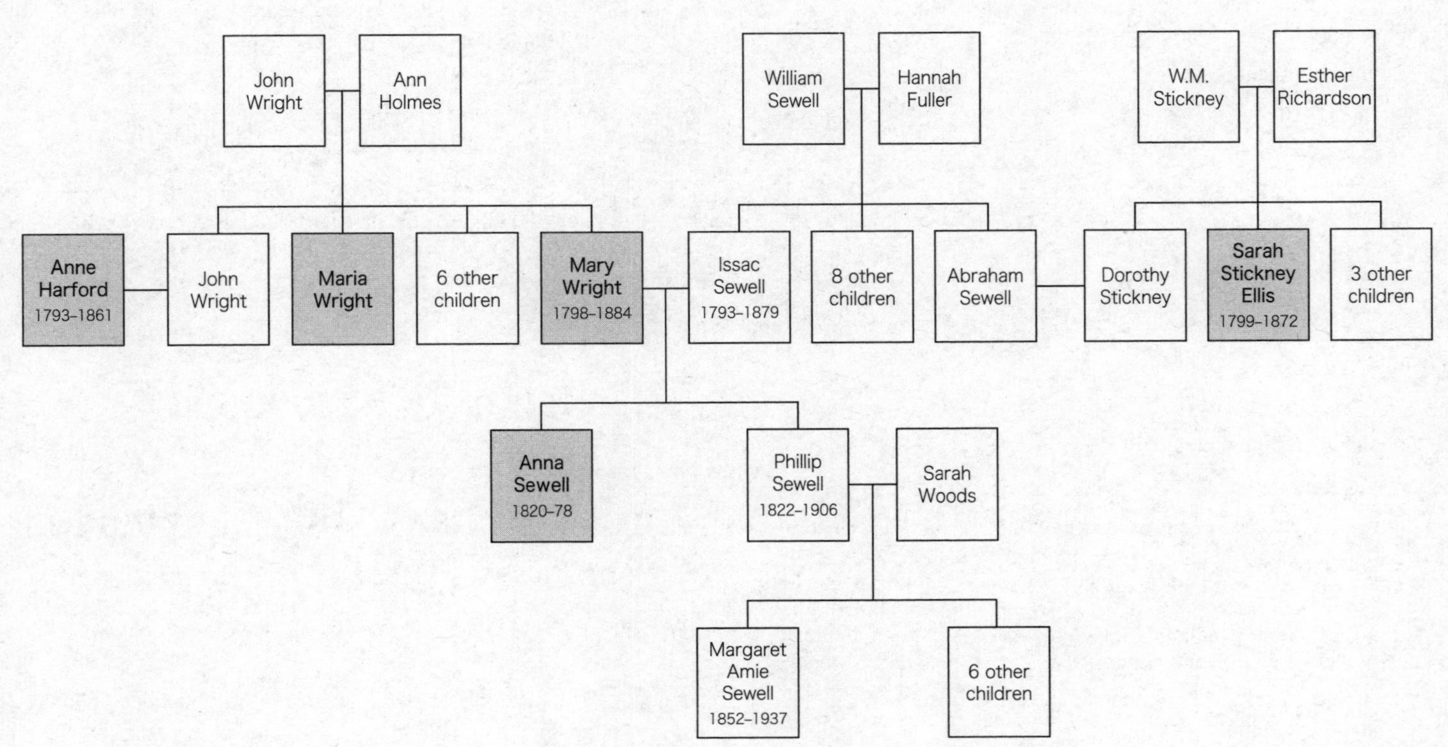

Introduction

On a raw spring day in 1871 a doctor visited The White House in the Norfolk village of Old Catton. He drove out in a small carriage along an unmade country road between water meadows and fields that were barely green with the new wheat. The land in all directions stretched away to the horizon with no hills to break the vista, challenge his horse or protect them from the biting wind.

His patient was Miss Anna Sewell, a character noted in the community for her sweet nature and air of serenity. She was the daughter of a well-known writer, her family had lived in the area for generations and most of them were Quakers. She had been disabled since childhood as a result of a foot injury, but recently she had been suffering from dizziness and fainting, and now she had severe abdominal pain that was getting worse. None of the treatment he had prescribed had helped. 'A troublesome case,' he admitted, with that carefully neutral face that spoke more than words ever could.

After he had left the bright white bedroom, where a vase of flowers and a few books were the only decorations, Anna's mother, an energetic, silver-haired woman of 75, asked his honest opinion about the prognosis. He told her that her daughter would be dead within eighteen months.

Pain and doctors had been Anna Sewell's constant companions since her early teens, since the day she ran home from school in the rain, slipped on some wet leaves and fell. She injured her ankle badly and overnight was changed from an athletic, outgoing girl into a woman living with permanently compromised health. This time, though, the pain was different, and Anna knew her body well enough to see through her mother's optimistic smile and the doctor's tactful opinion and recognise that now her life was limited.

There was one thing Anna wanted to do before she died, and that was to write something. Writing was almost her family business. Her mother, Mary Sewell, was a bestselling author of verse novels. One of her aunts had become famous for her natural history books, which even Queen Victoria had admired. Another close relative had seized the whole country's imagination with a series of 'conduct' books for women, which had really captured the mood of a nation ruled by a young queen. Another aunt had just started her career as a novelist, although she was well over 70 years of age.

Most of the visitors to the family home were her mother's writer friends and Anna herself had been her mother's editor and collaborator since the beginning of her writing career. Each day of the life that mother and daughter shared, from a morning reading of poetry or an essay to the word games they played in the evening, was saturated with literature. Nothing would have been more natural than for her to start writing.

At first, she was not sure that her notes and sketches would become a book. She was an astute critic of other people's work and not sure she could live up to her own standards, but that winter, in between making dolls and Christmas boxes for the village children, she began putting her thoughts down on paper. She also started keeping a journal, in which she noted, 'I am writing the life of a horse.'[1]

As her strength waned, her life contracted. With calm acceptance fostered by her Christian faith, she recognised that she would never again be able to ride, never drive her pony chaise, never visit her beehives. Soon she could not even walk as far as the garden gate. She was in so much pain that she could not sleep and, lying in bed or on a sofa in the sitting room, she thought back over her life.

She recalled the weary cab horses she had seen in London as a child, her grandfather's honest farm horses on which she had learned to ride, the carriage horses owned by the aristocratic visitors to the smart towns of Brighton and Bath, beautifully turned out but tortured until their mouths were bleeding by a cruel piece of harness called the bearing rein.

She thought of her own horses and remembered with gratitude how her world had opened up because of them. Although she often could not walk, her horses had made it possible for her to live a rich and fulfilling life. She could look back on happy times with family and friends, a teaching career in which she had been valued and long hours enjoying nature, all possible because of her horses. Now that she could no longer drive, she was forced to rehome her little grey pony, the sweet creature who had taken Anna everywhere but knew her own mind when it came to the stony streets of Norwich. Now the highlight of Anna's week was Sunday, when her brother Philip drove over with some of his large family and their restless mare, Bessie, whose cleverness provided him with entertaining stories for the children.

The doctor's prognosis proved too pessimistic and, after two years, Anna recovered a little and the pain became less overwhelming. With those celebrated women writers among her close relatives, she was at first reluctant to claim that her fragmentary sketches were a book, but gradually her writing took on that shape and she had the confidence tell her journal: 'From time to time I have, as I was able, been writing what I think will turn out a little book, it's special aim being to induce kindness, sympathy and an understanding treatment of horses.'

Her recovery was short-lived and she began to grow steadily weaker, sometimes able to write in pencil on little pieces of paper but often with only enough strength to dictate to her mother. Now, however, the work had a momentum of its own and she felt compelled to finish it.

For many years she had been her mother's editor and first reader, collaborating on the succession of popular verse novels that had made her an author of international renown. Now their roles were reversed, and Mary Sewell was the editor who transcribed her daughter's stories into a manuscript. From her bedroom, Anna could see the natural world that gave her so much delight: the wild birds pecking at a feeder on the tree in the garden, the deer in the park of the great country estate in the distance. From her balcony, she could watch the horses on the street outside and talk to their owners, asking about their lives 'because I am anxious, if I can, to present their true conditions and their great difficulties, in a correct and telling manner'.[2]

Four more years passed. By the time the book was finished, Anna was bedridden, losing weight and suffering a new pain in her back from pressure sores. By now a nurse had joined the household to help care for her. Her mother took the manuscript to her own publishers, Jarrold & Sons, in London and asked them to consider 'This little book of my daughter's'. They offered £20 for the copyright, which Mary advised Anna to accept. The proofs arrived in August 1877 and Anna's last journal entry about the book mentions 'very nice type'.

By November, when *Black Beauty: His Grooms & Companions – the Autobiography of a Horse Translated from the Original Equine* was published, Anna had a chest infection but was almost too weak to cough. She sent copies of the book to her family at Christmas. 'Step by step, day by day, the dear life seems to be slipping away,' wrote her mother to a friend in April 1878.[3] A few days later, at about seven in the morning, the nurse called Mary to Anna's bedside. 'I am not going yet, I am so strong,' her daughter assured her. Four hours later, Anna asked her mother and brother to pray, then said, 'I am quite ready', before taking her last few breaths.[4]

Her final resting place was with her ancestors in the Quaker burial ground in the next village of Lamas. Her grieving mother was infuriated when the undertaker's carriage arrived drawn by horses harnessed with bearing reins. She made them remove these cruel devices. In a few more years, thanks to her daughter's work, they would be illegal.

There was no hint then of what *Black Beauty* would become. In Victorian England, animal welfare was a minority interest entertained mostly by those who could afford it, while the majority of the population, living in poverty, had to choose between the welfare of their animals and their own survival. A few thousand copies of the book sold in the first year. Driven by grief, Mary Sewell demanded that Jarrold's try harder and market the book through the urban missionaries and animal welfare groups, notably the Royal Society for the Prevention of Cruelty to Animals (RSPCA).

CONTENTS

1

My Little Darling (1820–22)

Anna Sewell did not have an easy start in life. She was born on 30 March 1820 in a tiny, two-room house close to the twelfth-century church of St Nicholas, in Great Yarmouth in Norfolk, which was then a huge, bustling city, one of the greatest sea ports in Europe. The house, 25 Church Plain, is now protected by Grade II listing and has been embellished with a fake half-timbered façade with a painted inscription over the door identifying it as the famous author's birthplace. It dates from the seventeenth century and at the time of Anna's birth was a shabby little cottage squeezed between the ancient church and almshouses for 'decayed fishermen'.

Her mother Mary, a farmer's daughter who had married a young shopkeeper, had moved into this miniature home with determined optimism, saying it was 'very diminutive … but large enough to be happy in; able to take in a friend and enter on my first experience of housekeeping'.[1]

Mary recalls being immediately delighted by her daughter. 'On the thirtieth of March the little stranger came,' she wrote later. 'An unclouded blessing – for fifty-eight years the perennial joy of my life.'[2] The days of newborn bliss ended swiftly when Anna's father, Isaac, came home from his draper's shop to announce that he and his partner had been 'over-reached in business'[3] and he had to look for another job. Isaac was the son of a wealthy grocer, William Sewell, one of Yarmouth's most prominent citizens.

The town was one of the most prosperous places in England, the centre of the fishing industry on the east coast and an important supply port for the Royal Navy. The whole country was at that time enjoying an economic boom after the end of the Napoleonic Wars. Nevertheless, Isaac's shop had struggled. He had been forced out of the business by his commercial partner and now the young couple had to give up their home. While Isaac looked for a new business, Mary Sewell dressed her tiny daughter in the baby clothes she had hand-sewn herself and went back to the family farm at Buxton, an inland village 3 miles north of Norwich, a place which would be a second home to them both throughout their lives.

Mary Sewell had been a very reluctant bride and this setback only confirmed her misgivings about her husband. This failure was to be the first of many as Isaac demonstrated again and again that he had inherited nothing of his father's business acumen. William Sewell took exceptional interest in the education of Yarmouth's young men, including his own sons, and enrolled them in a Demonsthenian Society, which met every year for a reading of the members' essays.

Despite their father 'promoting in every way their intellectual studies',[4] both Isaac and his brother, also named William, proved consistently unwise, as if 'led by some unlucky genius'.[5] Some of Isaac's decisions were astonishingly wrong-headed, yet Mary, having committed herself to the marriage, never recorded a critical word about him, insisting that 'a kinder husband or better father could rarely be found'.[6] She was a relentless optimist, determined to see the best in everything and everyone, a mindset that would shape her daughter's life as well as her own. Reading the body of writing in which she recorded her life, it is clear that her memories are gilded with such a glow of positivity that one sometimes suspects a much darker reality underneath. She still had a genuine sympathy for her husband's struggles, later stating her belief that 'women should cultivate a spirit of great sympathy with men, who have to face the world and fight its battles'.[7]

Isaac Sewell had first proposed to her in the summer of 1815, when she was rising 18. She caught his eye during the stupendous street party staged in Yarmouth to celebrate the defeat of Napoleon at the Battle of Waterloo, when he and Mary's brother John worked together in the team of stewards charged with organising the crowds. The day began with a river pageant and a street procession, after which 8,000 people sat down at long tables on the quayside for a meal of beef, beer and plum pudding. William Sewell, Isaac's father, proposed toasts to the health of the Prince Regent, good fishing and death to all tyrants. The crowds were guided to the long golden beach to be entertained by donkey races and finally, as the summer evening drew in, a huge bonfire on which Bonaparte was burned in effigy until his head, packed with gunpowder, exploded.

After these spectacular festivities were over, Isaac Sewell tentatively suggested to Mary that he might be 'taken into her good books', an honour which she immediately declined: 'There was no spark upon the tinder.'[8] Isaac then moved to London, to learn the financial side of the cloth industry in the offices of a textile company, and Mary Wright, as she then was, continued to enjoy the life of a bookish, romantic girl, daughter of a prosperous Norfolk farmer, surrounded by loving siblings and without a care in the world.

The two families, the Wrights and the Sewells, already knew each other as they were both prominent in the Quaker community in Norfolk. Understanding Anna Sewell herself and the story of her life means understanding not only the beliefs of this Protestant faith group at that time but also the dynamics of the far-reaching and powerful Quaker network. William Sewell senior was the Elder of the Yarmouth meeting and had once censured Mary's mother for bringing all four of her young daughters to the meeting house in capes with swansdown trimming, going against the essential Quaker tenet of plainness in everything. Although Anna was to rebel against many Quaker customs and, in time, both she and her mother were to leave the movement, it would remain a dominant influence in their lives.

The Wrights could trace their ancestry back to the very first Quakers, who had followed the movement's founder, George Fox, a weaver whose spiritual vision led him to look for ways to express his Christian faith outside the practice of the Church of England in the late seventeenth century. At first they were persecuted, leading many Quakers to immigrate to America, but by Anna Sewell's time they were an accepted Nonconformist group. Many of those who remained in England had become prominent and wealthy citizens. The movement had settled in Norfolk and opened its first meeting house in Norwich. By the time Anna Sewell was born, the Norfolk Quakers were mostly ordinary folk distinguished by their ethical conduct and hard work. The Norwich meeting, however, included some of the richest families in England and also numbered among them some of the most famous women of the time. Within Britain's network of the wealthy elite, the 'solar-system' of successful Quakers formed a tightly knit inner circle.[9] Anna Sewell's family farm was only a few miles from Earlham Hall, the grand seat of the Gurney family, wealthy Quakers who had moved from farming to the wool trade and then into banking. They were such a byword for prosperity that the phrase 'as rich as the Gurneys' appears in Gilbert and Sullivan's comic opera *Trial by Jury* (1870). A Gurney daughter, Elizabeth Fry, had married another banker and, at the time Anna Sewell was born, had become a national heroine for her campaigns for prison reform and social work.

Elizabeth Fry was one of many Quaker women whose confidence in public life had been fostered by the principle of equality within the movement. Girls and boys received the same education and from its earliest days the movement had encouraged women to speak at meetings. It was a Quaker woman whom Dr Johnson derided in his often-quoted observation that 'A woman's preaching is like a dog's walking on his hind legs. It is not done well; but you are surprised to find it done at all.' However much outsiders scoffed, Mary and Anna Sewell both grew up with the benefit of a community that promoted women's equality in real terms, and knew Elizabeth Fry as a renowned reformer and popular orator who drew audiences of thousands to her lectures.

'Quaker' was a nickname; the movement's proper name was, and still is, the Society of Friends. They did not believe in religious institutions or ritual worship and the meeting was their shared expression of belief. On Sundays they gathered in the graceful, unadorned buildings, which can still be seen in many English towns and villages, to share personal spiritual experience in silence, a custom that had many of the elements of meditation.

For children, of course, it was intolerable to sit in silence for two hours. The teenage Anna Sewell simply dismissed meetings as 'useless' and, by her 20s, had dropped out of attending them. Her mother, as a girl, had learned banned novels by heart to entertain herself during meetings.

The larger meeting houses, including the original building at Goat's Lane in Norwich, held quarterly and annual events which drew people from far and wide to hear celebrated preachers. 'Goat's', as the light-minded Gurney girls called it,[10] was a place where Mary, and later Anna, would undoubtedly have heard Elizabeth Fry as well as the abolitionist writer Amelia Opie giving lectures. These meetings also brought the community elders together to discuss problem cases among them. Regrettably, these included Anna's father, Isaac Sewell, and, before him, Mary's father, John Wright.

When they met, Mary and Isaac had been of equal social status, both the children of wealthy community leaders. That was soon to change, as Mary's father made a number of bad investments with his younger brother, Richard, and also fell victim to a swindler. His bad luck culminated in an investment in a steam ship on the river at Yarmouth which blew up in 1817, killing thirteen people in front of the horrified crowds on the riverbank.[11] John Wright acted honourably as the Quaker community would have expected and personally compensated all the families whose loved ones had been lost in the explosion, which left him almost destitute. The remainder of the wider family fortune, a large farm at Buxton, had already been settled on Mary's brother, also called John, rather than her wayward father, and it was to a rented cottage on that land that the elder John Wright, with his four daughters and wife, went to live. The girls could no longer expect a life of leisure, ladylike pastimes and good works before marriage. They had to find jobs and almost the only positions for which they were suited were as teachers or governesses. Their exceptional Quaker education had at least qualified them for that, but it was 'a great descent in the social scale'.[12]

Mary's sister Elizabeth, to whom she was closest among her siblings, was taken on as a governess by Isaac Sewell's older sister, a move typical of the realistic support of a Quaker community but one which put the Sewells in the Wrights' debt and created a link of obligation between them. Anna, the oldest sister, was given a position by another Quaker family and Mary went to work as an assistant at a school in Essex. Her duties included teaching handwriting, which she was good at, and mathematics, at which she was not good at all and had to take extra tuition herself. Her own education had been largely at home with governesses, with the addition of a French master and a drawing master. Now, as well as teaching basic skills, she also had to mend the students' stockings and cut the quill pens which they used for their lessons, making forty pens a day for them. In addition, she had to get used to being treated as an equal by the school servants and addressed familiarly by her first name, when a few weeks earlier the staff would have curtseyed and called her 'Miss'. Nothing brought home the humiliation of her family more painfully.

During the Christmas holidays, which the Quaker community enjoyed although they did not celebrate religious festivals, the Wright family gathered at their cottage. Delighted as they were to be reunited, it was clear that their mother was struggling with depression, although she put on a brave face and tried to make the holiday happy and 'not let us feel the straitened resources of the house'.[13] To add to Mary's anxiety, Isaac Sewell came home from London and again asked her to marry him, which felt to her to be 'a great trial'.

At this time, the period depicted in great social detail by Jane Austen, young people from middle-class families were free to fall in love and marry as their hearts led them but were strongly influenced by their parents and other relatives, whose concerns were often for the financial survival of the kin group as well as the future happiness of the couple. Among Quakers, family pressure was particularly strong because this was an unhappy period in the movement's history and the number of adherents was shrinking. There were fewer than 20,000 Quakers in England, 500 of them living in or around Norwich.

Being a Quaker was a matter of birth. The faith did not proselytise but welcomed converts like Elizabeth Fry's friend Amelia Opie, although few outsiders were drawn to the sober and puritanical way of life. Quakers were expected to marry within the faith and a person who decided to 'marry out' was 'disowned' by their local meeting. This meant that the communities were becoming smaller, and there was corresponding pressure on young Quakers to marry and have families. Isaac would have already asked for the approval of his own father and of John Wright, so the pressure on Mary, within her family and in the wider community, was strong. She eventually agreed to a correspondence with Isaac once he was back in London.

Mary was not in love, and was not sure that she wanted to marry at all. She described herself as 'enthusiastic and sentimental, and my poetical reading as well as my nature had filled me with the idea that a very rare atmosphere was needed for wedded life'.[14]

Strict Quaker traditions forbade all the arts but had recently relaxed to allow poetry, and a few Quaker reading groups had been set up in London. Once their days of home-schooling were over, at the ages of 15 and 16, Mary and her sister Elizabeth had discovered poetry and revelled in it:

> My great delight was in poetry, and the works of Moore, Southey, Byron, Scott and others, continually coming out, gave me a perpetual feast. For two years I think I read little besides ... Quaker girls have little excitement in their quiet lives, and these works afforded to the craving imagination all the excitement and variety it needed.

Poetry quickly led the sisters to discover novels from the circulating library, 'and this being forbidden fruit, we devoured it in our bedroom'.[15] Thus Mary Sewell had begun an inner life of the imagination which was to sustain her through the trials of her marriage and which her daughter Anna would share from her earliest years.

Feeling that 'My heart had never been entangled and I was not at all ready to put on chains',[16] Mary returned to her job at the school, but there her love of literature sealed her fate. Of the two sisters who ran the establishment, one was also well read and introduced Mary to Shakespeare. The two young women formed a close friendship based on their shared love of reading, which the other sister resented. Mary felt that it was wrong to come between the sisters and decided that she ought to leave the school.

She knew it would be hard to find another job and refused to become a financial burden on her father. 'I wrought myself up to saying, "yes",' she recalled, adding that she did not regret her decision as long as she 'kept my castles in view', meaning that she consciously treasured the imaginative life created by literature as something that would sustain her through the difficulties that lay ahead. Mary was 22 and Isaac 27 years of age when they married at the meeting house at Lamas, a few hundred yards from the Wright family farm at Buxton. They spent a week by the sea at Cromer on the Norfolk coast before moving into their tiny house in Yarmouth.

After the failure of Isaac's first business, the meeting, dominated by his father, discussed the little family's future. At the suggestion of Isaac's brother William, the meeting decided that they should move to London, where Isaac was to open his own draper's shop. What little money Isaac had left was spent in buying a house at 38 Camomile Street, just off Bishopsgate in the city, a few blocks away from Drapers' Hall, the headquarters of the ancient guild of cloth merchants. Then, as now, this was the heart of the city's business district, although it was still a residential area, crowded with homes and shops beside the offices.

The grander houses were never far from areas of terrible poverty and already wealthy families like the Frys, whose London home was only ten minutes' walk from Camomile Street, were maintaining weekday homes in the city and escaping the dirt, stink and crowds to their country estates at weekends. Isaac used the last of his capital to convert the building so that the ground floor became a shop, and after six months at home with her parents, Mary and her baby daughter were able to join him in London.

It is entirely possible that the elder William Sewell promoted the move to London for his troublesome sons in order to distance himself from them. It is notable that, as Isaac Sewell's fortunes wavered and he struggled to provide for his young family, it was Mary's family, the Wrights, who stepped in with support in cash and kind. Quakers might have been compassionate to the failures of others, but they abhorred dishonesty and dealt sternly with those who had not maintained the highest standards during hard times. There was a hard-headed ruthlessness in parts of the community and the stern portraits of William Sewell suggest that he shared that tendency.

The strictures of Quaker belief limited their employment opportunities, so that many of the men went into trade or business. Although most Quakers read the Bible every day, they did not recognise it as a sacred book and would not take an oath on it, which meant that the law, politics and the newly founded police force were closed to them as professions. Most Quakers were pacifists, to the extent that as young women both Anna Sewell and Elizabeth Fry wrestled with their consciences if a military band was playing within their hearing, so a career in the armed services was impossible.

Quaker men had become prominent merchants and bankers, however, and in this sector the foundation principle of integrity had won them a glowing reputation for honesty and prudence, which they defended by expelling those in their communities whose action fell short of exemplary. The reputation of the elder William Sewell in Yarmouth would inevitably be tarnished if his sons' enterprises foundered.

London was the last place Mary wanted to live and the reality of this vast, teeming city shocked her even more than she had feared. 'I was taking my first lesson in fog, dirt, noise and distraction,' she wrote. 'Till then I had lived in the country and loved it with the ardent love of childhood and youth. I was a most rebellious scholar. I loathed and hated the place and I was nearly a stranger in it.'[17] Nevertheless, she set to work to support her husband. The miserable appearance of the shop alarmed her and she made some garments from his stock to put in the window and make it look more enticing.

The shop was close to a meeting house and Isaac had expected to rely on custom from the large number of Quaker families in the neighbourhood to get his business started, without taking account of the fact that many were also in the cloth trade themselves. In addition, there was already a flourishing Quaker draper a few streets away. They had a few customers and Mary did everything she could to support her husband, including helping in the shop itself.

'A lady called one day and asked if I knew of a needlewoman who could make some nightclothes for her.' Mary eagerly said she knew of exactly the right person, and suggested the customer leave the cloth with her to be made up. She then sewed the nightgowns herself, 'without telling'.[18] Thus the sewing skills she had learned as a rich young woman's pastime became a godsend when the family's survival was in danger.

The couple had the help of one servant in the house, and at first also an assistant in the shop. Isaac was soon forced to economise by dismissing him and hiring a boy instead. Mary and the maid took on the entire care of the household, including cleaning, cooking, shopping, looking after the baby and handwashing all the clothes, after which they struggled to dry them in a dark, cold house where the basement kitchen was the only warm room.

Anna was an easy, healthy child, but Mary worried that she was confined to the building's basement and felt guilty about making her wear dark, serviceable clothes which would need washing less often, whereas she and her sisters had been pampered babes in ruffled lace and satin ribbons. Energetic as she was, she began to slip into what would now be recognised as post-natal depression, in which a passionate yearning for the country made her feel guilty and uncontrollably anxious about her daughter:

> I thought it would be impossible for me to bring up my little girl among black houses and dirty streets, with never a flower for her little hand to gather nor a bird's song for her to hear. I used to sit and look over the roofs and the bits of blue sky, and cry like a child. Great London was to me like a huge cage with iron bars.[19]

To add to her worries, Mary found that she was pregnant again.

The animals that Anna Sewell saw most often in Camomile Street were the horses pulling hackney cabs who waited at a cab stand close to her home. The nippy manoeuvrable hansom cab that was to characterise Victorian London was not invented until 1834, so at this time the vehicles lining the road outside her house were simple, small carriages, each drawn by a single horse. The design had been imported from France and its name, cabriolet, shortened to cab. They also took their name from the village of Hackney to the east of the city, a traditional centre of breeding and training carriage horses. Some old-fashioned two-horse carriages for hire were still plying for trade and, as the post-war boom continued, the animals and their owners were not short of work.

A cab stand may have been picturesque and amusing for a little girl, and *Black Beauty* contains a vivid description of one and of the conversations that the cabmen had about the brutal economics of their business, but it can hardly have helped the passing trade for Isaac's shop. Another disincentive to customers was undoubtedly the gin shop on the corner of Bishopsgate, which survived as the Mail Coach pub until the buildings in the entire area were demolished and glass-walled high rises built there in 2011.

Mary described it as 'a dirty, disgusting looking place [that] ... often resounded with oaths, songs and quarrels'. As if in a trance of unhappiness, she watched a woman selling fruit from a stall on the pavement outside:

> A tall, haggard, white-faced woman she was, with black straggling hair, and a careworn countenance. In all seasons of the year there she sat – in the summer with her little bunches of cherries tied to sticks, and her small heaps of strawberries, gooseberries and currants piled up on leaves. In the autumn, her stall was covered with pears, apples and plums; in winter, with apples, nuts, oranges and slices of cocoa-nut. Hot or cold, wet or dry, there she was, often sitting in the rain, with her battered umbrella partially sheltering her and the fruit. Sometimes I have seen two or three children come to her, evidently her own; one of them, a baby, was brought in the arms of a little, lank, light-haired girl about eight years old. She would take the infant, kiss it, and give it suck; if it cried violently she would go into the gin shop with it, and presently bring it out pacified.[20]

If Camomile Street was rough, many of the smaller lanes and courtyards in the neighbourhood were far worse, and some of the urban areas newly settled by migrants from the country seemed like a dystopian nightmare to newcomers. London was the largest city in the world, the capital of the wealthiest country in the world, with about 2 million people at the time of Anna's birth. It would triple in size by the end of the century, swollen by people like the young Sewells who had tried to escape the poverty and uncertainty of life in the country by moving to what seemed to be an ever-growing centre of prosperity.

They quickly learned that the prosperity they sought to share had been achieved by the hard work of people and animals with nothing wasted on the welfare of either. The city had grown without planning, without public health legislation, and without any care or understanding for its inhabitants, human or animal. Fifty thousand people were homeless, sleeping in the streets or in the parks.

Many thousands more were crammed into jerry-built housing, ten people or more to a room, with no possessions except the ragged clothes they stood up in. One of the charities for which the Sewells' friend Mary Bayly worked kept an iron pot to loan out to families who had nothing to cook with, but many of them had no stove and no money for fuel either.[21]

Mary Sewell herself was to argue passionately the economics of soap, an unattainable luxury for people who had hardly enough money to feed themselves. Adults and children slept on straw or rags on the floor, with a chamber pot or, at ground level, a hole dug in one corner of an earth floor for a lavatory. In most of the city there was no piped water or sewage. Tuberculosis, pneumonia and cholera were common. Life expectancy was just 37 years – although it was much longer among Quakers, whose close communities supported their weaker members.

Unhappy as she was, Mary tried to help the people living in poverty around her. Her upbringing had emphasised 'a sense of duty and social responsibility, which implies that one is on earth to improve the lot of others'.[22] Unlike many of the middle-class women who undertook voluntary social work with their disadvantaged neighbours, she never attempted to foist a Bible on an illiterate family or offer the comfort of prayer or a sermon on the evil of drink when food, or soap, or the energy to scrub a floor were what was most needed.

Above all, she listened to people, wanting to know how she could help them. Later in her life, her friends remarked that 'in conversation she was careful not to smother the thoughts and observations of people with whom she was conversing',[23] and she seemed to have an instinct for the feelings that people were struggling to articulate. After listening, often the best help women like Mary could offer, besides food and clothing, was literacy as, in a time before state education, most of

London's poor could not read or write and relied on others to write letters and understand documents.

A visitor like Mary, who was hardly able to feed and clothe her own family, could still read and write letters for other people, decipher documents and put people in touch with agencies that could help them, from soup kitchens to orphanages. In particular, she befriended the family of a docker whose wife had died of cholera, leaving a number of small children. For a young mother expecting her second child, it was either brave or foolish to expose herself to an infectious disease that was often fatal. She was to continue in this kind of volunteer social work for most of her life and her experiences would inform her own writing as well as that of her daughter Anna.

Mary had a warmly sympathetic nature as well as a sense of duty and could readily put herself in the position of people like the desperate fruit-seller who resorted to calming her baby with gin. While this added to her own anxious state as her husband struggled with his failing business, she was to look back on this dark period and write:

> I was rebellious at having to live in that dingy place in London. I only existed on the hope of its coming to an end, and yet I am sure I should never have understood the poor and been able to help them as I have done, if I had not had that experience. The depths I was taken down to during those two years taught me more than any number of years looking on. And yet how I hated it.[24]

The little shop at last saw no customers at all and another meeting was called, this time more a Sewell family conference, which also suggests that the eminent elder William was anxious to contain the reputational damage threatened by his sons. Unfortunately, in Mary's eyes, the ideas of the younger William were again accepted and Isaac's little business was taken over by a much larger concern, run by a man who proved to be 'reckless and unsound in his trading principles'.[25]

The little family moved briefly to a large house with a number of servants 'and as it was a long-established business it was expected to do well, but before two years it was broken up, and so was I. It was a miserable failure; Isaac lost everything he had.'[26]

Anna's younger brother Philip was born in the depths of this disaster and the doctor who attended Mary insisted that she should leave London for the sake of her health. They rented two rooms in the village of Hackney and their furniture was sold to pay their debts. Mary 'grieved a little' to see her wedding presents auctioned, particularly the tea urn given to them by her mother, as it represented the death of her dream to entertain her family in her own little home. Her brother John and another friend bought some of the goods, which gave them enough money to rent a house in Dalston, only 3 miles to the north of Camomile Street, by then a new-built Georgian suburb in which houses had large gardens separated by communal green spaces. It was not the country, but it was to be a happy place for Mary and her children for the next nine years.

Isaac was declared bankrupt but somehow escaped expulsion from the Quaker community, perhaps because he himself had acted honestly and was clearly the innocent victim, while the blame for the collapse of the business was attributed to the wealthier partner, and perhaps because he moved from the catchment area around one meeting house to another. Either way, the elder William Sewell was spared the shame of his son's failure. Isaac took a job as a travelling salesman for a large lace manufacturer in Nottingham, and his long hours often left his young family alone until late at night. Anna and Philip grew up seeing their father only on Sundays and Mary settled down to home-school her children.

2

Hell for Animals (1822–24)

So many animals lived in Regency London that it was called an 'agropolis'.[1] As thousands of people migrated to the city from the country every year, their food, transport and power were largely provided by animals. The expanding settlement swallowed up outlying villages like Chelsea and Hackney with the most minimal planning, no regulation and no provision for infrastructure, so that paved roads, drains and access to clean water, natural light and ventilation were rarely considered by the landlords and speculative builders. Between the crooked medieval streets in the City and the elegant neoclassical terraces recently built to the west around Oxford Street and Regent Street, thousands of green spaces, from tiny yards to what are now the spacious inner-city parks, were home to cattle, donkeys, chickens, rabbits and pigs.

A typical street in central London would be crowded with horses, carrying individual riders or drawing cabs, private carriages, stagecoaches or carts loaded with everything from fine millinery to night soil. Once his youth is over and his luck runs out, Black Beauty spends a good portion of his life as a London cab horse and Anna Sewell gives us a detailed picture of good cabmen and bad, and the perils of rushing to catch a train through the teeming streets. An old former cavalry horse with whom Beauty works is fatally injured when a drunken drayman, driving too fast, crashes into the cab they are pulling.

Licences were given to cabmen for six or seven days, and the unlucky horses whose owners had seven-day licences could be worked day and night with no rest day at all. This is the fate of Beauty's former stable-mate, Ginger, who dies from overwork in a tragic passage that has been seared into the memory of millions of readers. The book also tells of Seedy Sam, a cabman who can't afford his own horses, so has to rent them and work such long hours that he too passes away in a hard winter.

The poorer traders, keeping market stalls or smaller shops, relied on donkeys. The mighty monarchs of the draught animals were the dray horses kept at the city's numerous breweries. The brewing industry in London was an economy of its own. The dray horses – massive creatures who towered over their owners at 7ft or more at the shoulder – were worked twelve hours a day in pairs or teams; a team of six could haul a load of beer in barrels weighing 1.5 tonnes. Breweries worked around the clock getting deliveries to shops, pubs and inns all over the city and could keep 100 or more horses in purpose-built stables.

These giant draught horses, mostly from a breed called Midland Black,[2] were prized and well-managed animals, descended from the war horses of earlier times and bred for their gentleness as well as their strength. A visitor to a London brewery was astonished to see that the horses knew their work so well that they did it almost without supervision. The waste grain, yeast deposits and gin lees from breweries were used to feed cattle and pigs in the city, a diet on which they thrived.[3]

A typical neighbourhood would have at least one butcher, who would keep a few pigs in a yard at the back of his shop. He might buy carcasses from the retail meat market at Newgate, or drive home sheep or cattle bought at Smithfield Market to slaughter behind the shop. Chop houses, pie shops and bakeries often kept pigs as well. Cows were kept in thousands of small dairies and milked in stalls at the back of the shop while their owners sold their butter and cheese at the front. St James's Park was virtually a picturesque dairy farm, home to dozens more milk cows who supplied the smart mansions around Piccadilly, while milkmaids walked single animals through the streets further afield, carrying their stools and ready to stop and serve customers directly from the udder.

The animals we now think of as domestic pets lived in London too. Feral dogs and cats roamed the streets but dogs in particular had roles to play. Indeed, many breeds of dog are still identified by their original function. Many small traders relied on at least one large, aggressive dog to guard their stock and their premises. Dog fighting was a popular entertainment, as was the baiting of many different animals from bulls to badgers, for which terriers and mastiffs were bred and deliberately brutalised.

The city teemed with vermin and, while small dogs were trained as ratters, numerous cats helped out with the mice. The number of animals kept as companions was much smaller but growing as people began to value the affection and fidelity of a pet. For centuries, the upper classes had kept companion pets prized for their beauty and breeding but ordinary city dwellers also kept animals, like the bull-terrier who was devoted to Bill Sikes, the brutal murderer portrayed by Charles Dickens in *Oliver Twist*.

Little caged birds, linnets or canaries, brought joy to the bleakest of tenements. Almost a century later, in his play *Pygmalion*, George Bernard Shaw portrayed the Covent Garden flower girl Eliza Doolittle sending home for her canary as she begins her adventure in social mobility. The music-hall song 'Don't Dilly Dally', made popular by Marie Lloyd in the early twentieth century, is sung by a girl whose family did a moonlight flit, running out on the rent and leaving their lodgings at night to avoid the landlord. All their belongings are piled on a van:

> My old man said follow the van
> And don't dilly-dally on the way
> Off went the cart with the home packed in it
> I walked behind with me old cock linnet.

But the singer stops at a pub, loses her way and wanders the streets in desperation, so hungry she is ready to eat the linnet's birdseed.[4]

By the time Anna Sewell was growing up in east London, the trade in animals in the city had attained an industrial scale. Smithfield, once located on the eastern edge of the town, had been the site of the animal market in London since AD 950, and while smaller towns and other

European capitals had moved their live markets and abattoirs out of the inner city, London had retained Smithfield as the hub of its meat trade. Streets of houses had grown up beyond it, so now the area was enclosed in a population centre.

A contemporary picture[5] shows it as a vast open space between the buildings of Clerkenwell and Farringdon, overlooked by the eighteenth-century façade of St Bartholomew's Hospital, with the medieval tower of the Church of St Bartholomew the Great behind it. As far as the artist's eye could see were cattle and horses tethered in rows beside pens of sheep. Once they were sold, some animals were slaughtered nearby but most were driven to and from the market through the streets of London. Smithfield was half an hour's walk away from Camomile Street, where the Sewells first lived, and by the 1840s market records show that over 1.2 million animals were sold there.[6]

The majority of these animals were sold for meat but herded away alive, as it was far cheaper to drive a live animal than carry away a dead one. The sellers therefore had an interest in getting them to the market looking healthy. Many, however, were older animals sold at the end of their working lives, their carcasses to be processed for leather, glue, bonemeal and dog meat. There was nothing to be gained by giving them food, water or shelter, so they ended their lives miserably.

Pigs, impossible to drive and demanding to keep, were not sold in large numbers at Smithfield. Pigs are omnivorous, quick to fatten and to reproduce, and pork was easy to preserve by salting or smoking. It was probably the most important meat for the poorer classes and was also bought in great quantities by the army and navy. The navy overall was the largest industrial client for food in Britain.[7]

A vast piggery had grown up at the western fringe of London, in Notting Dale, now known as Notting Hill and one of the most desirable residential districts in the capital. In Anna Sewell's time it was a semi-rural slum, home to 2,000 pigs and a smaller number of people. The community was an ad hoc recycling industry of its own. The pig keepers drove carts into the city to collect food waste from the houses of the wealthy. Back in Notting Dale, they kept the best scraps for themselves and fed the rest to the pigs. Animal waste polluted the watercourses in the area, and Mary Bayly describes it as one of the most wretchedly deprived places in England.

The city needed food, drink and transport, but it also needed power. The new steam engines were erratic, as Anna Sewell's grandfather had discovered. They were gradually installed, particularly to pump water, but the fuel for them arrived under horsepower. London consumed 1.2 million tons of coal a year, all of it collected at the docks and carried through the streets by horses and carts.

Traditional power sources like wind and water were difficult to manage there, more so as the city grew. Its low-lying and level situation meant that there was no consistent wind for windmills and the rivers flowed too slowly to turn watermills. Hundreds of horses were used to power machinery in treadmills or 'gins', milling steel, rags, bark or paper, powering jack-hammers, making bricks, weaving wool or silk, pumping the foul-smelling effluents of tanneries. These horses were old, suffering with harness sores and often blind, but they had once been young, well-groomed animals prized by their owners.

The life cycle of a horse was a tragedy played out on every street. As Anna was to describe in *Black Beauty*, many horses, even those from the finest bloodlines, declined through a cycle of maltreatment and exploitation until they dropped dead in harness. 'The High Mettled Racer', a popular song from a comic opera which inspired illustrations by a number of artists including Thomas Rowlandson, told the tale. In the last verse the horse, reduced to pulling a cart, collapses and dies in the street, the sad end Anna Sewell imagined for Black Beauty's stablemate, Ginger, in a famously poignant passage in the book. Even as a child, she would have seen many horses die in harness as the song described:

> Till at last having labour'd, drudg'd early and late,
> Bow'd down by degrees, he bends on to his fate,
> Blind, old, lean and feeble, he tugs 'round a mill,
> Or draws sand, till the sand of his hour glass stands still.
> And now, cold and lifeless, exposed to the view,
> In the very same cart which he yesterday drew,
> While a pitying crowd his sad relicks surround.[8]

This huge interreliant concentration of people and animals was the result of the accelerating transition from a rural to an industrial society. Many people loved, respected and cared for the animals they owned but many others simply could do no more than share a life of deprivation and hardship. The welfare of animals, in both city and country, was closely tied to the welfare of their owners. The poorer the owner, the more difficult it was for them to look after their livestock, and the less likely that they would have the education to understand how to manage them.

In a country village, the experience of older farm workers would be there to guide the less experienced, with principles of husbandry passed down the generations. In an urban setting, traditional wisdom was lost and animals were increasingly treated as commodities to be exploited. Animals needed feed, water and physical care. Horses needed shoeing, which cost money, and grooming, which took time. Without this care, a working horse's health was in danger. Black Beauty's decline begins with a stable boy who is too lazy to pick out his hooves. As a result his feet become infected and he goes lame.

Veterinary medicine was in its infancy but the remedies that there were also needed money. A wealthy brewer might build model stables for his prized dray horses, but his customer, the small innkeeper, would keep a sow in the old wash-house at the back of yard, feed her scraps and rubbish and get as many litters as he could out of her. As Tom Almeroth-Williams observes of the animal welfare movement in *City of Beasts*, his study of animals in Georgian London, 'the key characters in this narrative are, therefore, not clergymen, writers or politicians, but London's brewers, brick-makers, tanners, grocers, cow-keepers, coachmen, horse dealers, drovers, carters, grooms and warehousemen'.[9] Anna Sewell's gift was to understand this and appeal directly, not to the wealthy and educated, but to those who cared for animals at first hand: working-class men who were often either living in poverty or in desperate fear of it.

Brutality, cruelty and the abuse of animals were so common that few people remarked on them. The Smithfield Committee of 1828 was set up to consider the possibility of moving the market out of its central location. They called seventy-eight witnesses and heard about congestion, health hazards and the dangers of angry bulls who escaped and charged through the streets, killing or maiming people who did not get out of their way fast enough.

Only three of those witnesses raised concerns about animal welfare.[10] Local legislation often made a distinction between 'necessary' and 'wanton' cruelty, implying that there was an acceptable level of cruel treatment in the management of animals. Animals were routinely beaten to make them obedient, or to make them work harder or faster, but some owners were undoubtedly sadistic and, when an animal was no longer useful to them, beat it to death.

Contemporary prints often show cab horses with protruding ribs and visible vertebrae, standing as if they were lame. Chickens were often plucked alive, in the belief that the feathers came out more easily that way. Fox hunting had become the popular pastime for all social classes, and city dwellers would ride out to the country at weekends to hunt. This activity was so popular that it was immortalised in the character of Jorrocks, the Cockney grocer who goes hunting, who made his first appearance in the *Sporting Magazine* in 1838.

Even the most educated people accepted cruelty to animals as a necessary evil, like the medical students who learned by watching the dissection of live animals, usually dogs, at the Royal Society. For the more deprived social classes, animals were simply tortured for public entertainment. Large crowds all over England gathered to watch a dog fight or cock fight, or cheer on and place bets on dogs attacking a maddened bull, or bear, or badger, while children had fun torturing any stray animal they could catch.

Bull-baiting, in which a bull was attacked by dogs, was a particularly cruel sport, in which the crowd's amusement was in seeing dogs being gored, disembowelled, trampled or flung in the air. The dogs – bulldogs, mastiffs or terriers – were bred for their savagery. The bull was hobbled by cutting its leg tendons or even its hooves and enraged by stabbing it with knives or pitchforks, cutting off its ears or tail, burning it with hot tar or by blowing chilli powder into its nose or eyes.

Some researchers believe that this ritualised abuse has very ancient roots in pre-Christian water worship,[11] which developed into the custom of bull-running. This was recorded as early as the twelfth century and was still observed in country towns such as Stamford in Lincolnshire and Tutbury in Staffordshire. Here the chosen bull was chased through the town by a mob whose objective was to push it off the bridge into the river after cutting off chunks of its skin as trophies. The bull was then killed and its meat divided among the crowd.

People wore bizarre costumes and sang traditional songs during the festival, which has clear similarities with the bull-running traditions of France and Spain, but by Anna Sewell's time this had developed into a drunken frenzy of mass brutality. Unfortunately, a betting industry had developed around bull-baiting, dog fighting and cock fighting. The owners of successfully vicious animals made good money from them, as did the bookmakers who took bets from the crowds. The activists who opposed these 'sports' sought to deprive many people of good livings.

Supporters of these popular blood sports defended them as 'traditional, manly, English sport; inspiring courage, agility and presence of mind under danger'.[12] When a bill to ban bull-baiting came before Parliament in 1800, then Prime Minister George Canning opposed it, saying that 'the amusement inspired courage and produced a nobleness of sentiment and elevation of mind'.[13] *The Times* claimed that the issue was beneath the dignity of Parliament.[14]

Against this view, there was an increasing body of educated opinion that argued that cruelty to animals inspired not only cruelty towards people but a general moral degradation. William Hogarth's print series *The Four Stages of Cruelty* imagines a boy who progressed from torturing dogs to beating his horse, and then robbery and murder. In the foreground of the second print in the series, a carriage driver and a shepherd are both seen in a London street beating animals that have collapsed. Behind them, the drunken driver of a brewer's dray crushes a child under its wheels, while in the distance another man beats an overladen donkey and a mob of boys runs after a bull that is tossing a dog in the air.[15]

This everyday cruelty was a unique feature of British life and had been for centuries, at least since the reign of Mary I (1553–58), when the Mantuan diplomat Annibale Litolfi described the country as 'a paradise for men, a purgatory for servants and hell for horses', apparently quoting an old saying in doing so.[16] Cruelty as a public spectacle had been widely enjoyed for centuries and those who questioned it had been characterised as killjoys who tried to impose upper-class sensitivity on working people. Thomas Macaulay, whose multi-volume *History of England* first appeared in 1848, wrote, 'The Puritans hated bear-baiting, not because it gave pain to the bear, but because it gave pleasure to the spectators.'[17]

Many enlightened individuals, including the scientist Sir Isaac Newton, Samuel Pepys the diarist, the playwright Richard Brinsley Sheridan and the philosophers John Locke and Jeremy Bentham, had argued for change during the previous century. As early as 1800, a bill to end the 'savage custom' of bull-baiting was introduced to Parliament by the septuagenarian Scottish MP Sir William Pultney, and that debate clearly showed the vested interests of the opposition. They were led by a former Secretary of War, William Windham, who claimed that blood sports 'increased the vigour and manhood'[18] of the country and were essential to desensitise the young men who would be recruited into the services.

Windham cleverly dismissed the bill's humanitarian supporters as aristocratic liberals trying to impose their values on the working class. By deriding the hypocrisy of a patrician who enjoyed fox hunting yet was trying to ban ordinary people from enjoying their own form of blood sport, he astutely dragged the issue across the great divide between the working classes and the rest of society in Britain, a move that would empower the opponents of the animal welfare movement for the rest of the century. The House of Commons rejected the bill by one vote.

More general legislation was proposed by a radical lawyer and former Lord Chancellor, Lord Erskine, in 1809. In presenting his bill to the House of Lords, he told of stopping an overloaded greengrocer's cart on the street. The horse pulling it was a living skeleton, bleeding from harness sores and with a broken fetlock bone visibly sticking through the skin of one foot.

Erskine offered the man a guinea for the animal, but the man argued that he could work the horse for another three weeks and then sell him to a slaughterhouse for four or five pounds. Erskine bought the suffering animal at that price but made the point to his fellow peers that a lone act of kindness like this did nothing to prevent 'the sufferings of animals which meet our eye almost every day, and in almost every street of this metropolis'.[19] Erskine was a skilful diplomat and the Lords passed his bill on 9 June 1809, but in the Commons it was defeated by thirteen votes in a sparsely attended session, with one critic demanding, 'How can you legislate compassion?'

The cause was to find its champion at last in an Irish MP, Richard Martin. The Act of Union had brought Irish MPs to Westminster in 1800, and in 1809 this flamboyant statesman was elected for Galway County, although he did not have the means to take up his seat until 1818. Nicknamed the 'King of Connemara', Martin was in fact the largest landowner in Britain, but his estate on Ireland's west coast was a liability rather than a source of wealth.

The wild beauty of the region was to be praised by Oscar Wilde and W.B. Yeats, but it was poor, mountainous land that was largely uncultivable. Martin's 'kingdom' had been mortgaged for two generations even when he inherited it. When debt collectors were after him, he retreated to the most remote of his houses and relied on the appalling state of the roads and the loyalty of his tenants to protect him. He lived precariously off his tenants' rents and a succession of money-making schemes, the last of which was quarrying Connemara marble. Martin was the first person to have this beautiful green stone polished,[20] and when he finally arrived in London to take up his seat, he presented King George III with a fireplace made of it.

His own lifestyle was lavish and he was a generous landlord, giving smallholdings to tens of thousands of Catholic migrants from the northern Irish counties. It was said that he never charged a widow rent nor evicted tenants in difficulties. While he forgave debt, however, he banned cruelty to animals throughout his vast, wild estate.

In Westminster, Martin's greatest campaign was for Catholic emancipation, and he became a close associate of William Wilberforce, now also in his sixties and an MP for the past forty years. Wilberforce was the hero of the movement to abolish slavery that had led to the Slave Trade Act of 1807. Martin found him an ally and mentor in Westminster but his own interests extended at first to many other causes, not least those affecting his constituents. Connemara was one of the regions of Ireland hit hardest by famine in the early 1820s, and Martin brought in a bill for the improvement of land there.

In animal welfare, however, he found the cause which he could champion alone. He introduced the bill to Prevent the Ill-Treatment of Cattle on 1 June 1821, to a storm of ridicule and hostility. Nevertheless, he had lobbied persistently and engaged the support of outside authorities on animal management and welfare. He had also taken care to word the proposed legislation so generally that it was hard to disagree with it, and the blood-sport enthusiasts could believe that only working animals were covered by it.

Martin's colourful reputation opened as many doors as it closed. His speeches in Parliament and outside were always entertaining and his ebullient character generated a storm of anecdotes. At a reception given by the Prince Regent, when the conversation turned to duelling, he ripped open his shirt to show his scars.

In Westminster, Martin was always in danger of being dismissed as another crazy Irishman, although a journalist of the time observed that he was 'gifted with an abundant fund of sound common sense'.[21] Stocky, red-faced, his curly dark hair thinning and flecked with grey, he was 65 years old when his bill began its year-long voyage through the political process. Like Erskine, he was an experienced politician and persuasive in private conversation. The bill squeaked through its first reading on three votes then gradually gathered enough support to pass into law the following year, ever to be known as 'Martin's Act'.

Martin then embarked on a one-man mission to enforce his law. He sensed that his victory had been a narrow one and that the new legislation would be quietly ignored unless it was publicised and prosecuted. The first man he dragged before the courts was a stagecoach driver, John Wells, who raced another driver up Whitehall, the wide, straight road that links Trafalgar Square to Parliament Square, one summer evening, whipping his horses to make them go faster.

His lead horse fell, and he had started beating her to make her get up when Martin confronted him and had him arrested. In court the next day, he defended himself by explaining that the horse was lame and so needed to be beaten to make her move, a brutally ignorant argument that was put forward by many of the men Martin accused. The records of the cases he prosecuted are telling evidence of the suffering caused to horses by owners who were well meaning but did not understand their animals or know how to look after them – the everyday ignorance that Anna Sewell would set out to combat in *Black Beauty*.

Martin began to prowl the London streets, dragging offenders to court, making eloquent speeches in prosecuting them and then in many cases helping the bewildered offenders to pay their fines. His next victim was Thomas Worster, a greengrocer who had a mobile street stall that was drawn by a donkey. On Fleet Street, another recklessly driven coach frightened the animal and it bolted, tipping the stall over and scattering its produce in the street. Worster flogged the animal so viciously with a leather belt that passers-by intervened even before Martin made his arrest.

Worster brought the animal to court with him, inviting the magistrate to see that it was well fed and 'fat as a mole', and argued that he only beat the animal because it was so 'timersome'.[22] Since punishment would make the animal even more frightened, his reasoning demonstrated his own ignorance. Martin made a witty speech in prosecution and paid the man's fine for him, believing that the publicity he generated for his new law was worth the effort and expense.

He acquired a new nickname, 'Humanity Dick', and became a gift to satirists, music-hall comedians, balladeers and caricature artists,[23] who often enjoyed reporting his exploits at the expense of the truth. While in general he regarded all publicity as good publicity for the cause, he was occasionally maddened by the misrepresentation inflicted on him and once stormed into the Press Gallery at the House of Commons to confront a journalist from *The Times* who he felt had defamed him.[24]

One publication pursued a vendetta against him. The *Morning Chronicle* raged:

> That Irish jackass Martin throws an air of ridicule over the whole matter by his insufferable idiotism. I hope to see his skull, thick as it is, cracked one of these days; for that vulgar and angry gabble with which he weekly infests the Public Offices of the Metropolis, is a greater outrage to humanity, than any fifty blows ever inflicted on the snout of a pig or the buttocks of beeve, blows which, in one and

> the same breath, the blustering and blundering blockhead would fain prosecute, punish and pardon ...[25]

This editorial highlighted the demand made in *Blackwell's Edinburgh Magazine*, 'Why don't they murder him?', although it alluded to the threat rather than quoting it directly. The 'they' in question were the drovers at Smithfield, a mob of whom had attacked Martin when he stopped a youth from beating a donkey. Martin took the *Morning Chronicle* to court for making a death threat. The case was eventually settled but lasted for three acrimonious and occasionally violent days, which, as Martin triumphantly explained to his attackers, was all good publicity for the cause.

Another campaigner for animal welfare, Anglican clergyman the Reverend Arthur Broome, had been using the London press to find like-minded activists. Broome was a gentle, unworldly man, a graduate of Balliol College, Oxford, who had entered the Church of England after leaving university. He wrote pamphlets and essays on animal welfare, which was an issue that divided Christians. Some asserted that man's dominion over animals, described in the Old Testament book of Genesis, gave them the right to use the natural world as they wished according to their superior judgement; others argued that the Bible denounced cruelty of every kind and Christ's teachings required mercy and compassion of his followers.

Broome had published an early essay on animal rights, *The Duty of Mercy* by Humphrey Primatt, and was to publish Lord Erskine's speech to the House of Lords as well.[26] He bombarded newspapers with anonymous letters under the pseudonym 'Clerus', which he now followed by a notice in several different newspapers that read:

> An Individual who feels for the sufferings of the Brute Species, and laments, in common with every benevolent mind, the wanton cruelties which are so frequently committed with impunity on this unoffending part of God's Creation, earnestly appeals to the Public in their behalf. He suggests the formation of a Society by whose united exertions some check may, if possible, be applied to an evil, the toleration of which is equally repugnant to the dictates of humanity and

> to the spirit and precepts of the Christian religion. Persons whose sentiments accord with those of the Writer, on this subject, and who are willing to promote the object he recommends, are requested to address a few lines (free of postage), to 'Clerus', 25, Ivy-lane, Paternoster-row.[27]

Many of the anti-slavery campaigners were also concerned about cruelty to animals, notably Elizabeth Heyrick, who was to have an influence on Mary Sewell. She was another Quaker, a wealthy widow and an influential pamphleteer who had supported Wilberforce and was now arguing that the act of 1807 did not go far enough and that more wide-reaching laws were needed. She also prepared a report on the conditions at Smithfield Market in 1823,[28] which was published anonymously and criticised the police and legislature for not enforcing Martin's Act. It also argued that Smithfield could no longer be left to regulate itself, with a few elderly and ineffectual inspectors.

The following year Broome was able to call a meeting of twenty other supporters, including Wilberforce, Martin and two other MPs, at Old Slaughter's Coffee House in St Martin's Lane on 16 June 1824. Among the company was Lewis Gompertz, the fifth son of a wealthy diamond merchant. He was a noted inventor with a prototype bicycle among his designs – decades before the bicycle as we know it came about. Gompertz was also before his time in lifestyle politics. He was a vegan before the word was invented, and refused to wear leather or silk because cruelty to animals was involved in their production.

The group resolved to set up an organisation, which Broome named the Society for the Prevention of Cruelty to Animals (SPCA), and began by employing two inspectors at Smithfield Market. Broome, who by now had resigned his post as a curate and hoped to make a living by writing and publishing, took on the role of the society's secretary, and shortly afterwards made the unwise decision to guarantee its debts.

Martin continued to blanket-bomb Parliament with follow-up legislation, introducing bills to ban bull-baiting and ensure humane treatment of horses by slaughtermen. He pursued his cause relentlessly but two years later, at the general election, Martin lost his seat in Parliament and with it the protection from his creditors which his status as an MP had provided.

To escape a debtor's prison he fled to Boulogne in France, joining a large community of British fugitives there. He lived in modest comfort on the proceeds of Connemara marble and continued to fire volleys of inspiring letters to the society's activists until his death in 1834. The Reverend Arthur Broome was not so fortunate. The SPCA, paying for inspectors, an office and publications, ran into debt and in 1826 Broome was declared bankrupt and sent to prison.[29] The great step forward in the animal welfare movement represented by Martin's Act proved to be a false dawn.

3

'I Think We Were Exceedingly Happy' (1824–32)

When Anna and her family moved to Dalston in 1822, the village was already partially urbanised but still green, airy, open and pleasant. It lay a few miles to the north-west of Hackney, and slightly closer to the centre of London. They lived at No. 12 Park Road, now renamed Parkholme Road, one of the web of new-built side streets that swallowed the fields on either side of the main thoroughfare, the Old North Road. It was still a green area, although much farmland had been sold off for development. There were market gardens sending vegetables and fruit into the city, and brickworks supplying the speculative builders in open spaces between the housing, and all of this produce was moved by horsepower.

The house in which Anna and her family lived no longer stands but on the evidence of the rest of the terrace it was a small, stucco-fronted home built over three floors with two rooms at each level and gardens front and back – slightly bigger than the flat-fronted artisan cottages built for industrial workers but still very modest by the standards of the time. Isaac had escaped expulsion from the Quaker movement and found a job as a salesman travelling between drapers' shops with samples of lace from a manufacturer in the traditional lace-making town of Nottingham in the Midlands. It was hard work. He was typically on the road from 8 a.m. to 8 p.m., Monday to Saturday, and sometimes came home so late that Mary could only leave out bread and cheese for him on the kitchen table before she went to bed. The only day on which the family was together was Sunday, and much of that was taken up by the Quaker meeting.

The family was poor, but Mary Sewell threw herself wholeheartedly into making virtues out of necessity. 'It will easily be supposed that strict economy had to be practiced,' she recalled,[1] 'but there is no hardship in plain, simple food and clothing. Trouble often comes when these are superabundant, but as long as there is *enough*, without carking care, there is freedom; and I believe this is the best atmosphere for a child's mind and body.'[2] It is worth noting the emphasis Mary placed on freedom, suggesting that she believed children were inherently good (rather than inherently naughty and in need of discipline), thinking that chimed with the philosophy of Jean-Jacques Rousseau and the more liberal Quaker educators. The expression she used, 'carking care', is now archaic but implied the stress and anxiety of poverty. Anna and her brother Philip lived largely on bread and milk, porridge and what could be grown in the garden. They had no toys and few home-made clothes. There was no question of sending them to school, as free education for all was many decades in the future.

Their mother's imagination, however, was a luxury in itself. Was it expensive to light the house with candles in the long winter evenings? Well then, 'as very little children I accustomed them to playing in the dark. Many a game of hide-and-seek have I had with them in a room bordered by a dressing room and two closets, and admitting of all kinds of surprises.'[3]

To any parent familiar with the philosophy of Maria Montessori, the revolutionary Italian educator who opened her first school in Rome in 1907 and whose legacy proliferates in early years schools all over the world, Mary's approach to educating Anna and Philip, born of her own instincts and guided by Quaker doctrine, seems almost prophetic, particularly in its principles of respect and auto-education.

She described letting the children sit at a table and amuse themselves stringing beads or building things with wooden blocks as long as their interest lasted. Anna, Philip and their mother were alone together for days on end, and the children naturally helped with the household tasks: 'They shared with me in household occupations. They were always with me. We were workfellows and playfellows, and wished no greater happiness.'[4]

Her approach to discipline was informed by the Quaker belief that God lives in every being, and was in direct opposition to the prevailing Anglican and Catholic doctrines of original sin which led to harsh discipline, physical punishment and often outright brutality in many schools. Mary Sewell favoured kindness, patience and allowing a child to discover the consequences of their actions rather than any kind of punishment. Later in life, she recalled, 'The children had very happy dispositions and fine tempers; we knew nothing about punishments – to have a kiss withheld was too severe for either of them. How beautiful their young lives seem to me now, as I look back upon those promising young plants.'[5] Given that her daughter became one of the most original writers of her time, her educational approach seems to have produced a highly creative mind.

The study of nature, from an ecological perspective, is also a key Montessori value. Maria Montessori was to write:

> We must study the correlation between life and the environment. In nature all is correlated. This is the purpose of nature. Nature is not concerned just with the conservation of individual life or with the betterment of itself. It is a harmony, a plan of construction. Everything fits into the plan: rocks, earth, water, plants, man, etcetera.[6]

This was exactly what Mary Sewell believed more than 100 years earlier.

Anna and Philip were taught to approach the natural world with kindness and respect. They observed flowers, trees, animals and insects but, after one experiment, never killed specimens or shared the fashionable mania for collecting birds' eggs or pinning butterflies. 'We never compassed death to make a collection,' their mother remembered.[7] Her natural inclination was to teach her children to be tender-hearted, again something opposed to prevailing orthodoxy in schools where, as Dickens wrote in *Nicholas Nickleby*, 'every kindly sympathy and affection [was] blasted in its birth'.[8] She justified her approach by arguing that 'the habits of insects were observed much more accurately'[9] if the creature were only trapped in a glass for an hour or two while the children described it and she made a drawing of it, than if it were killed and pinned up in a glass case. In time, the children themselves drew their specimens from life and Anna in particular proved to be a gifted artist. She could use this talent only in making drawings and watercolours in the process of her education, according to Quaker teaching, which remained sternly suspicious of all creativity.

Their father, absent though he was for most of their early years, brought back seashells if his travels had taken him to the coast and, when they could afford it, Mary took the children by horse tram to the British Museum to identify their finds. In this constant study of the natural world, Anna was also taught by her aunt Anne, who she spent time with on her many visits to the family farm in Norfolk and who also wrote letters to both Anna and Philip. Anne Wright, called Aunt Wright by the children, was married to Mary's brother John, who had inherited the larger family farm at Buxton after his own father's financial crash. John Wright the elder, Anna's grandfather, still lived in the cottage on the estate and was a great favourite with the children.

Aunt Wright had no children of her own. She was a charming, vivacious woman without whom, in her neighbourhood, 'no party was complete', and she was known throughout her community for 'Mrs Wright's Stories', the tales she made up to amuse her pupils. When her frail health permitted, she worked as a teacher, in later years at The Red House Reformatory School, set up by her husband to provide free education for poor boys in the area and which was to become as much a part of the family's heritage as the farm itself. Anna no doubt had the same pupils on her mind when she wrote *Black Beauty* which, as its subtitle *His Grooms and Companions* promises, is richly peopled with stable boys, grooms, coachmen, ostlers and cabmen whose progress through life is recorded with as much empathy as that of the horses. The Red House boys, sent to the school as an alternative to prison after they had been convicted of minor crimes, were trained for most of these jobs and the book is an excellent guide to horse-mastership.

Mary Sewell recalled that Aunt Wright:

> Enchanted children, instructing them with the utmost simplicity. She could interest a company of children anywhere; her interest

> and affection flowed out to them so intensely that she never felt the burden of self-consciousness and the plentiful store of her imagination always seemed within reach.[10]

The two women taught children about nature so that they would learn to understand, respect and protect wild things. During her bouts of illness, Aunt Wright continued to pass on her passion for the natural world in letters to Anna and Philip. In a few years, these letters would be collected into a book and Anne Wright would briefly hold the title of the most celebrated author in the family, but in Anna's childhood she was simply one of the many fascinations of her mother's family farm.

The 'Christmas Hamper from Buxton' arrived every year. The excited children stood by as it was opened, greeting every carefully labelled package with shrieks of delight. Their Christmas presents were not toys, however, but food from the farm to help out in those lean times. Their grandmother sent ducks, sausages and mince pies, while apples, pears and walnuts came from their grandfather. The labels read 'for my dear boy' and 'for my little maid', and the much-needed food parcels were accompanied by letters from all the family.[11]

The farm was a permanent source of happiness and abundance. In her early childhood, Anna and Philip were sent there for holidays and called it 'the Paradise of children'.[12] When Mary could save the money for the coach fare, she and her children made the long journey up the Great North Road, which followed the route of the Roman Ermine Street. The railway that would eventually link London and Norwich was not begun until 1839, so they travelled by stagecoach. Four or six heavy horses pulled these coaches over the unmade roads, carrying five people inside and as many as could hang on outside, with luggage strapped to the roof. At the front, a coachman drove the team and next to him sat a guard to protect them all. They travelled as fast as 12 miles per hour and each 'stage' was 10 or 15 miles at a steady trot, with stops only for toll booths. At each stage the tired horses would be unharnessed, stabled and rested for a day, while a new team was hitched and the journey continued.

It was at the farm at Buxton that Anna learned to ride and drive horses. Aunt Wright was famously, perhaps notoriously, a fearless coachwoman and went out in all weather in her pony and chaise, without even a groom as escort to help her open gates. Anna's first rides were on the patient farm horses, far too large for a child to control, but while she was learning, her grandfather or uncle would have led them. Anna and Philip were also taught to care for animals, to help with hay nets and water buckets, to groom their coats, pick out their feet, wash and polish their harnesses and give them the benefit of blankets in winter. The family encouraged physical as well as mental courage in the children.

The only shadow that crossed Anna's life in this period was an accident in which she dislocated her elbow. This is a common childhood injury but with her it took unexpectedly long to heal. The pain was extreme but 'I bored it well,' she told her aunt proudly and was praised for her 'cheerful, patient courage'.[13]

Anna also learned to keep bees, something that gave her delight throughout her life. Bee-keeping was considered a good occupation for a woman and a leading expert in the field, Samuel Bagster Jr, in his book *The Management of Bees with a Description of the Ladies' Safety Hive* (1834), was to propose a custom beehive design for women and also men who preferred not to be stung. This, his own invention, Bagster introduced with a poem:

> Let not my love disdain these truths to hear
> Which please alike the learned and the fair:
> ...
> But these pursuits will honeyed fragrance bring
> Without the danger of the treacherous sting.[14]

The children learned to swim at Buxton, where the River Bure meanders slowly though the fields, and were given as much freedom as possible, something Mary believed was important in fostering independence and courage. Philip also learned to shoot, not to equip him to take part in the mass slaughter of specially bred game birds which was becoming an entertainment for rich landowners, but to be useful in the 'rough' shooting to control the predators that menaced the farm livestock and which were called 'garden thieves', such as magpies, crows and foxes. Shooting for pleasure was something the family detested and Anna's earliest recorded words were prompted by a man who shot a blackbird near their house. The dead bird fell into their front garden. 'The man came to the gate to get possession of it,' her mother remembered. 'Anna rushed to the door. With an obsequious smile, the man said, "If you please, Miss, will you let me take my bird?" "No," she said, "thee cruel man, thee shan't have it at all."'[15]

Here and for the rest of her life Anna used 'thee' and 'thou', the Quaker form of address, which was the normal mode of speech when the movement was founded in the seventeenth century. As spoken English evolved, people started to use the second-person plural 'you' and 'yours' when talking to one person, instead of the singular 'thou', 'thee' and 'thine'. The early Quakers found this new plural form too fancy and grandiose, so stuck with 'thee', even though, by Anna's time, they were absurdly quaint to non-Quaker ears. 'Thee' and 'thou' also preserved the language of the King James Bible, giving ordinary conversation a religious tone.

The nature walk was an institution in Anna's little family. Her mother believed that being in the natural world would:

> bring bloom to the cheeks of the little ones and sunshine to their spirits. These would be the days which [they] would look back upon in after life. They would remember them as festivals when they sat upon the green grass under the spreading trees ... making all kinds of discoveries among things whose beauty never wears out. It was through the beauty of nature that God spoke first spoke to my own heart when I was a child of not more than four years old ... When children have once got hold of Nature ... they want no toys.[16]

She gave an illustration of what she meant, suggesting that children should take 'a little basket' on these walks to bring back 'treasures for examination'. As an example, she suggested that if they found a bird's nest – meaning one from an earlier year that had fallen out of a tree, rather than depriving the nesting bird – it could be brought home to study in a practical experiment, with teaching materials collected on their excursion:

> What little things will make fairy days of enjoyment for children. Take two intelligent little children who have been accustomed to prove all things as far as they can, and give them a chaffinch's nest and a summer afternoon to collect materials similar to those of which it is composed, and then try their skill at making one … Imagine the delight of that search for wool, moss, hair, grass, etcetera; fancy the many thoughts that will occur to them … life may have many joys afterwards, but that long summer afternoon will stand out radiant amongst them. And then the nest-making – the ineffectual attempts, the bungling performance, and then a lesson upon the exquisite faculty of instinct preparing the way for a hundred thousand more.[17]

The time came, however, when seashells and birds' nests had provided Anna and her brother with all the learning they could extract from raw nature and Mary wanted to buy them books. Although Isaac was working long hours, his wages had not increased and the household budget would not stretch to books for the children. Mary's solution was to write a book herself, based on her nature walks and devised with words of one syllable only, so children themselves would readily read them.

She sold *Walks with Mama* for £3 – about £300 at today's value – 'a little fortune to me then'. It was published in 1824 and was one of the first cloth-bound books for children. Her publisher, based in Norwich, was Jarrold & Sons, making it one of the very first books from a publishing house that, fifty years later, was later to see its fortunes transformed by the success of *Black Beauty*. In 1824, when Anna Sewell was 4 years old and her mother was desperate to buy books for her, the firm of Jarrold's was a former agricultural merchant which had newly moved to Norwich and diversified into book publishing. It was undoubtedly through the Quaker network in which her family was so prominent that Mary made contact with them.

The company that was to play such a central role in *Black Beauty*'s success began life in 1770 as a grocer and draper in the little market town of Woodbridge in Suffolk. The founder, John Jarrold I, was of French

Huguenot stock – his Protestant forefathers had immigrated to England a century earlier and the family firm would remain friendly to religious dissenters ever afterwards.

Early in the nineteenth century the company diversified into farming, but the collapse of food prices in 1815 prompted the founder's son, John Jarrold II, to expand his business into printing. By 1823 he had decided to leave sleepy Woodbridge and move to Norwich, a busy, bustling and cosmopolitan city. John Jarrold II set up as a bookseller, publisher and printer at 3 Cockey Lane (now London Street), opposite the firm's present premises and around the corner from the Quaker meeting house on Goat's Lane. Mary Sewell, the eager young Quakeress with extensive local connectionsand a passion for teaching children, could have been his ideal debut author, given that all her extended family shared her interests and were ready to buy her first book.

Mary did not buy dreary textbooks with her earnings. Instead she chose from the output of Maria Edgeworth, one of the most famous authors of the day, who was to have a decisive effect on Mary's subsequent writing and on Anna's education. Maria Edgeworth was an Irish novelist who was as popular as Fanny Burney or Jane Austen in the early decades of the nineteenth century and at the height of her success outsold Sir Walter Scott.[18]

Jane Austen herself inserted Edgeworth's 1803 novel *Belinda* in a tart exchange in *Northanger Abbey* (written in 1803 but not published until 1817). The heroine protests ironically, when asked what she is reading, 'Oh, it is only a novel … It is only Cecilia or Camilla, or *Belinda*; or, in short, only some work in which the greatest powers of the mind are displayed …'

Edgeworth's first novel, *Castle Rackrent* (1800), would have been among the volumes of forbidden fruit from the library which lured the teenage Mary Sewell away from the dreary volumes approved by the Quakers. It is a subversive story that satirises the failures of English absentee landlords in Ireland and, for all its sparkling humour, is an overtly political work that appeared as the Acts of Union, which added Ireland to the United Kingdom, passed into law. She followed quickly with the three-volume *Belinda*, a 'society novel' with a spirited 17-year-old heroine that nevertheless portrayed mixed-race relationships in subplots, although they were subsequently censored by Edgeworth's father.

Maria Edgeworth was the second of twenty-two children born to her father, Richard Lovell Edgeworth. An inventor and founder of the Royal Irish Academy as well as a wealthy landowner, he had four wives, only one of whom outlived him. Maria herself was childless and, after her fiancé was executed as a spy, devoted her life to the care and education of her half-siblings.

Her first book, which Mary Sewell eagerly bought as soon as she could afford it, was *Practical Education* (1798), a pragmatic, Rousseau-inspired manual for home-schooling parents written jointly with her father. Edgeworth *père et fille* proposed that educators should 'adapt both the curriculum and methods of teaching to the needs of the child; the endeavour to explain moral habits and the learning process through associationism; and most important, the effort to entrust the child with the responsibility for his [*sic*] own mental culture'. This chimed exactly with Mary Sewell's own impulse to foster independence of mind and spirit in her children.

Maria Edgeworth was to have a decisive influence on both Anna and Mary Sewell as writers-to-be. She was prolific and her literary output extraordinarily diverse. While Mary Sewell readily absorbed the advice in *Practical Education*, Anna and Philip grew up reading Edgeworth's books for the young, intended for 'innocent amusement and early instruction'.[19] These, even more than her adult fiction, were vividly charming but still didactic and moralistic collections of lively tales in which bad manners, selfishness and pride were always the downfall of their characters while honesty and hard work were rewarded.

The little family absorbed not only the lessons of the books themselves but also the template created by their author, of entertaining stories drawn from real life which educated their willing readers almost by stealth. This model informed *Black Beauty*, although Anna's highly creative approach was far more subtle than Edgeworth's. The same model was to evolve and endure in the work of the greatest children's writers of succeeding centuries, including Enid Blyton, Malorie Blackman and J.K. Rowling.

On Anna's 9th birthday, her mother wrote a portrait of her, which Mrs Bayly, Mary Sewell's biographer, quoted, adding annotations of her own:

'Anna Sewell has this day completed her ninth year, and is in many respects a delight and comfort to her mother, who, that she may be able to test her progress from year to year, wishes now to write a short account of her attainments and her learning, and of the qualities of her mind, etcetera.'

There follow entire approbation of her truth and candour, and her progress in some branches of learning. But the mother, with her intense love, has withal a high standard of perfection, not easily satisfied. She goes on to speak of Anna's want of persevering industry.

'Much disposed to idle over lessons and work. She needs to get the habit of a cheerful surrender of her own will – to give up entirely telling tales of her brother. She begins to be useful to her mother but is not tidy. In everything her mother hopes she will be improved in another year.'[20]

Mrs Bayly, writing in 1888, four years after Mary's death, describes patiently putting into order the 'old, faded papers, looking as if they had not seen the light for many a long day' and searching for the birthday memories for succeeding years, which were shorter and increasingly critical of both the children. Through the double layer of interpretation, we can see Anna as a girl with an independent mind and a strong will who nevertheless enjoyed an exceptionally close bond with her demanding mother.

Philip, her brother, was not spared either, although he appears to have been an absolutely normal boy of about 7. In many families of the time, the only son would have been treated exceptionally, but on the evidence recorded it seems he was regarded simply as the less interesting younger sibling.

More persevering in play than in work: he has an awkward habit of repeating what other people say; can neither sit nor stand still; takes no pains to speak distinctly. Altogether he is a nice little boy and his mother hopes that by this day twelvemonths he will have lost all his bad habits and increased his good ones.[21]

Mary Sewell also responded to the rebellious streak in Maria Edgeworth's writing, her robust challenges to educational orthodoxy and her bold political intent, which were voiced at a time long before women could vote or hold public office and when women were publicly criticised for any evidence of political thought. Although, as Anna witnessed, the family 'read Mama's Bible every day to make us good', and the family also attended one, and sometimes two, Quaker meetings every Sunday, she clearly felt the need for more than Christian orthodoxy in developing her children's minds.

After their move to London, Mary and Isaac Sewell first attended the Gracechurch Street Meeting of the Religious Society of Friends, where they shared their silent meditations with some of the most illustrious members of the group. Gracechurch Street is in the City, only ten minutes' walk away from the shop in Camomile Street. London was home to the largest community of Quakers in Britain and once a year they convened at Gracechurch Street for the Annual Meeting, a social as well as a spiritual event. 'Many parties were made up for visiting exhibitions of painting, and other London sights ... It had the feeling of a great family meeting ... Many of the rich Friends kept open house,' Mary remembered, 'and invited large companies to dinner between the meetings. Mildred Court, where Elizabeth Fry presided, was very popular.'[22]

Mildred Court was a huge turreted mansion on the street called The Poultry, but the generous hospitality of Elizabeth and Joseph Fry was soon to be curtailed as Britain descended further into financial crisis. W.S. Fry, the bank founded by Joseph, had twice been saved by his wife's family, the Gurneys, but they would not step in a third time. The bank failed and in 1829 Joseph was judged to have fallen short of the scrupulous standards required of a Quaker and was disowned by the society. The couple had to sell Mildred Court and moved with their ten children to The Cedars on Upton Lane in West Ham, about 5 miles to the east of the Sewells in Dalston.

When Anna and her family first moved to Dalston, they travelled to Gracechurch Street for Sunday meetings by a horse-drawn coach hired for the purpose. A Quaker school for girls opened in 1824 and four years later a new meeting house was built a few miles to the north of Dalston, in Stoke Newington, with almshouses for poor elderly women alongside. The journey to Gracechurch Street was no longer necessary and the route of the horse-drawn coach which had bussed in Quakers from the eastern suburbs became the route of London's first horse-drawn tram.

The congregation at Stoke Newington was almost as illustrious as that at Gracechurch Street, and included the banker Samuel Hoare of Paradise Row (Stoke Newington Church Street), whose son Jonathan built Clissold House, and William Allen, a wealthy chemist, educator and philanthropist. The hero of the abolitionist movement, William Wilberforce, was so taken with the leafy tranquillity of the area and the simple, neoclassical meeting house that he asked to be buried there. Wilberforce's wish was not granted and he lies in Westminster Abbey, but his sister is buried at Stoke Newington.[23]

Wilberforce's visits were an indication of how dominant the Quaker community was in the movement to abolish slavery. The Quakers had led in this campaign in Britain from its outset, setting up their first abolitionist organisation in 1783 and forming the majority of Wilberforce's Committee for the Abolition of the Slave Trade, formed in 1787. Their activism, lobbying and raising of public support had led to the Slave Trade Act 1807 and the Slave Trade Felony Act of 1811, which banned the trade – though not the ownership – of enslaved people throughout the British Empire. There was then considerable pushback from the plantation owners in America and by the time Anna Sewell was born it was becoming clear that the campaigners' belief that slavery would die out if no more enslaved people were transported had been optimistic.

The impetus in the movement, the final push for the abolition of slavery in every form, spread out into women's groups, inspired by the critic of Smithfield Market, Elizabeth Heyrick, a convert to Quakerism and one of the most prominent activists of her day. In 1824 Heyrick wrote and published a pamphlet, *Immediate, not Gradual Abolition*.[24] She advocated civil activism, the boycott of sugar and cotton that had been produced by slave labour. She also believed that women had an important part to play in opposing slavery as they were able 'not only to sympathise with suffering, but also to plead for the oppressed'. Since women were so often the primary educators of their children, they could also spread the abolitionist message to rising generations.

Amelia Opie, a fashionable novelist who was a close friend of the Gurney family, put her literary career behind her when she was received into membership of the Society of Friends in 1825[25] and immediately wrote an illustrated poem for children, *The Black Man's Lament*, which Anna would certainly have read during her childhood. Simple as the verses are, they are absolutely direct in their presentation of the reality of an enslaved person's life:

There is a beauteous plant that grows
In western India's sultry clime,
Which makes, alas! the Black man's woes,
And also makes the White man's crime.

For know, its tall gold stems contain
A sweet rich juice, which White men prize;
And that they may this sugar gain,
The Negro toils, and bleeds, and dies.

But, Negro slave! thyself shall tell,
Of past and present wrongs the story;
And would all British hearts could feel,
To end those wrongs were Britain's glory.

Elizabeth Heyrick became a founding member of the Birmingham Ladies Society for the Relief of Negro Slaves in 1825 and, despite Wilberforce's misgivings about them, women's groups quickly sprang up all over Britain, including in Dalston which Mary Sewell enthusiastically joined and where she had her first taste of activism.

Quaker meetings were mostly, but not completely, silent. At the beginning of the meeting, an extract from the Bible was often read and also perhaps one of the 'Queries', a series of questions devised by the movement's elders to prompt meditation on the congregation's faith and practice. Supporting people in poverty and opposing slavery were among Queries current during Anna's childhood. Query No. 10 demanded, 'Are the necessities of the poor among you properly inspected and remedied, and good care taken of the education of their offspring?'[26] As children were always included in meetings, Anna would have heard this question and perhaps answered it silently for herself. Mary Sewell and Maria Edgeworth were both in agreement that children should not be left to the care of nursemaids but included in all the life of a household. So Anna was aware from earliest childhood of her mother's activism.

Mary continued to visit the poor and recalled later in her life calling on a desperate young mother who had pawned her shawl to pay her rent and could only fantasise about having a stove, hot food and water. She also started a local campaign to help the boys doing the dangerous, unhealthy and often deadly work of sweeping chimneys, another abuse that Charles Dickens highlighted in *Oliver Twist*, which first appeared as a magazine serial from 1837 onwards, some years after Mary stepped in to save boy chimney sweeps in Dalston.

Oliver narrowly avoids being apprenticed to a sweep when the magistrate deciding his fate discovers that the man 'did happen to labour under the slight imputation of having bruised three or four boys to death already'. These children, often orphans like Oliver, were bought by the sweep from a workhouse under the false offer of an apprenticeship. They were lowered into chimneys to sweep out the soot, and died of suffocation or lung disease.

Mary Sewell discovered that it was possible to clean a chimney using a long, flexible brush instead of a child, but this new equipment was too expensive for the local chimney sweep to buy. Mary then went round her neighbourhood knocking on doors and managed to collect the £10 that was necessary to buy their local sweep a longer brush.

When Anna was 9, as Mary recalled, an appeal for poor people in Ireland reached their local meeting. She wanted to contribute to the fundraising campaign for them but the only money they had was what she had managed to save for a seaside holiday. Although they had been looking forward to the trip for weeks and talking of little else, the children readily agreed to donate their holiday money to the cause.

This is a story worthy of Louisa May Alcott's *Little Women*, who unhesitatingly donate their Christmas breakfast to the poorest family in their neighbourhood. While it is not unthinkable that Mary Sewell could have embellished her memory of Anna's childhood, her daughter was 9 in 1829 and the first Irish Potato Famine struck in 1845, when she was 25 and the Sewells were living on the coast at Brighton. Ireland's tiny Quaker community made extraordinary efforts, from running soup kitchens to setting up model farms, to help people during the famine, which today would be classified as a humanitarian disaster, and in which a million people died and the same number were forced to leave their native country as refugees. Mary Sewell's recollection was no doubt related to an appeal launched sixteen years earlier. In the event, her children's sacrifice was rewarded by coincidence as their uncle William, Mary's husband's brother, paid for the family to have a seaside holiday at the village of Sandgate, near Folkestone in Kent, although he was unaware of their donation.

William Sewell, Anna's uncle, had gone into banking and was doing well. Towards the end of Anna's years in Dalston, her father was able to give up his ill-paid and demanding job as a travelling salesman and join his brother as his assistant. He earned more and worked shorter hours, and an end to the years of 'strict economy' seemed to be in sight.

Mary Sewell also recalled doing 'a good deal of visiting the poor' during the Dalston years, and also, following the example of Elizabeth Fry, visiting at the prison in Shoreditch.[27] London at this time was a teeming, chaotic megapolis more like a supercity in today's developing world than any modern European capital. The 1830s were known as the 'age of reform' in which many organisations, both in and outside government, addressed the intensifying social problems of the country. George Eliot wrote of the optimism that characterised the early part of the century, 'those times when reforms were begun with a young hopefulness of immediate good', in the finale of the novel *Middlemarch*. In the political sphere, the poor were completely marginalised.

The Representation of the People Act of 1832, called the first Reform Act, finally broke the link between property ownership and the vote, extending the franchise to 'ten pound householders', meaning men paying £10 or more in rent, which still excluded more than half the population. Ten pounds a year was well beyond the means of a manual worker whose annual average wage would be between £20 and £40 for a family.

The Sewell family in their daily lives could not have avoided the tragic effects of the poverty that existed all around them. Dalston bordered the East End of the city, which had a long association with its poorest people and worst living conditions, and these had only intensified with industrialisation. The Poverty Maps created by a late Victorian reformer, Charles Booth, which colour areas of extreme poverty black and grey, show the entire eastern swathe of the city, from the Thames to the southern half of Hackney, in dark colours with substantial pockets between the more comfortable streets further north.

This deprivation had deep, historic roots. Because the prevailing wind in the south of England is from the west, and the River Thames flows eastwards, industries that generated pollution and foul smells, such as tanning and fulling (wool preparation), had long been established on the eastern edge of the old city. The poorest of the poor lived there and the opening of the London Docks in 1801 only increased the proportion who were casual, unskilled workers. Every ounce of cargo collected at the dockside to distribute throughout the country was, of course, carried away by horses, many of whom were as half-starved as their owners.

In his famous collection of essays, *London Labour and the London Poor* (1851), the journalist Henry Mayhew described the environment:

> roads were unmade, often mere alleys, houses small and without foundations, subdivided and often around unpaved courts. An almost total lack of drainage and sewerage was made worse by the ponds formed by the excavation of brickearth. Pigs and cows in back yards, noxious trades like boiling tripe, melting tallow, or preparing cat's meat, and slaughter houses, dustheaps, and 'lakes of putrefying night soil' added to the filth.[28]

The new-built streets of Dalston and Hackney were dotted with institutions set up to help and house the homeless and destitute, some funded by the parishes and others run by religious or philanthropic institutions, the Quakers among them. The Quaker meeting house on Park Road had a much larger block of almshouses for the poor beside it. The parish workhouses, where the most desperate were sheltered and put to work breaking stones or picking apart old ropes for use in caulking ships, were often deliberately run to offer only the barest chance of survival, lest they become a softer option than life outside. In his novel *Oliver Twist*, Charles Dickens portrayed the board of governors as they 'established the rule, that all poor people should have the alternative … of being starved by a gradual process in the house, or by a quick one out of it'.[29] The death rate within their walls was astounding and in addition workhouses usually separated couples and broke up families as a deliberate disincentive to those who needed help. Young as she was, Anna could not have avoided the sight of people dying of malnutrition in the open street, the death that Dickens depicted for Oliver's mother. The coach that took the Sewell family to the Gracechurch Street meeting followed a route through areas of severe deprivation. She was never shielded from the harsh truths of poverty and gained a deep understanding of the desperate lives led by millions all around her.

Some years after Anna and her family left Dalston, a couple living only a few streets from their former home were prosecuted for child neglect. The starving family was found with their dead and dying children on Christmas Eve 1855. The father, a casually employed bricklayer, had been imprisoned for child neglect before and the family had been separated in different workhouses. He and his partner – the biological mother of the children was presumed dead – lived in one room with a single mattress. While the father struggled to find work, they had begged help from the Hackney Workhouse and were finally given two loaves and some oatmeal on condition the whole family came to the workhouse the next day. They never arrived. When his children started dying, their father asked his landlady for help. She found that the children 'were quite skeletons – there were not any bedclothes, there was a thin covering over their faces'. Reporting to the court when the father and his partner were prosecuted, a South Hackney surgeon described finding the 9-year-old daughter cradling a baby in her arms and two other children, aged 5 and 7, lying dead or dying in the corner. In his report of the post-mortem examination of the children, he stated: 'I found all the organs of the body quite healthy, except that they were entirely devoid of fat – there was no fat about the body at all – I found no food of any kind in the stomach.'[30]

In years to come, Mrs Sewell would mine her memories of visiting the poor to urge her more comfortable readers to join the great groundswell of determination to go beyond the bread grudgingly given out at the workhouse door and rebuild society itself to support even its most vulnerable members. Social reform was the true passion of her life, and one that Anna would grow up to share. Unlike her mother, however, she embedded political ideas in her book and, without naming names or parties, made her political allegiance clear.

4

Troubled Waters (1832–36)

Anna was about 12 years old when her father at last recovered from the disastrous beginning of his business career and became a junior banker, working with his brother, William. Unfortunately, he did not seem to have taken in the essential lessons of his early business failures. As soon as his earnings increased, he began to exhibit the eccentric optimism that was to lead him into further errors of judgement and his family into more precarious financial situations and consequent anxiety.

Isaac was described by his son as a man with 'a very lovable nature, with a keen sense of humour'.[1] Although Mary Sewell never pretended that her marriage was a love match, she accepted her husband's authority as the head of the family without question. Isaac had good qualities. Mary described him as 'unselfish' and 'exceedingly kind and patient',[2] a man who was never censorious and seemed to have inherited nothing of his own father's stern nature, who always respected her concerns and took time to talk through her anxieties with her.

His grandchildren – Philip was to have a large family – remember him as a delightful old man who was always happy to play with them, dream up little games and imagine little fantasies to make the most ordinary aspects of life entertaining, such as putting little pieces of cheese on biscuits and calling them riders on horses, and making them gallop over the kitchen table.[3] With adults he was genial and tolerant: 'Never bigoted or pronouncing harsh judgment on others, his spirit was truly catholic and charitable.'[4] Loyally, Philip also described his father as a 'shrewd man of business',[5] but the evidence of Isaac's career does not really prove that. Without the support of the Quaker network, the family's fortunes would have been miserable. In his adult life, Philip was to surpass his father considerably as a businessman.

The downside of Isaac's benevolent nature was that he often took an unwisely rosy view of his own situation. No sooner was he established in his new career than he decided that the family should move to a bigger house. And not just a bigger house, but one that was half-ruined and needed substantial restoration to make it habitable. As Mary was to observe, he 'delighted in places which afforded scope for alteration and improvement'.[6] He discovered Palatine Cottage, a neglected building that had once been the coach house and stables of the much larger Palatine House, a gracious little mansion in Stoke Newington, an area a little closer to the city centre than Dalston. Palatine Cottage (now confusingly Palatine House) and Palatine Road still survive. The name was given to them in the eighteenth century because the area became home to the refugees from the region of west Germany known as the Palatinate. Many thousands had fled the invading French and settled here, some before moving on to the New World. In London they were called the 'Poor Palatines', while in the New World they became the 'Pennsylvania Dutch'. Many buildings in the area were first constructed to house them, while others, including Palatine House and its gatehouse, were built by wealthy businessmen. Mary remembered the family's first sight of it:

> I shall never forget the morning when [he] first took us to see it. The traces were there of what had been beautiful when cared for; it was now quite ruinous. A broad, straight piece of water, in which goldfish were swimming, divided the garden from the meadow; the old damask rose was growing wild; there was a fine acacia and a tulip tree besides walnut, apple, pear and plum trees. I and the children were almost beside ourselves with delight.[7]

One of Isaac's uncles, also named Philip Sewell, lent the family the money to restore the house and after six months of rebuilding walls and making good the worm-eaten woodwork, Anna and her family moved into their 'very pretty and pleasant home'.[8]

Palatine Cottage also came with 4 acres of land and Isaac's idea was that the family could make money by establishing a smallholding. The prettiness of the tumbledown old coach house and this enticing potential of returning to their farming heritage enchanted them all.

A letter from Anna to her grandfather, written when she was 12, describes her organised approach to keeping chickens: 'My hens have layed [*sic*] exceedingly well. I keep a regular account so that I know who is the best, and how many eggs I have, one hen began to lay before Christmas.' It is clear from the rest of the letter that, young as she was, Anna considered her chickens to be contributors to the family budget.[9]

Mary, meanwhile, had resolved to keep cows and sell their milk. Even the prospect of starting a dairy seemed romantic and entirely suitable for a young wife. Since time immemorial, there had been a traditional association of women with dairying in farms and this persisted even in Regency London,[10] where dairymaids were a common sight leading their animals through the streets and an established dairy farm sold milk direct to customers at the heart of the most exclusive neighbourhood in St James's Park, one of the Royal Parks whose green fields bordered the walls of Buckingham Palace. Cow-keepers' shops had been a feature of city life since the late seventeenth century and a contemporary drawing shows one in a terrace of shops, designed with a clean, tiled dairy at the front storing fresh milk in metal churns, with a sales counter at one side and a shop window displaying butter, cheese and other produce for sale. At the rear of the building were stalls for one or two cows and hay and feed was stored in the basement.[11]

Not that Mary planned to do all the milking herself, although she soon found herself churning butter after she realised that the family budget would not stretch to indoor help. Her son Philip 'often milked a cow'[12] and loved seeing the milk measured out in the morning, but the Sewells employed a couple to look after the cows and help generally with the smallholding that they rapidly established. The 4 acres soon welcomed pigs, ducks, hens and rabbits, and Anna was able to set up her own beehives – probably the traditional domed skleps made of coiled straw.

There was money to send the children to school, too, and it had arrived at exactly the moment when their young minds were ready for intellectual space and a wider circle of friends, so they were eager pupils. Philip had been first sent to Hackney Grammar School and now moved to the Quaker school in Stoke Newington where French was taught, but only to older boys. Philip immediately memorised La Fontaine's fables in order to persuade the teachers to let him join the senior class.

Anna went to a local day school that was relatively close to their new home and her world expanded dramatically. It seems likely that this was not a Quaker establishment because her curiosity was clearly no longer imprisoned by Quaker suspicions of creativity and her mother's limited horizons. She too learned French easily, discovering a gift for languages that was to add to her independence in a few more years. Her artistic talent was free at last, and she learned to paint in oils. The Quaker ruling was that this was a dangerous indulgence of the imagination – drawing and painting in watercolour as an aid to scientific study were all that was sanctioned. For the rest of her life she was an accomplished artist whose paintings were cherished within her family.

A likely product of her art lessons was the picture of her in this book. It has the direct gaze of a self-portrait, and it is hard to imagine a category of painting less likely to find approval with the Society of Friends. The portrait is of a clear-eyed young woman with a bold, independent stare and a firm nose and chin. She isn't noticeably thin, which suggests that it was done before her weight became a source of anxiety. Her dark auburn hair curls strongly away from a wide forehead, and it has not yet been tamed into the ringlets of her later portraits.

This suggests that she was still a girl, only just considered to be of marriageable age. Throughout the nineteenth century, and into the twentieth until women began to wear short hair in the 1920s, a girl would 'put up her hair' to mark her transition to womanhood and consequent marriageability. The girl's long hair was literally pinned up in a chignon and, in Anna's time, styled with ringlets around the face. Quaker women, in addition, covered their hair with a bonnet similar to those worn today in Amish or Shaker communities. But in this portrait Anna's hair is a tomboyish mop, which gives us a clue to her age and suggests she was in early adolescence at the latest. In Jane Austen's

Northanger Abbey (1817), for example, Catherine Morland is 15 years old when she puts up her hair.[13] In the portrait, Anna is wearing the traditional Quaker costume for women and girls: a pleated, wide-necked dress which she probably made herself.[14] The colour is dark green – the preferred colour was grey, but many Quaker women interpreted this prescription widely. Some people considered the Quaker costume attractive despite the fact that it was intended as an antidote to both vanity and lust. Amelia Opie favoured a lavender silk gown worn with a lace and muslin bonnet and was admired as a great beauty despite the utilitarian design of the garment.[14]

Mary and Isaac Sewell were 32 and 36 respectively when they moved to Palatine Cottage with their children, ages considered mature at the time but which still marked them down as a young couple with more enthusiasm than experience in the world. Trouble very swiftly came to their door. The husband and wife who they had employed to care for the cows, milk them, measure the milk and then load it on to a cart and deliver it around the neighbourhood were dishonest. Cow-keeping was in any case not a guarantee of financial success and about a fifth of London's cow-keepers ran into difficulties.[15] Perhaps this couple had lost their own business through poor management and had been forced to find employment but harboured resentment against their unwary employers. Mary noted that 'the cows were not very remunerative' and accepted the woman's assurance that she had allowed customers credit and expected them to settle their accounts in due course. She did not immediately worry but as time passed and no payments were forthcoming she began innocently to wonder if all was well with her customers.

The majority of the people who bought milk from the Sewells were, of course, fellow Quakers, about whose honesty there could be no question. One Sunday after a meeting, Mary got up the courage to mention payment to one of them and discovered that 'her account had always been kept close paid up'. She asked others and 'found the same story'. The couple had been cheating her, charging the customers and pocketing the money themselves. To make things worse, Mary must have hinted at her suspicions because the swindling pair 'decamped, leaving not a trace behind them'.[16]

Worse was soon to befall the household. Anna was a 'day boarder' at her school, which meant she stayed there for lunch and returned home in the late afternoon after lessons were finished. One afternoon she was caught in the rain on the way home. She had no umbrella or other protection from the downpour and so ran as fast as she could to get home before she was soaked to the skin. Palatine Cottage was entered from the garden gate, down a sloping lane at the side of the main house. Here Anna slipped on some wet leaves and fell.

Her mother could never forget the event that was to limit the rest of Anna's life. 'I can scarcely bear, even now, to recall the beginning of this life of constant frustration,' she wrote, after her daughter's death. 'Just as she reached the gate she fell and sprained her ankle. It was a very bad sprain. She called out, and I helped her indoors, little thinking that henceforth her dear life was to be coloured by this event.'[17]

A sprained ankle is an excruciatingly painful injury. Having both sprained and broken bones in this joint, in my own experience the sprain was more painful than the fracture, although the joint will not bear weight in either case. Once indoors and out of the rain, Anna would have had to rest with her leg up but, as a sprain will heal itself in time, and medical attention was expensive, Mary did not immediately call a doctor. If she had, he might well have made things worse. Medicine in this era was almost entirely a male field and was a science in its infancy at a time long before modern diagnostic aids. A fracture would not be suspected unless the broken ends of the bone had pierced the skin, or unless handling the limb produced decrepitation, the sinister feeling or sound of the broken surfaces of the bone grinding together. X-rays were not discovered until the end of the nineteenth century and not used clinically until 1896, so at the time of Anna's accident the only way to make a diagnosis of her injury was by looking at her ankle, touching and manipulating it.

So what had happened? Later in Anna's life she had periods in which she could walk and ride almost normally, although these grew fewer and shorter after her twenties. At other times, she could only manage a few steps and sometimes could not walk at all. She often had pain in her injured foot, and sometimes in her good foot as well, perhaps because she inevitably favoured it. In addition, she was to experience a serious and debilitating illness as a young woman, which may have been unrelated. Initially, she was in pain and unable to walk after her fall, and all agreed that she had injured her ankle.

The ankle joint, which normally can bear the whole weight of the body, is composed of three bones – the tibia, the larger of the leg bones; the fibula, which is the thinner leg bone; and the talus, the foot's knucklebone, which is thick and flat. A network of seven ligaments binds the joint together and also connects it to the heel bone, the calcaneus. The ligaments attach to knobby protrusions of the bones, called malleoli. In an adolescent, the cartilage covering the bone ends would still have been forming, the ligaments would have been relatively soft and the whole joint, particularly in a girl, would have been much more supple than that of an adult.

The most common ankle fracture is of the lower end of the fibula, with damage to the end of the tibia also common. These breaks in the long leg bones would probably have been diagnosed, however, as the broken ends of the bone would have been evident. It is also common for one or more of the malleoli to shear off, leaving a ligament torn or unattached, but this would not have healed without setting and splinting.

Ankle injuries can be complex, with multiple fractures and loose bone fragments. Damaged ligaments can compound the problem. Less common but a good candidate for Anna's injury is a fracture of the talus bone. This is typically the result of considerable force, such as a fall or car accident, but is also seen in snowboarding and other dynamic sports. Both the long bones of the leg are connected to the talus, which bears the whole weight of the body on occasion. It has a humped shape like a long narrow turtle, and most commonly breaks at its narrowest point, known as the neck.

Because this bone has a poor blood supply, it is often slow to heal. Without trained medical attention and a definitive diagnosis prompting those caring for Anna to immobilise her ankle, a broken talus would not only have healed slowly but probably with some distortion, known as a malunion. This would have been less stable than the natural joint, and so liable to break again. Untreated, a talus fracture can also lead to the death of the bone, or to arthritis in the joint and difficulty in walking. Bone spurs could also develop after an injury and in time the dead bone becomes brittle and can break again, leaving the injured person unable to walk and in considerable pain. Given Anna's lifelong disability, a fractured talus bone that healed badly and perhaps even succumbed to necrosis seems a strong possibility.

If diagnosis was difficult, much conventional medical treatment of the time was absolutely misguided and this too was something that affected Anna's long-term health. While most authorities did advise rest, they often also suggested pouring hot water on the injury or applying a hot poultice to stimulate the circulation – the opposite of modern treatment which favours ice to reduce swelling and inflammation. Then, as now, the injured limb was often strapped up in a supportive bandage or even splinted. As a countrywoman, Mary would have been familiar with herbs considered to have healing properties for sprains and fractures, such as comfrey, whose folk-name is 'knitbone', mare's tail, a common weed, and arnica, derived from sunflowers. Doctors would also advised more exotic treatments, but a doctor was in any case beyond the family's means at this point.

Their hopes of making money by keeping cows had been dashed, which Mary called a 'great discouragement'. Instead of welcoming friends and family to stay at their spacious new home, they took in lodgers, which 'proved neither pleasant nor profitable'.[18] She admitted frankly that 'we could not make both ends meet'.[19] In desperation, Mary and Isaac decided that their last resort was to leave the home that they had restored and decorated with much loving care and rent it out, renting somewhere smaller themselves.

Anna was still unable to walk. They no doubt remembered the slow recovery from her dislocated elbow and took it as evidence that she was just a child who took longer than average to heal. Friends in Bridgemont in Lancashire invited her to convalesce with them, and after a few weeks there, she went to stay with her grandparents on the farm in Norfolk while Mary and Isaac packed up and moved their home. She endured the agony of jolting over the rough road in a stagecoach for twenty-four hours or more, and later a long but less painful ride to the home of her kind hosts. Evidently the rest did her good and by the time she moved on to her uncle's farm she was well enough to ride their horses again.

On 23 September 1835 Anna wrote her longest surviving letter to her mother,[20] first asking for clothes for her uncle Richard and for her own trousers, then telling her about a sea trip from Yarmouth. 'This morning I have been doing some French exercises and I rode over to Rippon Hall on Bob. He is very rough to ride after Balaam,' she wrote.[21] Rippon Hall was about 2 miles away, not a long ride but not one that she would have attempted if her injury was causing pain. Being out in the beautiful countryside had also inspired her to paint, which had evidently become a matter of conscience and a source of argument with her mother, for she went on to tell her:

> Pray do not congratulate me on my wise resolution about not going on with my oil paints for I have heartedly repented of it since I have been here and seen all the fine old oakes [*sic*] and elms with the bright colours of Autumn … I have never seen anything so beautiful … I could not have believed, if I had found it myself, how entirely just painting that view of Lancaster has altered the way in which I look at scenery. I am now always looking for something to make a picture of, what tints will harmonise together, what colours will do for this oak and ask and what for the distances. In fact, I never enjoyed looking at the country so much before. It seems like another sense, I shall send my 3 attempts at oils soon with the carrier.

The letter includes news of her height and weight, so it seems that Mary had asked her family to make sure that Anna was eating properly and gaining weight normally. Given the family's poor diet in earlier times, and the constant Quaker emphasis on self-denial, Anna may well have been underweight, especially if the pain of her injury had diminished her appetite.

She wrote of making herself a 'stuff dress' and of making wax flowers, a popular craft of the time. Her bees, in their straw skleps, needed to be kept dry over the winter, so she suggested, 'Now for the poor Bees. I think the dairy would be a good place for them in a few more weeks if they can be kept dry. Aunt Ellen feeds hers. I cannot yet think calmly on that sad affair with those dear little industrious Bees.'

As a child on the farm, Anna would have ridden astride like her brother. As a woman, she would have been expected to ride side-saddle, as it was considered immodest for adult women to ride astride and, although the concern was too delicate to be voiced in public in Victorian England, also considered, inaccurately, to pose a threat to the hymen, the internal membrane which was believed to indicate virginity. The design of side-saddle still in use today emerged in the 1830s and holds the rider firmly in place with something like a double pommel. The fact that she asked for her trousers does not indicate that she was riding astride, because women usually wore trousers under an overskirt when riding side-saddle. It does suggest, however, that her right leg was the one that had been injured, as a side-saddle rider's right leg is only used for balance while the left foot is in a stirrup and is used to 'cue' the horse as in riding astride. A switch or stick in the right hand gives the aids on the right side.

Before the letter closes, Anna also asks, 'Dost thou not find a great many Is in my letters? I afraid thou wilt think they are quite Egotistical.' The question, and the tone in which she broke the news that she was painting again, demonstrates her impatience with the constant injunction towards modesty and self-effacement that framed the Quaker way of life and also the affectionate discussions that mother and daughter had about everyday morality. The fact was, however, that Anna's injury, coming after years of hardship and the frustration of the family's hopes, had challenged her mother's faith.

Mary Sewell recorded that her spiritual doubts had developed during the family's years in Stoke Newington. Her brother John and his wife Anne stayed for seven weeks at Palatine Cottage in their early days there. Mary described her brother, who had discovered another movement, Unitarianism, as almost radiant with a new understanding of Christianity. Like Mary, he had felt frustrated by the silent, inner-directed way in which Quakers were left to discover their personal faith without formal doctrines to guide them. He had read the work of the American Unitarian leader William Ellery Channing, who in 1815 defined the core beliefs of this Protestant faith group: the goodness of God, the use of reason in understanding the Bible, the centrality of Jesus's moral message, and the tolerance of religious differences.[22] More controversially, the Unitarians traced intellectual descent from the earliest Christians and maintained that God the Father was the only deity and Jesus Christ an ordinary mortal sent by God to teach his ways. John bored his sister every day with his new ideas but she noted, enviously, that he was ecstatically happy: 'He had rest, peace, and joy overflowing.'[23]

Mary, on the other hand, was feeling 'very unsettled in my religious views'. She too wanted something more concrete than private meditation on the Queries at the silent meetings. She became uneasy because she had never been baptised. Anxiously, she reread the New Testament, 'day after day, month after month'.

Amplifying her personal doubts was the menacing truth about her beloved daughter. 'Nannie', as she called her, had relapsed and was again in constant pain and unable to walk. Anna and her mother were throughout their lives the very embodiment of positive thinking but no amount of prayer, patience and injunctions to resignation could suppress the growing fear that her beloved daughter might never recover nor ward off the guilt that she could have done more to prevent her suffering. In later life, Mary wrote:

> Recurring again and again to the treatment of this first injury, in which many mistakes were made, how often have I unavailingly said, 'Oh, if I had done this!' 'Oh, if she had not done that!' 'Oh, if the doctors had been wiser!' or, 'Perhaps if we try this or that, she may be cured.' And we tried everything, as far as our circumstances would allow, for I always kept alive the hope that the healing-time would come.[24]

She was clearly beside herself with anxiety. Mary and Anna were united in the belief that the accident that had disabled this vibrant girl was God's will, part of the divine plan for their lives, even though there was no way of knowing or understanding that plan. Many decades later, Mary was to write: 'I conclude *now* that the Blessed Lord saw that He could make a more exquisite character out of that noble, independent, courageous, capable creature by imprisonining it within the stricted limitations. But oh, how often did my heart yearn over those apparently wasted faculties.'[25] Comparing them as writers, it is worth noting that, while Mary's books have an overt religious tone, there is almost no mention of God in *Black Beauty* and no attempt to persuade readers to go to church or accept Christian beliefs. In her diaries, Anna mentions her difficulty with faith several times and it is clear that she struggled to understand the divine purpose in her suffering.

Mother and daughter alternated between trying to resign themselves to the divine will and hoping that Anna would get better. The influential analysis of the grieving process, *On Death and Dying*,[26] by the psychiatrist Elizabeth Kubler-Ross, published in 1969, identified 'Denial' as the first stage and described it as a state of shock or numbness, in which the bad news is denied and the person who is grieving clings to their hopes. It is considered to be a phase in which natural feelings are suppressed for fear they will be overwhelming. It seems that Anna and Mary stayed in denial for almost a decade after her accident.

This was an unhappy time in the British Quaker movement, which was beset by schisms, and a number of people left the movement to found an alternative breakaway sect. This did not last, and Mary did not join them, but she was aware that she was not alone in her alienation, not from Christianity itself but from the stern practice of it in which she had been raised. Her Bible study gave her the idea that she should be baptised – ritually cleansed of sin by washing or being immersed in water – and that she should take Communion, the sacrament which acknowledged Christ's death and resurrection, both of which were impossible for a Quaker.

She could not keep her doubts to herself and decided to share them with her husband. One evening, when her anxiety was unbearable, she waited up late for him to come home, eventually going to bed but listening out for his arrival. At last she heard him open the door, take off his coat and boots, and eat the cold supper she had left out from him. Finally he climbed the stairs to their bedroom and found his wife wide awake and in distress.

She stammered out the agony of conscience which she was feeling and he listened patiently. They prayed together and then discussed the practical steps which Mary should take. He advised her to withdraw formally from the meeting rather than wait to be excluded,[27] which she did, writing to Gracechurch Street. She wanted to continue attending some meetings, alternating with visits to services in other churches, but he advised a clean break. Thereafter, on Sundays, while they remained in London, Philip went to the Stoke Newington meeting with his father while Mary stayed at home and 'dear Anna, being lame, could seldom go anywhere'.[28]

The personal cost of following her conscience was terrible. 'Exceeding pain' was how she described it:

> Oh, I was very lonely – almost all my friends and acquaintances were Friends, and there was, as might be supposed, much misjudging. Some thought I wanted more liberty, and that I … wanted to get rid of the Quaker bonnet. So far from this, it was quite a trial for me to give it up. I thought then, and think still, that the Friends' dress is the prettiest a woman can wear.[29]

Her son, Philip, would later describe his mother as a 'woman of [a] very strong and original mind'.[30] The fate of such a woman in a puritanical, bourgeois community is not hard to imagine – she found herself an outcast.

In addition to her daughter's sudden disability and the pain of cutting herself off from her friends, Mary had to confront another financial crisis. Even allowing for the fact that they would not have to pay Anna's school fees because she could no longer walk to school, the family's plan to rent out Palatine Cottage did not work. They had found cheaper lodgings in Shacklewell, another area within the parish of Hackney, not 500 yards from Dalston, but the profit promised by making this move was no more than £20 a year, which should have told them at the outset that the enterprise was too marginal to succeed. They then sublet Palatine Cottage to some young newlyweds in the community, and Mary felt a little better about being forced to give up her happy home when she pictured another couple's happiness there. However, this tenancy lasted less than a year and then once again financial ruin was staring Mary and Isaac Sewell in the face.

5

'I Am Very Miserable' (1836–46)

Once again, the Quaker community stepped in to save the Sewell family fortunes. The wealthiest Quaker families in England were the lynchpins of a network that supported its less successful members. Although barred from mainstream politics and the judiciary by their beliefs, Quakers still formed a parallel elite to the highest levels of British society at this time. Their families were closely linked by marriage but also brought into constant contact by the annual, monthly and weekly cycle of meetings which brought the whole community together in the same rooms year after year.

The biographer Victoria Glendinning identified the most prominent Quaker dynasties: 'Mostly prosperous bankers and merchants … Names are many but they recur: Barclay, Hoare, Buxton, Seebohm, Tuke, Ransom, Lucas, Wheeler, Gillett, Rowntree, Exton, Leatham, Fry, Clark. They still intermarried and visited each other constantly.'[1] This wealthy network also mingled frequently with less prosperous Friends at the big London meetings, where bankers and industrialists met shopkeepers and clerks on equal terms and the resolutely egalitarian Quaker values meant that snobbery had no place among them. The 'dinner book' kept by the Seebohm family reveals that they entertained some Sewells,[2] so it was fortunate that Anna's father had never felt the same spiritual doubts as her mother and so could, in all sincerity, benefit from his Quaker connections who now came to his rescue again. Just as their tenants left and the Sewells found that they could not make ends meet, Isaac was offered a new job, as the manager of the London & County Joint Stock Bank in Brighton.

The London & County was a brand-new bank, established that very year. Joint-stock banks were an innovation in themselves, so for Isaac, with his healthy (or perhaps unhealthy) appetite for risk, the offer was more than tempting. Banking was a booming business as new industries demanded more and more investment, although general financial instability, with dramatic peaks and troughs, had caused the Bank of England much anxiety. Their solution was the Banking Co-partnership Act of 1826, an attempt to stabilise the banking system and change the structure of banking in England and Wales by permitting the establishment of joint-stock banks outside a 65-mile radius of London. The banking industry exploded immediately and 138 new banks were created under this legislation before it was repealed in 1844.

The new joint-stock institutions established themselves in direct competition with the old private banks. The beauty of joint-stock companies was that they were owned by a large number of shareholders and had limited liability, so that shareholders were liable for a company's debts only up to the value of their investment. Until then, a company's owners had been liable for all its debts, meaning a failure could bankrupt them.[3] This new freedom made enormous sums of capital available to businesses, fuelling vast expansion. It also distanced these new banks from the shared principles of the old Quaker bankers, but many young Quakers, such as Isaac, were enthusiastic about the new order.

While she was still recuperating at the family farm, Anna's parents packed up and set off for Brighton, then the most fashionable seaside resort in Britain, a settlement of over 40,000 people and dedicated to pleasure of every kind. It was, and still is, a beautiful town where the white domes and minarets of the Royal Pavilion gleam above gracious squares and sweeping neoclassical terraces, all bordered by the sea. In 1832, William Cobbett had claimed that it 'certainly surpass[ed] in beauty all other towns in the world'.[4] The Royal Pavilion rose at its heart, a fantasy Oriental palace designed by the great architect of Regency England, John Nash. It had been built over several years from

1815 for the decadent Prince Regent, later King George IV, who made Brighton a mecca for his pleasure-loving courtiers. His successor, King William IV, who was the reigning monarch at the time the Sewells moved, extended this little palace still further and so Brighton continued to enjoy the status of a favourite royal resort.

Her new home tempted Anna with every kind of enjoyment. Brighton was a town dedicated to entertainment – a culture shock for the 16-year-old who until then had known little more than the sober existence of a Quaker girl. Between the soaring white stucco terraces lay pleasure gardens where people could stroll in search of amusements, and their frenetic history gives us a good idea of how dedicated the town was to giving visitors a good time. There were assembly rooms for dances or for lectures, greenhouses full of tropical plants, a zoo displaying exotic animals and tea rooms with tempting displays of cakes and patisseries.[5] While gambling was a private, rather than organised, pastime, the atmosphere of blatant and dedicated entertainment must have been like that of modern Las Vegas, with the added features of the beach and the seaside. In good weather people walked up and down the Chain Pier, once nothing more than a landing stage for the fishing boats and the ferries to France, but now the prototype of an amusement venue which was at first unique to the English seaside. For 2p, visitors could stroll out over the sea on a wide wrought-iron walkway, looking down on the restless waves and breathing in the sweet sea air charged with health-giving ozone. The pier was lined with decorated kiosks where visitors could buy sweets, pass the time with a fortune teller, sit for a silhouette artist or marvel at the camera obscura which captured the panorama of the sea front.

On land there were theatres, art galleries, concert halls and bandstands, all brandishing their temptations. At the centre of the famous 10-mile beach, a sweep of round grey pebbles where bathing machines were crowding out the old fishing boats, a promenade had been built to offer yet another social space. But even the inescapable pleasure of walking, meeting and chatting with new neighbours was a guilty one, as mixing with 'society' was a practice frowned upon by Quakers, many of whom at that time believed that the simple way of life was incompatible with socialising.[6]

Worse than its reputation for pleasure was Brighton's name for scandal and immorality, which was enhanced by enormous army barracks built there during the Napoleonic Wars to house 1,000 horses and whole regiments of single young men. When Jane Austen wanted a destination to which Lydia Bennett could escape in the hope of encountering the raffish George Wickham in *Pride and Prejudice* (1813), Brighton was the obvious choice:

> In Lydia's imagination, a visit to Brighton comprised every possibility of earthly happiness. She saw, with the creative eye of fancy, the streets of that gay bathing-place covered with officers. She saw herself the object of attention, to tens and to scores of them at present unknown. She saw all the glories of the camp – its tents stretched forth in beauteous uniformity of lines, crowded with the young and the gay, and dazzling with scarlet; and, to complete the view, she saw herself seated beneath a tent, tenderly flirting with at least six officers at once.[7]

Anna would have been horrified at this prospect and found life in Brighton a constant trial. She and her family had been brought up as 'Plain' Quakers, the strictest members of the movement, in contrast to the 'Gay' Quakers of whom their Norfolk neighbours, the wealthy Gurney family, were typical. The fact that Anna used the old pronouns 'thee' and 'thou' and had worn the Quaker dress clearly identified them as Plain, and this was a way of life just as much as a belief system. While Mary had formally withdrawn from the movement, and Anna had grown impatient with the 'useless' hours spent in silent meetings, they continued to live as Plain Quakers for the rest of their lives, striving to love the perfection of God in every creature, human or animal. Frugality was a major virtue in day-to-day life and they were careful not to take more than they needed and to give away as much as they could spare – in time, energy, money, goods or talent. Philip Sewell's biographer noted that he believed in 'simplicity of life, abstemiousness and self-denial'.[8]

Most pleasures were considered a waste of God-given resources and self-denial was a shining virtue. Plain Quakers specifically forbade 'dancing, music, cards and the theatre',[9] all activities for which Brighton had a reputation. Flirting was an activity so obviously wicked that its interdiction was assumed without question. For Anna, a young woman trying to follow these doctrines of self-denial, every day in that town was a moral torture. Elizabeth Fry wrote of the daily dilemmas she also faced. If musicians took to the park bandstand, was it permissible to listen? Perhaps if they were a civilian group but, if a military band struck up, the double interdiction of music and militarism meant that a good Quaker should walk briskly away.

For Anna here was no possibility of withdrawing from this fun-loving world because her father's bank was at 167 North Street, at the corner of Prince's Place, at the very eye of the hedonistic storm. The family lived above the shop. The Royal Pavilion was only a block away to the east, the pleasure gardens and tea rooms were directly opposite and the theatre almost as close in a westerly direction. It must surely have been the most fashionable bank in the most fashionable town in England. Between North Street and the seashore lies the area known today as The Lanes, an enticing warren of narrow, quirky streets that twist downhill towards the sea and were lined with shops of every kind.

Pubs and beer halls also abounded there, but at the heart of the area stood the Quaker meeting house, a destination for the substantial Quaker community which had, against all odds, established itself in the town. The meeting house still stands on Ship Street, and a ghost, a lady in grey, is said to use the rear doors on Meeting House Lane.[10] The windows are set high in the front wall so that the Friends were not distracted by the riotous crowds outside, but the meeting house was so close to a pub that the noise still disturbed them, even on Sunday.

Anna was 16 when the family moved to Brighton and travelled there directly from her stay at the family farm in Buxton. She was to live there for ten years, and for the last five of them kept a diary which suggested that she still enjoyed considerable periods of good health. The close relationship between Anna, Philip and their mother began to loosen as the children became adults and claimed their independence.

Escorted by her brother, Anna began to build her own life, following her interests and making friends. Some of Brighton's pleasures were educational, even intellectual – talks on history, science or politics, art exhibitions and musical recitals. She took lessons in art and music, and showed considerable talent at both, consolidating skills which were to give her great pleasure throughout her life. Five years after the railway line opened in 1839, she went up to London with a group of friends to visit the Royal Academy Summer Exhibition.

A significant friend Anna made at this time was Robert Folthorp, a publisher and the proprietor of the Royal Library, a bookshop almost next door to her father's bank. Perhaps through him they met another young publisher and bookseller, Henry S. King, who started a bookselling business in Brighton with his brother, Richard, in 1838. Henry would later become a partner with George Smith in the firm Smith, Elder & Co., which was to publish Currer Bell's *Jane Eyre* in 1847, and was eventually subsumed into the giant publishing house of Routledge.

At this time, however, he was an ambitious, young, single man who was three years older than Anna. King was to be an influential figure as Mary and Anna developed as writers and remained a family friend for some years. Her mother described him as a 'most refined man … in everything his taste was perfect'.

This happy, stimulating life was not enough for Anna. If she found pleasure in something, after the long childhood years of self-denial, she felt guilty and could not reconcile her enjoyment with the Christian ideals of her upbringing. Equally, on the threshold of adulthood, she felt her fragile identity threatened by the demand that she surrender herself to the will of God. In her diary, she wrote of her continual struggle against 'the irresistible charm of worldly things'.[11] She wrote down a prayer for the strength to resist enjoyment:

> Lord, break my bondage for I have not the strength to do it myself. I have not the strength to give myself up to Christ nor the sense of being willing that his perfect will should be fulfilled in me, lest it should mean entire crucifixion of self.

She was strong enough to work as a teacher and took a Sunday school class. Sunday schools, while usually run by religious institutions, were doing the job of general education at this time and had originated in the late eighteenth century when so many children were at work during the week that their only opportunity to learn to read, write and do arithmetic was on Sunday. Significantly, Sunday schools were also free, while day schools charged fees and were largely used by the middle classes.

By the mid-nineteenth century it was estimated that as many as three-quarters of working-class children had attended a Sunday school at some point in their lives.[12] Adults also went to Sunday schools. In 1840, 33 per cent of men and 50 per cent of women were illiterate, the poorest sections of the population.[13]

Sunday schools were also the only opportunity that working-class people had for spiritual learning. When Britain was largely a rural society, and most people were farm workers, the church in each town or village was a natural destination on Sunday, but industrialisation had swept away the traditional structure of rural communities leaving millions of working people in anonymised, rootless and often also homeless masses. Britain might claim to be a Christian country but the majority of its citizens had no meaningful contact with any kind of religion. A Sunday school, offering a Bible story and a prayer as well as basic education, would be their only chance of spiritual or moral education, and one which most churches were eager to offer.

Anna's pupils in Brighton were children but, even so, as she noted a few paragraphs later in her diary, her sense of guilt affected her ability:

> Last Sunday was the first time I took my class in the afternoon. I did not get on very well, for in the morning I had given way to sin, and there did not get near to Christ, for I sinned wilfully, knowingly resisting the voice of the Spirit in my heart, and so the sting was left behind. The darkness returned for two or three days.

She did not specify the 'sin' she had committed, which could have been as trivial as enjoying her breakfast or taking pleasure in a new bonnet.

Beyond such simple feelings of guilt, Anna was aware of a deeper sense of emptiness. She wanted something to 'satisfy the soul' and interesting history lectures could not do that. As a child she had lived in unthinking certainty of belief. As a young woman she questioned everything and found no answers. In these days of spiritual struggle, she never directly connected her disability with her loss of faith, and nor did her mother – a telling omission which indicates the degree to which they sought to deny the impact of her disability on their entire lives. On the contrary, Anna wrote that she was thankful for her suffering:

> I would not be without this dispensation, and pray Thee, Lord, to do with me what Thou seest best. I thank Thee for my lameness. I am sure it is sent in love, though it be a trial. I should without it have too much pleasure in the flesh, and have forgotten thee.[14]

Despite this protestation, it is clear that it was hard for Anna to live with constant pain and day-to-day uncertainty about her health. Added to these natural sufferings were those inflicted by doctors. She fell ill while staying with some friends, who called a doctor who bled her 'severely'.[15] This ancient practice, in which blood is drawn from a patient either by opening a vein with a scalpel, taking it with a syringe or pipette, or by applying leeches, was becoming controversial by the mid-nineteenth century but was still used to treat conditions from pneumonia, stroke or yellow fever to a sore throat or excess of 'nervous energy'.[16]

A severe bleeding implies the loss of litres of blood, when a healthy adult has only about 5 litres in their entire body. Afterwards, her mother traced Anna's bouts of overall weakness to this event. At times, her strength seemed to simply drain away, and with that came the growing realisation that her health was permanently compromised and she would never feel whole and healthy again. It seemed possible that she would be confined at home for the rest of her short life, unable to walk, to ride, to make a journey to school, or to think of marriage or children.

In her memoir of the family, Mary's friend Mary Bayly reflected:

> Although [Anna's] sweet and helpful influences were felt wherever she might be, there is no doubt that a considerable portion of her life was spent mainly in repression. Her very varied capacities enabled her to enter with unfeigned interest into a great variety of subjects. She could see at once how a picture should be composed, a fact or sentiment expressed, a garment cut out; how flowers should be arranged; what a committee should or should not do – but with all these mental

> resources, the frail body refused to do its part, and days and weeks had often to be spent in enforced idleness. Her hungry nature longed for food of many kinds – political, social, philanthropic – all these departments teemed with interest to her; yet there were periods when to read a short paragraph in a newspaper … for days together was an impossibility.[17]

In modern language, Anna was often depressed. She called her periods of low mood 'the darkness', which graphically describes the hopelessness and despair that sometimes threatened to overcome her. Her mother, unhelpfully, called Anna's bouts of depression 'visiting Doubting Castle', a reference to Milton's *Paradise Lost* which, coy and euphemistic as it sounds, in fact alludes to a state of extreme distress. In Milton's poem, Doubting Castle was owned by Giant Despair, who imprisons the pilgrims Christian and Hopeful in a dungeon, abuses them, beats them up and tries to drive them to suicide.

Both mother and daughter were searching for a new spiritual home. Mary had formally withdrawn from the Gracechurch Meeting of the Society of Friends, and Anna was often too lame – or simply disinclined – to get to the meeting house in Brighton, but Mary in particular was still drawn to Quaker beliefs and the records show they both occasionally joined Isaac and Philip there. Mary was effectively shopping for a new faith but failed to find one.

Anna often accompanied her mother to a range of Protestant places of worship. They tried services at chapels of many denominations: Baptist, Methodist, Unitarian, Moravian and Plymouth Brethren. None of these provided the comforting certainty which they craved. They also visited Anglican churches. At first, like many newcomers, Mary was confused by the layout of the Book of Common Prayer. At one church she was also horrified to see the choirmaster prodding the choir boys with a long cane to keep them awake and dutiful.

After many more experimental visits, and advice from Henry King, they arrived at the chapel-of-ease at St James's in Brighton, where the curate, Charles Maitland, was formerly a medical officer in the army[18] and a man remarkable for his evangelical style as well as his artistic sensitivity. The chapel was a simple 'preaching box' with a neoclassical exterior which had been built hastily as a satellite church to the parish church of St Nicholas, a modest medieval building that had been the only Anglican church serving this seaside Sodom and Gomorrah at the start of the nineteenth century.[19] Maitland was a popular preacher, engaged in a public argument with another well-followed Brighton priest, Edward B. Elliott. He was also a gifted artist and both he and his wife Julia were published authors – Julia followed a memoir of her early life in India with some charming books for children. Their son, Edward, four years younger than Anna, was also to become a respected humanitarian author and animal welfare campaigner whose views would influence Gandhi.[20] So the Sewells found them congenial neighbours as well as a source of new inspiration.

Before they discovered Charles Maitland, however, Mary fell under the spell of another fashionable Brighton cleric. She was so embarrassed about her attachment to this 'false prophet' that she never named him. 'We came into a world of very varied interest at Brighton,' she recalled, 'and I was not as quick as I might have been to see that all is not gold that glitters. I am afraid I wasted a good deal of my time on people and theories that gave me nothing worth having in return.' She also accused herself of making false idols of clay and 'I have bewailed that worship'.[21]

While her mother was swept away, however, Anna remained unimpressed and the slow reversal of roles between mother and child began at this time. They became close friends as well as close family, but Anna was the one who held back, advised caution and spoke from experience and common sense, while Mary remained as impulsive as a child to the end of her life. Mrs Bayly observed:

> In many respects the lives and interests of Mrs Sewell and her daughter were so closely associated that the story of one describes the other. It has been shown that the usual relative positions of mother and child were reversed in them. I cannot say that the daughter led, for the impulse to action came usually from the mother, but the daughter pronounces judgment on it. The enforced sedentary habits of Anna's life were favourable to early maturity of judgment, and Mrs Sewell was by nature quick to bend to the opinion of one she trusted.[22]

Congenial as the Maitlands were, it was at a Baptist service that Anna finally found the spiritual comfort she needed. In her journal for 7 January 1845, she wrote:

> At the beginning of this month we went on Sunday morning to Clarence Chapel. Mr Warren preached from the text, 'Christ has redeemed us from the curse of the law, being made a curse for us.' It was a powerful sermon, and the Lord mercifully used it as the conveyance of His good Spirit, to bring again life and light to my dark soul. As I listened I truly felt Christ precious. I believed, and was justified from all things. I was made to sing as in years long past. This is not, I trust, a transient revival. I do now trust in none but Jesus.

Two months later, on her birthday, her recovery was still strong: 'This is my birthday. Oh, what a happy one compared to any I have had so long! I feel as if I had exchanged a rough, stormy sea for a calm, smooth river.'[23]

Her mother, meanwhile, was finding a sense of purpose as a workhouse visitor. She was drawn into the occupation by a young woman who had just left a workhouse. She came to Mary to ask her to find a place for her in a penitentiary – the implication being that she was afraid of being coerced into prostitution by one of the many pimps active in the town once she was no longer able to stay in the workhouse. Mary investigated and found that the workhouse ward in which women were held was 'the general receptacle for the miscellaneous cases of sin and poverty which could not easily be classified and admitted to other wards. It was looked upon as an ignominious place of punishment.' This was despite most of the women who were there being simply destitute and not criminals. The institution's chaplain was too scared to visit it and if a woman rebelled she was confined in the 'black hole', a dark, underground cell.

These years were known as the 'Hungry Forties' in Europe, when a succession of poor harvests, brutal new laws and the collapse of stable rural communities meant that more people than ever lived in poverty and near starvation. The editors of middle-class media such as *The Times* newspaper were challenged to describe the everyday suffering of the disadvantaged without putting their readers off their lavish breakfasts.[24] In 1834 the English government, concerned at the soaring cost of handouts to the destitute, brought in the Poor Law Amendment Act, which became known as the Workhouse Act because it increased the number of these institutions. The most desperate of the poor could be housed and given enough food to keep them alive in return for gruelling manual work if they agreed to enter a workhouse. Welfare payments were thenceforward handed out only to the old and ill.

The living conditions in a workhouse were shameful. The people who were reduced to these institutions could be kept like animals, sleeping on straw in wooden stalls. Orphans and widows were crammed into huge dormitories alongside vulnerable people who were mentally ill or physically disabled. Vermin and maggots infested the rooms; hygiene was impossible. Even if people were healthy when they arrived, the frequent outbreaks of cholera or smallpox, the meagre diet and the dangerous conditions in which they worked might well end their sad lives within a few months. In a Reading workhouse, where the men worked crushing bones for fertiliser, a riot started when the inmates fought like animals for the shreds of sinew still attached to the bones.[25]

Undeterred by the chaplain's tales of rioting and violence, Mary insisted on visiting this notorious ward alone:

> It was a large, bare, barn-like looking place with no furniture but two rows of beds. 'Dear Friends,' I said, 'I have heard that many of you are in trouble and difficulty. I have come to see if I can help or comfort any of you. I have been advised not to come; it was thought you would not receive me well; but I did not believe that.'[26]

One of the women immediately said they were glad to see her; a group clustered around her, sitting on the beds, and Mary continued, 'Come then. Let us sit down and talk together; tell me your troubles and let me see if I can help you.' The women immediately began to tell her the stories of their unhappy lives, and Mary, always delighted with practical tasks, set about helping them. She found places in the penitentiary for some girls, and persuaded others to return to their families, or persuaded the families to take them in again. She wrote to the clerks in faraway parishes asking for financial help on behalf of some of the sufferers, and wrote letters to friends or sweethearts for others.

One woman, however, held back from approaching her and remained in a corner, rocking to and fro in anxiety but listening when Mary read from the Bible. Eventually, the woman took her aside for a private conversation. She was Irish and Catholic, a widow concerned that her dead husband's soul would be trapped in purgatory because she had been unable to pay for a proper funeral. Her only son was in prison, and she would not abandon him in England and go back to her family in Ireland.

Mary discovered that this desperate widow could cook a little and so volunteered to take her into the family home and train her as a cook herself. This she did, and in addition, persuaded some Friends with naval connections to find her son a job aboard a ship, as it was his ambition to go to sea. The mother eventually moved on to become cook in 'a clergyman's family'. As the icing on this benevolent cake, Mary noted that she also became 'a sincere Christian'.[27]

Although Anna and her mother eventually found peace in Brighton, they were ready to move out of the town as soon as the new-built railway lines would allow Isaac to commute to his job every day. Mary, ever nostalgic for green fields, said, 'It was all dead in Brighton, houses and stones.'[28] She lived for occasional weekend excursions into the country with her husband and remembered bursting into tears of joy at the sight of a bank of wood sorrel with its little starry flowers. She had the lifelong habit of an early morning walk but craved to hear woodland birds sing in place of seagulls squawking in Brighton.

A passage in one of her books, *Thy Poor Brother*, imagines a woman consumed by anxiety taking an early morning walk on the Chain Pier, on a stormy day when 'the wind was wild, the sky was leaden grey and the sea rolled its heavy, discoloured waves with an angry growl upon the shore'.

The woman watches a flock of wild ducks fly straight into the tempest and then notices one weaker bird fall out of formation and into the water. She watches it struggle up into the air again, disappear from her sight and then dart forward with increasing speed and catch up with the rest of the flight. In this passage, Mary projected all her anxiety about her disabled daughter and drew a lesson that 'He who guided these trustful voyagers across the billows to their haven of rest, would assuredly guide His children across the rough billows of their life's journey, and not suffer the feeblest amongst them to fail, or be overwhelmed'.[29]

6

No Idle Passing Patronage (1837–61)

Early in the morning of 20 June 1837, Britain's old king died and the Princess Victoria, who was barely 18 years old, became queen. Anna Sewell, almost exactly Victoria's contemporary, felt the effect of this change as much as every other woman in the country. While in later life Victoria was noted for her vitriolic condemnation of the suffragettes, her accession alone galvanised women's awareness of their role in society.

The simple fact that a young woman was the head of state brought the issue of a woman's role into question. While women were denied the vote and played no role in government, the laws from whose creation they were excluded were signed into statute by a woman. The fact that this woman was an animal lover was also to have a decisive effect upon the cause of animal welfare.

Almost immediately women writers and activists began to question the norms that had limited their lives, while those who were opposed to the old, militaristic culture of brutality were delighted to discover that the young queen not only loved animals as an individual but was fully prepared to exercise her power as sovereign to improve the lives of animals in her empire. Victoria's influence marked Anna Sewell's life, and her future writing, in several important ways.

The nation's entire identity shifted shape within a few years. While the Duke of Wellington remained a national hero, in the period covered in this study industry, engineering and technology offered new sources of national pride, while inequality, and the social and political forces that maintained it, became the focus of reformers.

William IV had been a popular king for his easy-going nature and down-to-earth ways. Although he had supported slave owners in the abolitionist struggle, he accepted the electoral reforms that made the voting system fairer but also diminished the power of the Crown and edged his position towards that of a constitutional monarch. Being the third son of George III, he had never expected to become king and had enjoyed his earlier life either at sea as a naval officer or at home, getting drunk, running up debts, living with an actress and fathering at least eleven illegitimate children. His accession at the age of 64 was a delightful surprise to him and, from the evidence, he seems to have spent a good proportion of his nine-year reign posing for portraits that show him as a white-haired, red-faced, rotund figure lapped in ermine, swathed in satin and clanking with jewelled regalia.

Late in his life, when it became clear that both his older brothers were going to predecease him, William gave up drinking and started to take care of his health. Given his age, however, his reign was never expected to be a long one and he had no legitimate children, so the spotlight fell on Victoria from her childhood. Astute lobbyists attempted to penetrate the protective barrier of the 'Kensington System' erected around her by her mother, the Duchess of Kent, and the duchess's 'advisor', Sir John Conroy.

Today the Kensington System, named after Kensington Palace which was the princess's home, would be condemned as the worst degree of coercive control. The young Victoria was substantially isolated and denied most of the innocent pleasures of childhood. She saw no one but her mother, her governess, two selected friends and Conroy. She even slept in the same room as her mother and had almost no privacy or independence.

Victoria loathed Conroy, a figure who would be universally condemned by history as a self-serving bully, and refused to be cowed by his oppressive demands. Yet his relentless campaign to dominate her life and that of her mother produced one of her greatest joys. When she was 13, Conroy gave her mother a dog. Victoria's mother, a princess of the

German house of Saxe-Coburg, had lost her beloved husband just seven months after their only child was born and was a conciliatory, rather insecure woman who Conroy controlled with little effort. His loyalty to her was transparently venal and his stated aim was to be appointed as Victoria's private secretary once she was queen. Grudgingly, and with irritation, he did whatever seemed necessary to keep the duchess on his side.

The dog Conroy chose was a Cavalier King Charles spaniel, mostly black and white with tufts of brown as eyebrows. He belonged to a small breed with strong royal associations, one which had been popular with successive British monarchs since King Charles II, who was often observed playing with his dogs rather than paying attention during councils of state.[1] With an affectionate nature, a soft, long coat and silky ears, the breed emerged in Europe in the sixteenth century and, although called spaniels, probably owe more ancestry to the Chinese Shi-Tsu or the Pekinese than to the energetic working spaniels used by hunters for centuries.

By the early 1700s the Cavalier King Charles was so iconic that it was being immortalised in porcelain and, later in Victoria's reign, a pair of Staffordshire pottery statuettes, often modelled with a gold collar and chain, and with markings picked out in lustre, were the most popular items on a patriotic middle-class mantelpiece.

Victoria, the lonely little princess, immediately fell in love with the spaniel. His name was Dash and they adored each other. By their first Christmas she was wrapping presents for him.[2] In her journals she wrote of him as 'DEAR SWEET LITTLE DASH'. She moved on from dressing her enormous collection of dolls to making outfits for the dog.

Conroy, seeing a means to ingratiate himself with the increasingly hostile mistress of his fate, commissioned a life-sized portrait of Dash for Victoria's 14th birthday. It was to be the first of many paintings of the dog. He became Victoria's constant companion and was so devoted to her that when, during a visit to the seaside, she went on a boat ride without him, he ran into the water to swim after her.

Victoria was also an excellent horsewoman. Horses, either ridden or driven, were by far the most common means of transport at that time and most people who could afford to keep a horse learned to ride as children. Future sovereigns, however, were expected to be exceptionally good riders as they faced many public ceremonies in which they would take part on horseback.

Many a European prince was traumatised by a sadistic riding master in the cause of preparing them for what was to come. Even so, any rider can have an accident and royalty was never any guarantee of safety on a startled horse. Victoria's grandson, King George V, was in France during the First World War, inspecting troops on horseback, when his mount was startled by the men cheering, slipped, unseated the king and fell on him, leaving him in agony with a broken pelvis.

The young princess had been eager to learn to ride. When a very young child she was given a donkey by one of her uncles and was so fond of it that her guardians worried that she was neglecting her lessons. When she was 9, her mother took her to Captain Fozzard's riding school in London, where, by chance, the actress Fanny Kemble had gone to enjoy a ride out with some friends. Kemble recalled:

> My riding-master was the best and most popular teacher in London. … Fozzard's method was so good that all the best lady riders in London were his pupils, and one could tell one of them at a glance, by the perfect squareness of the shoulders to the horse's head, which was one invariable result of his teaching. His training was eminently calculated to produce that result, and to make us all but immovable in our saddles. Without stirrups, without holding the reins, with our arms behind us, and as often as not sitting left-sided on the saddle, to go through violent plunging, rearing, and kicking lessons, and taking our horses over the bar, was a considerable test of a firm seat, and in all these special feats I became a proficient.[3]

Captain Fozzard took advantage of the happy coincidence by asking Fanny Kemble to demonstrate her skills, with the result that Victoria was enrolled immediately with 'Old Fozzie' and her mother was soon being billed for the 'kicking lessons' mastered by the most advanced of his pupils.

Victoria rode side-saddle, which was far less dangerous than it appears, thanks to the modern design that was widely adopted around this time, in which a double pommel holds both the rider's legs so firmly in place that even if the horse fell she would not be thrown clear. While ordinary young women like Anna Sewell were expected to ride side-saddle for reasons of propriety, Victoria, as a princess with dynastic responsibilities ahead of her, was firmly prohibited from riding astride following a lingering suspicion in royal circles that the practice would induce infertility. This mistaken belief was articulated forcefully by the Empress Maria Theresa of Austria when writing to her daughter, Marie Antoinette:

> Riding spoils the complexion, and in the end your waistline will suffer from it and begin to show more noticeably. Furthermore, if you are riding like a man, dressed as a man, as I suspect you are, I have to tell you that I find it dangerous as well as bad for bearing children – and that is what you have been called upon to do; that will be the measure of your success.

The empress could not have foreseen, however, that after the Revolution her daughter's preference for riding astride would give her prosecutors grounds to accuse her of lesbianism and an unnatural lust for power.[4]

The prejudice against riding astride, and the association of side-saddle riding with the upper classes, lasted well into the twentieth century, with a *Times* correspondent covering the 1931 Royal International Horseshow noting with approval that the women riders showing rode side-saddle: 'How much better it looked, and how much safer, than the astride method which, however it may appeal to some people, can never make a lady on a horse look like a lady on a horse.'[5]

At barely 5ft tall, Victoria was considered too short to look imposing on horseback but her ability as a rider was obvious in her 'beautiful seat and a light hand. [She was] always was a most courageous horsewoman.'[6] A daily ride soon became part of her household routine and she always enjoyed riding fast. On horseback, she could get away from her hated would-be guardian and, as she was a much better rider than most of her household, she could be alone for a few precious moments with only her mount and nature for company.

All these details were of great interest to the directors of the Society for the Prevention of Cruelty to Animals (SPCA), who now counted the banker Samuel Gurney, Elizabeth Fry's brother, among their number, as honorary treasurer. Lewis Gompertz had taken over as secretary and settled the society's debts himself, but policy disagreements were starting to fragment the movement as a whole.

In the year of the society's birth, Gompertz had written his first book, *Moral Inquiries on the Situation of Man and of Brutes*, which was influential but far more radical in its approach than the views of many supporters of this infant animal welfare movement. A rival organisation, the Association for Promoting Rational Humanity Towards Animal Creation, attacked the book, alleging that Gompertz held anti-Christian views. Some of the SPCA's members hoped that the two organisations would merge, so this opposition disturbed them.

Britain at that time was an overtly antisemitic nation. It was not until 1850 that the law was changed to allow Jews to become Members of Parliament, and racial abuse and the stereotypical characterisation exemplified in Charles Dickens's creation of Fagin in *Oliver Twist* was commonplace. Gompertz was Jewish. In a shameful manoeuvre, the SPCA voted to endorse a statement announcing that the society was based solely on 'the Christian faith and on Christian principles'.[7]

Lewis Gompertz resigned and formed a third and more radical campaigning group, the Animals' Friend Society for the Prevention of Cruelty to Animals. All three struggled financially and within a few years both smaller societies had collapsed. Without William Wilberforce, however, the SPCA badly needed friends in high places as well as money. At their lowest point, they had been forced to give up their offices, auction off their furniture and meet in a coffee house.[8]

They had appointed two inspectors at Smithfield Market, to bring prosecutions under Martin's Act against those who abused the millions of animals who passed through the market every year, either to be sold or slaughtered there. Lewis Gompertz had been much in favour of this move but the idea that cruelty to animals was a crime had not won popular support, and even magistrates dismissed cases brought by the inspectors on the grounds that they were 'paid informers'.[9]

Furthermore, the act also outlawed 'wanton cruelty', but 'wanton' was not a legal term and proved almost impossible to demonstrate in court. The inspectors were therefore retired and the society reduced once more to printing pamphlets and looking for different ways to achieve its aims.

Astutely, the SPCA invited the Duchess of Kent, as Victoria's legal guardian as well as her mother, to become one of their patrons. This manoeuvre allowed them to penetrate the cordon of the Kensington System and appeal at the same time to Victoria. Swiftly, they were informed by her secretary, on 4 July 1835, that:

> I have laid before the Duchess of Kent your letter of the 2nd inst. And its enclosure, relating to the Society for the Prevention of Cruelty to animals and Her Royal Highness very readily acceded to your request that her name and that of the Princess Victoria be placed on the list of Lady Patronesses.[10]

The patronage of the heir apparent had an immediate effect on the society's fortunes, and public donations picked up. Wealthy patrons also showed interest. In August the following year, they felt confident enough to open a fund to buy 'decaying and worn-out horses' and received a donation of £5 from a young woman who would later be referred to in their annals as 'the ever benevolent Baroness Burdett-Coutts'.

As Baroness Burdett-Coutts, this extraordinary woman would be the most significant of all the society's benefactors, but when she sent her £5 to them that was all in the future. She was then merely Angela Burdett, the shy, willowy youngest daughter of a popular and liberal MP, Sir Francis Burdett. The following year, at the age of 23, she would unexpectedly inherit the enormous fortune amassed by her maternal grandfather, the banker Thomas Coutts, and add his name to her own in recognition. Queen Victoria was to elevate her to the rank of baroness in 1871, after a lifetime of spectacular philanthropy in which, with due caution and prudence, she gave away the equivalent of about £130 million in today's money to an impressive range of causes all over the world.

Also in the summer of 1837, Queen Victoria came to the throne a few weeks after her 18th birthday. It was immediately apparent that her love of animals were never a childish indulgence to be put away, but would continue throughout her life. She at once confirmed her patronage of the society, which then became the Royal Society for the Prevention of Cruelty to Animals (RSPCA), the title by which it has been known ever since. They were suddenly a fashionable cause, which allowed them to expand their base of supporters in the highest echelons of society.

Again displaying considerable diplomatic skill, the RSPCA then invited Angela Burdett-Coutts not to give them more money, but rather to become more closely involved with their expanding operation. The young heiress had been besieged by every fortune hunter in Europe and begging letters had arrived by the sackload every day once the news of her inheritance was made public. The RSPCA, by appealing to her intelligence rather than her fortune, won her patronage for life. In 1839 she became vice patron of the Ladies' Educational Committee, and at her induction 'her slight figure and pleasant conversation charmed everyone'.[11]

While the young queen was popular in most quarters, her passion for animals did not endear her universally. Charles Greville, then Clerk to the Privy Council but destined to become a notorious diarist, recorded in horror an after-dinner conversation at which the queen first asked him if he had been riding that day, then asked if his sister rode, and only showed animation when talking about her own ride that morning and her 'very nice' horse.[12]

She fell into a routine of meeting her Prime Minister, Lord Melbourne, at eleven o'clock every morning to discuss state affairs. Melbourne, a childless widower, was by then 58 years old, silver haired, flushed and well covered after a lifetime of good living and not an enthusiastic rider. The young queen was markedly oblivious to the physical limitations of her companions.

She rapidly became so close to Melbourne that there were rumours of an affair. She expected him to accompany her for most of the day, including her afternoon ride. Soon Lady Holland, the wife of one of the royal doctors, was observing:

> She has a small, active, safe but very fleet horse, nor does she undervalue the last quality or allow it to rust for want of using: the pace at

> which she returns is tremendous ... I am startled by the thinness of Lord Melbourne. It is too much; but it may be partly ascribed to the hard riding of those who are attendance of the Queen.[13]

A painting of the scene shows the young queen in her black velvet riding habit, with Melbourne beside her on a noticeably quieter horse, and Dash playing with her West Highland terrier, Islay, among the party.

Queen Victoria's coronation ceremony at Westminster Abbey lasted five hours, and she appeared to be the most composed and confident participant in it. She spent a further hour changing her ceremonial robes and struggling to remove the coronation ring, which the nervous archbishop had placed on the wrong finger. Carrying the orb and sceptre and wearing the heavy crown, she then rode in the Gold State Coach through streets lined with cheering crowds to Buckingham Palace.[14]

According to the painter Charles Leslie, as the State Coach drove up to the palace steps, Victoria heard her dog barking and exclaimed, '"there's Dash", and was in a hurry to doff her crown and royal robe, and lay down the sceptre and the orb, which she carried in her hands, and go and give Dash his bath'.[15]

Victoria married Prince Albert of Saxe-Coburg-Gotha two years later. One of the few traits that the young couple had in common was their love of animals. Prince Albert had a devoted greyhound, Eos. Like Victoria, he had been a lonely only child, and was given Eos as a puppy when he was 14. An animal 'remarkable for sagacity and beauty', Eos was never banished to the kennels but allowed to live indoors, and on occasion fed from a fork by her owner. Black with one white paw and a white streak down her nose, she too accompanied her owner everywhere and was sent ahead to Windsor to greet the bride before Albert himself arrived for the wedding.[16] She was to be a great comfort to him in the awkward early days of the marriage.

Dash died ten months after the royal wedding, and a tearful Queen Victoria wrote the epitaph for his headstone. Eos survived a shooting accident and lived until 1844, whereupon the grieving Albert commissioned a memorial statue. A few years later, the royal couple created a cemetery for their household pets at Osborne on the Isle of Wight, and Eos's memorial was moved there. The two dogs, and their successors, were frequently included in portraits of Victoria, Albert and their family, which record a significant shift in the whole relationship between people and animals in the developed world at that time – the keeping of animals as pets, for their companionship.

While often dismissed as evidence of 'Victorian sentimentality', the move to value companion animals led to a shift in the way all animals were considered. Royal and aristocratic portraits had included animals for centuries, but rarely as the sitter's pets. Animals were symbolic, like the little dogs embodying fidelity in Early Modern portraits.

Later, animals like pedigree hounds and horses were included to show off the owner's prestige bloodstock in eighteenth-century portraits. The pictures commissioned by Queen Victoria and her circle mark the first time that royal portraits positively indicated that these were animal companions, pet creatures who were treated as part of the family. From the finest painters in Europe, Victoria commissioned solo portraits of many of her animals, even her favourite Guernsey cow, Buffy, who was depicted with her calves.[17]

Pre-eminent among Victoria's animal painters was Edwin Landseer, who she knighted in 1850. An extraordinarily prolific talent, who also created the four bronze lion sculptures that flank Nelson's Column in London, he not only painted portraits of both Dash and Eos, and many royal family scenes, but also animals with far humbler owners.

Edwin Landseer was the youngest child of an engraver, John Landseer, a choleric and disappointed man who was elected as an associate engraver to the Royal Academy in 1806 and campaigned ever after on behalf of his growing profession for full membership. Engraving was an art that had grown with the printing industry and with the European middle class, who delighted in hanging on their walls the mass-produced prints of great paintings owned by the wealthy. Newspapers, in these days before photography, commissioned imaginative reportage drawings of great events of the day and engravers worked through the night so that those pictures could be splashed over thousands of pages the next day.

Landseer was also a vital public advocate for animals. He had been a child prodigy and his earliest drawings, done when he was hardly 5 years old, are all of animals. At 16, he was exhibiting at the Royal Academy, where one of his tutors called him 'my little dog boy'[18] because of his passion for painting dogs in particular. Good-looking, diminutive and capable of wit and charm, he was very quickly taken up by the aristocracy of both England and Scotland but his work was also loved by thousands of ordinary people, who bought the prints made by one of his brothers, who had followed their father into the business. Thus, when Queen Victoria first commissioned him he was already famous and successful. His work popularised the queen's love of animals throughout the country, probably doing more to waken the nation's conscience to animal welfare than the entire efforts of the RSPCA up to that time.

Landseer's abundant imagination captured the emotional response each animal inspired, making his most popular portraits too cute for modern taste, although in a pre-photographic age his images were extremely powerful social statements. Landseer loved to depict animals in heroic or noble acts, saving lives or, in the case of his famous stag picture *The Monarch of the Glen* (1851), merely striking an inspiring pose.

Anna Sewell was certainly aware of Landseer's animal paintings: in fact, she copied two of them and the pictures were among those later inherited by her niece, Margaret Sewell, although by the early 1970s they had vanished.[19] Significantly for the story of *Black Beauty*, Landseer also often attributed human traits to his animal subjects, opening the door to the anthropomorphic tone of Anna Sewell's novel.

One of his most popular pictures was of two dogs, *Dignity and Impudence* (1839), and contrasts a dignified bloodhound with a cheeky West Highland terrier. A year later came *Laying Down the Law*, a anthropomorphic satire in which he imagined a group of dogs gathered around a legal textbook and apparently obedient to a large French poodle in the role of Lord Chancellor. His idea came from the dinner party quip[20] – Landseer enjoyed a glittering social life – but, as with many of his most popular pictures, it linked the upper, middle and working classes in shared feelings. In this case, it was the feeling that the judiciary was far from independent.

A love for Scotland was another passion that the queen and Landseer shared. Scottish aristocrats had been among his first patrons and he painted stags several times, always depicting them as majestic and noble animals, even when savaged and brought down by hounds. Clearly, he also shared his royal patron's distaste for stag hunting, which Prince Albert nevertheless enjoyed at the new royal retreat of Balmoral in Scotland, but which Victoria abominated.

She also deplored fox hunting, which in consequence did not become a fashionable field sport until her son and heir, the future Edward VII, took it up to spite his mother, although his corpulent physique did not fit him for sport of any kind. Otherwise, while they famously disagreed on many other issues, Victoria and Albert were united in their approach to animal welfare.

In the early days of their marriage, Albert's distaste for fox hunting gave rise to the malicious rumour that he was a poor horseman, so at a large gathering at Belvoir, home of the country's oldest fox hunt, whose hounds lived at Belvoir Castle, he consented to ride out with a hunt to set the record straight. His secretary triumphantly reported, 'We had a capital time and the Prince rode admirably, to the amazement of most, who were not at all prepared to find him excel in the art.' Victoria was exasperated: 'The absurdity of people … Albert's riding so boldly has made such a sensation that it has been written all over the country and they make much more of it than if he had done some great act!'[21]

Anna Sewell also hated hunting, and very early in *Black Beauty*, in the second chapter, a hare hunt passes the field where Beauty and his mother are grazing. It is a violent episode which makes it clear to the reader that this book will not be a sun-kissed sentimental fantasy of animal life. Later in the book, two horses die in a stable fire and an old cavalry horse gives a graphic and gory description of a cavalry charge during the Crimean War.

In the hunt sequence, the hare is killed but so too is a rider, the only son of the local squire, and his horse, who breaks a leg and is shot. Beauty's mother observes:

> I never yet could make out why men are so fond of this sport. They often hurt themselves, spoil good horses and tear up the fields; and all this for a hare, a fox or a stag, that they could get more easily some other way. But we are only horses, and we don't understand.

Placing this scene so early in the book was a bold choice by Anna, as she risked alienating both her more sensitive readers and people who enjoyed hunting, but she intended the book to be read by adults and curiously, apart from criticism from hunting fans, this scene is rarely mentioned as distressing.

The almost obsessive public interest in the royal couple's lives and their animals had plenty to feed upon. As soon as he was married, Prince Albert immediately applied himself to improving the royal farms, with the overt aim of using royal wealth and privilege to improve farming throughout the country. Victoria's grandfather, King George III, had been nicknamed Farmer George because he established these two farms over 1,400 acres (566.5 hectares) at Windsor, but by Victoria's time they had been neglected.

Albert had the farm buildings renovated with many modern improvements for the welfare of the cattle. He added the truly palatial dairy at Windsor Castle, which still stands. With marble counter-tops and walls decorated with thousands of Minton tiles, it was justly described by an early visitor as 'more like an apartment in fairyland than a dairy'.[22]

Prince Albert became Governor of the Royal Society of Agriculture and in his annual speeches always talked about the introduction of new breeds of animal or the trial of new methods of husbandry. He showed his livestock every year and was delighted if his animals won prizes. The enthusiasm and earnest commitment which he brought to farming impressed even fellow farmers, one of whom remarked:

> His was no merely idle passing patronage or casual aid, but it was rather a pursuit he delighted in ... The most practical man could not go that pleasant round from [the royal farms] without learning something wherever he went.[23]

Less respectfully, *Punch* magazine caricatured him as 'Prince Albert, the British Farmer' wearing a smock embroidered with the royal coat of arms and munching a turnip while Victoria gives their children milk fresh from the cow.[24]

Albert did not limit his influence to farming, however. The exotic water fowl on the lake in St James's Park in London, where flamingos and pelicans still live a few hundred yards from Buckingham Palace, were first established there by him.

While her husband set about the advancement of British farming, Victoria unhesitatingly used her power and influence to promote the cause of animal welfare. Hunting deer and shooting game birds had been courtly entertainments since time immemorial, despite the death of King William II in 1100. Now, however, these were no longer acceptable aristocratic pastimes and Victoria openly criticised those who enjoyed them.

When legislation came before Parliament to protect wild birds or ban vivisection, she instructed her secretary to inform the House that she was taking a close interest in its progress – the most that a constitutional monarch could do to exert influence. Her patronage of hospitals and medical schools was granted only on the undertaking that they would not experiment on animals.

Prince Albert became president of the Royal Zoological Society and oversaw many improvements to the zoo at Regent's Park and its opening to the public for educational purposes. Until Albert's early death in 1861, the royal couple were the most illustrious champions the cause could have had and as a widow Victoria continued in her support.

As a woman of 19 on the throne of England, who was to use the power of her position decisively throughout her long reign, Victoria's existence alone was enough to shift the country's self-image from that of a military state which still worshipped the Duke of Wellington in the first half of the century to an industrial and colonial power which, for all its many faults, embraced progress in science, exploration, social organisation and many other fields.

Victoria's influence, coming as industrialisation destroyed the ancient, stable communities of rural England, focused women's thinking on their role in this new society. The first evidence of this fresh thinking came from a writer remarkably close to Anna Sewell and her mother.

Two years after the young queen's coronation, a relative of Isaac Sewell, Sarah Stickney Ellis, also a lapsed Quaker, wrote a series of books which became instant bestsellers. Sarah's sister Dorothy, whose son Joseph nearly inspired Philip to become a missionary, was married to Isaac Sewell's brother Abraham and all the family had spent many days together at Great Yarmouth in Norfolk, where Abraham still owned the draper's shop he had inherited from Anna's paternal grandfather.

Sarah and Dorothy Stickney, the daughters of an innovative farmer in Yorkshire, had enjoyed an unconventional childhood in which 'individuality had been allowed free play',[25] so it is no surprise that Mary had found them congenial company and as young women they became good friends. Sarah was the second wife of William Ellis, a missionary who was also celebrated as the author of several books based on his work in the South Pacific. She met him through her own work for the London Missionary Society. He soon retired in order to spend more time with her and took a position as a Congregationalist minister in Hertfordshire, but not before she had formed the habit of writing books in his absences. Suddenly, in 1842, she departed from the travel memoirs and essays she had produced up to then and wrote an immensely successful series of books about the role of women. First was *The Women of England* in 1843, followed smartly by *The Wives of England*, *The Mothers of England* and *The Daughters of England*.

The Women of England: Their Social Duties and Domestic Habits is prefaced by a painfully apologetic introduction in which the author anticipates censure for putting forward her opinions at all. Within a few pages, however, she abandons this tentative tone and enthusiastically accepts Napoleon's description of the British as 'a nation of shopkeepers', then argues that it is indeed the women of the middle classes – meant in the contemporary sense of the petite bourgeoisie rather than as the modern euphemism for the elite – who truly embodied the national character.

She then goes on to argue that the time is ripe for women to assume moral leadership of the nation: 'The British throne being now graced by a female sovereign, the auspicious promise of whose early years seems to form a new era in the annals of our nation and to inspire with brighter hopes and firmer confidence the patriot bosoms of her expectant people.'[26]

Sarah Ellis addressed ordinary women – women like her sister, a shopkeeper's wife, or like Mary and Anna Sewell – who she considered bore the responsibility for righting wrongs, for social reform and for educating the next generation. She dismissed 'ladies' as belonging to an international caste of aristocracy that promoted as an ideal the 'morbid listlessness of mind and body' which men admired and society approved. Her clarion call was for women to reject these aspirations of frivolity and idleness, to become active citizens, to demand education and assume moral leadership in an increasingly profit-driven age. More than a century before popular feminist authors pursued the same themes, she argued against women who lost their identity in an excess of 'agreeableness' and criticised women who constantly apologised for themselves.

While second-wave feminists were to condemn Ellis for her emphasis on the domestic sphere and her portrait of the submissive Victorian wife, later scholars describe her as 'progressive or even proto-feminist'.[27] She was the first popular author to open what became known as 'The Woman Question', the national debate about women's role in society.

Around ten years later, more decisively feminist authors were to emerge. In 1854 two key works were published, *Remarks on the Education of Girls* by Elizabeth Rayner Parkes and *A Brief Summary in Plain Language of the Most Important Laws of England Concerning Women* by Barbara Leigh Smith, and these two authors, both Protestant Nonconformists, went on to found the Langham Place Group and launch *The English Women's Journal*, the foundation enterprise of the suffragette movement.

Sarah Ellis took a much less radical tone and was clearly concerned not to 'frighten the horses' – in other words not to alarm her readers, both men and women, by demanding reforms. Nevertheless, she asserted that women were equal and in some respects superior to men, flatly advised her readers to remain single and enjoy their independence rather than marry a man who was their moral or intellectual inferior and counselled that a bride should make her moral position clear to her future husband before their marriage.

She also went against the prevailing wisdom of the time and encouraged women to be physically and intellectually active, specifically suggesting that horse riding was ideal exercise and that both social reform and animal welfare were worthwhile causes that a woman could support, taking note of 'the droves of weary animals, goaded, stupefied or maddened, none of which would ever tread again the greensward on the mountainside or slake its thirst beside the woodland brook'.[28]

Among the growing middle-class readers in the expanding suburbs, this message was empowering. *The Women of England* ran to at least eleven editions. In the estimation of the British Library, the subsequent books, *The Wives*, *Mothers* and *Daughters of England*, followed within three years. And of all the women in England, none admired the literary success of this free-thinking minister's wife more than her niece and sister-in-law, Anna and Mary Sewell, both ripe for her unassertive brand of radicalisation. Mary enthused to a friend, 'I have read Mrs Ellis' book and advise every mother to read it ... I have been to see her and we had many earnest talks together.'[29] Before long, those earnest talks would encourage Mary to begin her own literary career.

7

'She Consciously Studied for *Black Beauty*' (1846–56)

The story of Anna Sewell's family is the story of many of the great changes in British society, as their lives were successively transformed, first by the flight from the countryside to the city, part of a great population shift in response to industrialisation, and then again by the age of steam, in which the whole country was, within a few years, linked up by the railway network.

In 1846 the prospects for the Sewell family were excitingly improved by the opening of the London, Brighton and South Coast Railway, which merged two smaller railway companies and upgraded the rather basic railway connection between Brighton and the little seaside town of Shoreham, to the west. Soon the route was extended even further westwards to the gracious cathedral city of Chichester. For the Sewells this meant that at last the country life for which Mary yearned was possible because her husband, Isaac, could continue to work in the bank in Brighton and commute by train every day. The railways also offered Anna's brother Philip an exciting future, and a significant role to play in building Europe's rail network.

This was an age of 'railway mania', the dizzying expansion for the rail network, one of the many forces that revolutionised daily life for millions in this small country. Between 1836 and 1844, 2,210 miles of new railway lines were opened, making travel and transportation faster, more comfortable and less expensive, and facilitating the new phenomenon of commuting.[1] The Sewell family spent the next eight years moving westwards to a succession of country homes, and Isaac Sewell became the embodiment of the modern man of business, commuting every day to his office.

He boarded the train every morning near his home, spent the day at his desk at the bank in central Brighton, and arrived back at the same station every evening, marvelling at the magnificent feats of engineering and technology which had given his family the best of both worlds. The move also brought Anna together with the horses who were to win her a place in history, because, like many other rail passengers, her father needed to get to and from the station, and so the family added a pony chaise, a pony, a groom and a stable to their establishment.

Like Black Beauty, their horse would have been trained for both a rider and a carriage, and in her book Anna also describes the new addition to a horse's education: training them not to be afraid of trains. Beauty's breeder sends him to a farmer who has a railway line running through his land:

> I shall never forget the first train that ran by. I was feeding quietly near the pales which separated the meadow from the railway, when I heard a strange sound at a distance: and before I knew whence it came – with a rush and a clatter, and a puffing out of smoke – a long black train of something flew by, and was gone almost before I could draw my breath. I turned, and galloped to the further side of the meadow as fast as I could go; and there I stook snorting with astonishment and fear.

Anna revived her driving skills and became the family coachman. A pony chaise, also called a pony trap, would have been a simple open carriage with two or four large wheels, seating between two and four people on benches, with a footboard against which the driver could brace. It is the simplest and most basic carriage design, light enough for one small horse to pull it and to bounce easily, if uncomfortably, over unmade roads. A woman by herself could easily drive one, as Anna's aunt often did. Anne Wright, although often in poor health, would drive herself over farmland to The Red House School where she taught, jumping down to open gates unless one of the pupils ran beside her to save her the trouble.[2]

Riding and driving undoubtedly played a part in improving Anna's health. While she was to visit spa towns in Germany for the sake of her health, and these long holidays gave her the separation from her family which allowed her own identity to develop, riding in particular must have improved her physical health.

When a person who cannot walk rides a horse, they respond to the animal's movement very much as they would if they were walking themself, using their abdominal muscles for balance and stability. A disabled rider on a moving horse strengthens these core muscles that also maintain an upright posture, hold the spine in a firm but flexible wrapping and support the large organs of the body. The ligaments and tendons, the nervous tissue and all the bodily organs also respond to the animal's movement, which increases the blood supply and develops a healthy tone in the tissues.[3] Small studies have shown that equine therapy can help a variety of conditions, including cerebral palsy and paralysis. It can also act as an analgesic simply by distracting people in pain.[4]

The modern exploration of equine therapy dates from an extraordinary Olympic victory in Helsinki in 1952, when a disabled Danish rider, Lis Hartel, won a silver medal in Individual Dressage. She had contracted polio at the age of 23 and was so badly affected that she had to be helped to mount her horses. Hartel's medal was the first won by any woman in any individual sport when in direct competition with men, and she went on to win again in 1956.[5]

Hartel's inspiration spread worldwide and many small organisations began to offer horse-based therapies to people experiencing illness or with disabilities. In the US, the Professional Association of Therapeutic Horsemanship International, known as PATH Intl, was founded as the North American Riding for the Handicapped Association in 1969 and in the same year the Riding for the Disabled Association was founded in Britain.

Small research studies began to confirm the health benefits of equine therapies, and also investigated the mental health improvement achieved by riding, driving and interacting with horses. In 1994 one researcher observed:

> Horse riding is a therapy full of pleasure, where deep emotions can be experienced. The feeling … of being able to perceive oneself and of being able to establish a relation with one's surroundings is essential for a way out of the psychic illness.[6]

This implies that, if there was a psychological or emotional element in Anna's most severe illness, it could have been alleviated eventually by her contact with the family's pony.

Her progress towards better health was still very slow. Mary's dream of living in the country once more was finally realised when the family moved to the picture-postcard village of Lancing, nestled close to Shoreham among the rolling hills of the South Downs. Perhaps because she wanted to live among green fields again, or perhaps because Isaac was a hopelessly impractical man, their new house was a few miles from the railway station.

The family needed their pony chaise to get about, and Mrs Bayly writes that Anna 'consciously studied for *Black Beauty*' in driving her father to and from Shoreham Station every day.[7] She was able to keep bees again, and to plant and enjoy a garden, but was still suffering severe pain in her feet. Her injured foot seemed to be getting worse. If her original injury had caused the death of a bone, this would have become more brittle over time and may have fragmented, making her ankle joint unstable and releasing chips of bone into the complex structure of the ankle to cause further pain and loss of function. Her good foot had taken the strain of carrying her whole body weight and now also began to hurt.

Worse, she began to suffer bouts of overall weakness. The first occasion on which she felt ill, shortly after the family moved to Brighton, was one on which she was bled severely by a doctor, which suggests that she may have had a fever, or that she was showing signs of a heart problem, for both of which bleeding was a favourite treatment. Indeed, it had been a 'worldwide panacea' since the days of Hippocrates.

With modern medical knowledge, bleeding seems a bizarre treatment. When the blood carries oxygen, removes waste and potentially toxic substances and brings infection-fighting cells to the site of injury or infection, removing a substantial volume of it from the body seems more likely to make an illness worse than to cure it. A few medical conditions do respond to reducing the volume of blood in the body – there is evidence that symptoms of congestive heart failure, atrial fibrillation, congenital heart disease and even eclampsia of pregnancy have been relieved by bleeding.

By the time of Anna's illness some doctors had begun to question the practice, but it remained a standard, even popular, treatment which some patients actually requested.[8] It was even used on horses, and Black Beauty is bled after an inexperienced stable boy nearly kills him by letting him get cold after a hard ride.

Once the family moved to Lancing, Anna's periods of illness became more frequent and more worrying. As well as pain in her feet, she had pains in her back and chest. Sometimes she was so weak she could hardly move and her newly discovered talent for driving and her role as the family coachman were often beyond her strength. Her father was prosperous now and there was money for doctors, so 'many infallible cures were tried, and proved most fallible. Much was spent upon physicians, but the poor patient was nothing the better.'[9]

While Anna's illness restricted her life, her brother was growing up and beginning his own adventures. Brighton became a major railway terminus and the building of the new line that would change his family's style of living was also an inspiration for his choice of profession. As he grew up, he witnessed many extraordinary feats of engineering.

Brighton is encircled by the South Downs, a beautiful chalk escarpment, the backdrop to much of England's south-east coast, which is now a national park and a protected habitat for rare plants and wildlife. At the time that the railway was built, however, the need to run the line through these steep hills was a major engineering challenge. Thousands of men with picks and shovels dug out the New England Cutting, a huge trench excavated from New England Hill.

Thousands more men laid millions of bricks by hand to construct the imposing viaducts around Brighton Station; just one part of the station complex required a workforce of 3,500 men and 570 horses.[10] Aggregates, rails, ironwork and sleepers either arrived by rail or were unloaded from ships at the harbours at Brighton and Shoreham, from whence they were carried by horse-drawn carts to the construction sites.

Of the tens of thousands of spectators watching this massive enterprise, none was more enthralled than Philip Sewell. He was 14 when the family moved to Brighton, and four years later went to work in the bank with his father, which he found stifling. Although he was a loving son, he wanted adventure and independence and the prospect of a desk-bound life like his father's appalled him.

Altruistic and warm-hearted, he flirted briefly with the idea of becoming a missionary, inspired by his uncle, Sarah Stickney Ellis's husband William, who was famous for his accounts of living in the South Pacific. Philip's cousin Joseph, the son of Abraham Sewell and Dorothy Stickney, was similarly taken with the idea, but the Society of Friends did not train or fund missionaries.

William Ellis had been sent on his travels by a Church of England institution, the London Missionary Society.[11] Philip boldly withdrew from the Quaker movement and wrote Anna an ecstatic letter celebrating his freedom and happiness. He resolved to take orders as an Anglican minister and was accepted at theological college in Cambridge,[12] but before he could begin his studies he fell ill. As with Anna, the struggle for an independent adult life after a childhood so closely bonded with their mother seems to have taken its toll physically as well as mentally and emotionally.

Both the Wright and Sewell families put maximum pressure on Philip and also on his cousin Joseph to reconsider their ambitions. Philip capitulated and gave up his dream. His father still attended meetings every Sunday and Anna and his mother both lived a Quaker life even when no longer officially members of a meeting. Philip's subsequent career took him abroad for many years, which seems to have satisfied his yearning for independence. He later rejoined the movement formally. His anonymous biographer observed, 'Anything connected with the well-being and elevation of those around him, physically, mentally or morally, excited his warm interest.'[13]

This interest had been equally excited by the new railway, however, and Philip now resolved to become a civil engineer. He learned with two of the greatest men in engineering history, Thomas Brassey, the father of railway mania, who is credited with the construction of a third of Britain's railway network, and Charles Edward Vignoles, who was then teaching at University College London, although in 1846 he began work on the Nicholas Chain Bridge over the Dnipro in Ukraine.

Engineering was then the most international of professions, and both men were extensively involved in railway building all over Europe, which was expedient as railway mania in Britain ran out of steam in the late 1840s. Philip's early projects sent him to Cumbria, to work on the railway between Carlisle and Settle,[14] and then to France, where a railway across Provence required some of the famous salt marshes of the Camargue to be drained.

Here the sound teaching of French he had had in London came into its own, as he overheard two of the boatmen hired by the engineering team to carry them across the Rhône plotting to rob and perhaps even murder them. He reported this to his chief and the programme of works was altered to keep them safe.[15] This would not be the last time Philip's thirst for adventure put his life in danger, however.

Anna, Philip and their mother had a close and loving bond all their lives, despite Philip's absences. Isaac was a more distant figure, because he was at work all day, and also because he was a practical, unimaginative man who could not share the pleasure that Anna and Mary in particular took in literature.

Mrs Bayly described him as a man with a 'downright, matter of fact view of things', and observed that, 'although he sympathised with their works of kindness, I do not think he cared much for the books they read'. Philip, on the other hand, seemed to have inherited his mother's mercurial charm, was highly intelligent and soon began to develop a good business brain. His letters to his father are full of investment tips and news of new opportunities. He was also a charming and captivating man who easily found his place among the pioneering engineering teams with which he worked as well as the Norfolk Quaker grandees among his family connections.

His 'simplicity of character and cheerful and optimistic way of looking at life'[16] made Philip popular wherever he went and when he was at home he was the sunshine of his family's life. The days when the three of them had stood against the world in Dalston had formed a tie between Anna, Philip and Mary that would never be broken. Philip also had 'a very strong feeling that families should not be divided'.[17] But his new career nevertheless divided the Sewells. The dynamic of their home changed as Philip made a life of his own, and Anna and her mother grew even closer.

Accustomed as Anna was to talking herself out of negative feelings, she would not have been human if she had not felt the loss of her brother's companionship as an emotional blow. It must also have been very hard for her to see her younger sibling suddenly become a mature man, exploring the world and consolidating his adult identity. Anna never expressed regret for the limitations of her disability, but in *Black Beauty* the horse constantly yearns for 'liberty' and, dutiful as he is, reacts with horror when he is first harnessed. Philip certainly found all the adventure he could have wished for as a railway engineer, while Anna was condemned to stay at home.

Philip was also making plans to get married, something which Anna would have realised that she would be unlikely ever to do. The possibility of her marriage is something that her mother never mentions, another of her telling omissions. Given the close bond between mother and daughter, it is likely that Mary was not anxious to lose Anna to an independent life.

Anna's independent nature must also be considered. While the view of Jane Austen's heroines is that marriage is desirable above all things for a woman, Sarah Stickney Ellis firmly advised a woman who could not find a man with good qualities to choose a single life rather than a bad marriage, and Anna had the awkward example of her parents' vexed relationship before her. We must also consider that the disabled daughter of a rather flaky bank manager was not an attractive prospect in the hard-headed mercantile society which surrounded them, and the fact that both Anna and her mother had an equivocal relationship with the Quaker movement meant that it would not rally round to find her a true-believing husband.

Looking at the pattern of Anna's ill health, it seems linked to stressors such as moving to a new home and particularly to the loss of her brother's companionship – on both the occasions when these factors combined she became most severely ill. Stress is recognised now as something that diminishes the immune response and worsens many different medical conditions. A post-viral syndrome, or an auto-immune condition, would be exacerbated by the stress of major life events and even today these can only be managed, not cured.

Anna continued to link her suffering to her faith, to see it as something sent by God, and something that could be relieved by prayer. She left a record in her diary, dated just after the family moved to Lancing, of these beliefs in action:

> Mother went to Brighton, and I stayed to attend to the planting of seeds in the garden; my feet were very weak, and I prayed that they might be strengthened sufficiently for me to attend to what was necessary. The Lord most graciously heard me, and gave me more strength than I have had for some time, so that I am able to see after the garden properly.

Philip was already in France when the rest of the family moved to Lancing. He returned to work on the harbour at Shoreham and the family were briefly reunited. Philip, Anna and Mary then made a trip to a spa town in Germany, together with Mary's youngest sister Ellen, in the hope that the new hydrotherapy cure would improve the health of Anna and her aunt.

They went to Marienbad, the beautiful resort in the mountains of Bohemia, a place which was destined to become a legendary centre of European spa culture, whose wedding-cake architecture and colonnaded terraces were celebrated by Alain Resnais in a classic film of the New Wave era, *Last Year in Marienbad*. The film's characters drift through sumptuous baroque interiors and haunting, mist-wreathed gardens, and the strange spirit of dissociated calm must have been close to the experience of the spa's fashionable clientele in its heyday, a few decades after the Sewells' visit. Encircled by forested mountains, it was becoming the most fashionable of all the destinations in the new craze for hydrotherapy and the family must have invested heavily in the trip in the hope that the two would overcome their illnesses.

Marienbad is now in the Czech Republic and is known by the Czech name of Mariánské Lázně. The thermal springs on which its reputation rests were owned by the Tepia Abbey and towards the end of the eighteenth century the monastery physician wrote papers to demonstrate the curative powers of the spring water which were soon noted by the founding fathers of the hydrotherapy movement. When Anna Sewell visited in 1846, the town was just becoming fashionable and must still have had the atmosphere of a mountain village, 2,000ft above sea level, encircled by pine forests, with clear air and brilliant light.

Most of the hydrotherapy treatments being developed at this time would have appealed to Anna with their emphasis on simplicity, purification and contact with nature. The foundation myths of many European spas involve stories about animals that instinctively healed themselves in thermal springs, such as the boar wounded by hunters at Salies-de-Béarn or the Roman soldier's elderly dog at Dax, both in France.

Vincenz Priessnitz (1799–1851), the Austrian founder of nineteenth-century spa culture, was the son of a peasant farmer who, as a child, observed a deer bathing a wound in a pond near his home and tried the same cure successfully when he was run over by a cart and suffered broken ribs. From his own recovery, he developed the basic theory of hydrotherapy and set up a clinic which was extremely successful.

By 1840, Priessnitz had 1,600 patients in his clinic, including many physicians as well as important political figures, members of the aristocracy and prominent military officials. A large part of his treatment was based on living a simple lifestyle, eating wholefoods, gentle exercise, especially walking, and, of course, drinking plentiful quantities of spa water at regular intervals during the day.

Priessnitz's successor was Sebastian Kneipp (1821–97), whose treatments Anna would have enjoyed even more. He rejected the more extreme therapies, such as cold-water baths or wrapping patients in cold, wet sheets, and instead recommended medicinal herbs, massages, balanced nutrition and 'regulative therapy to seek inner balance'.

His patients were invited to walk barefoot in the snow or over pine needles. Like Priessnitz, Kneipp had no medical training. He explained his theories in layman's language, writing about strengthening the body, calming the mind and removing toxins in language ordinary people could understand. For a patient such as Anna, chronically ill and disillusioned by the conventional doctors of the day, a large part of the appeal of hydrotherapy was that it was an alternative practice.

Of course, many other activities were typical of Marienbad and the other spa resorts which Anna visited. Marienbad offered many of the same entertainments as Brighton, with assembly rooms and pleasure gardens, music, theatre and shopping – all with the crucial difference that Anna was, by implication, allowed to enjoy them for the sake of her health.

People stayed at spa towns for months on end, and many of them were not ill but suffering from bereavement or anxiety, loneliness or boredom. Spa culture in Victorian times also embraced a whole range of diversions provided to make the patients' stays as pleasurable as possible. Marienbad is one of the great spa towns listed as a World Heritage Site by UNESCO, which notes that the whole resort could be considered a 'therapeutic landscape'.[18] In a therapeutic context, Anna could go to concerts and play the piano without the eternal shadow of Quaker guilt.

Similarly, she enjoyed painting and the company of like-minded amateur artists. She learned German and a whole new repertoire of *lieder* which her niece, Philip's daughter Margaret, remembered her singing for the rest of her life.[19] Her mother wrote, 'She has made dear and valuable friends, and gained a great deal of experience, and seen much variety which, to such a prisoner as she is, is a great advantage.' This noting of 'dear and valuable friends' is significant. In Mary's euphemistic mode of writing, it may well have suggested a romantic attachment which, while it evidently came to nothing in the end, no doubt brought Anna some happiness and strengthened her sense of adult identity.

She also read poetry, devouring new works by Wordsworth and Tennyson and learning them by heart in order to recite later, which she did with great emotion, as her niece remembered. Her annotated copy of *In Memoriam* (1849) was found among her papers. Importantly, Anna made many new friends and could really establish her own life, her own interests and her own identity, despite the restrictions of her disability – and without the constant rain of advice from her family.

Anna stayed behind in Marienbad after Philip, Mary and Ellen returned to England. In Brussels, her aunt was taken so ill they thought she would die, which suggests that the spa cure had not helped her, whereas it had clearly been of benefit to Anna. Her new sense of autonomy and freedom may have been as therapeutic as the physical healing achieved by the waters themselves and the skilled practitioners who cared for her. As a young woman, Anna had clearly rejected the lifestyle of the classic Victorian 'invalid', the stereotypical woman – this phenomenon seemed to be predominantly a female one – who was confined to her bed for years with a malady beyond the understanding of contemporary medicine.

This has been called the age of the 'great malingerer', with both men and women attracting public and personal sympathy for their unspecified illness. Charles Darwin and the poet Elizabeth Barrett Browning were prominent among other great figures in intellectual life whose output was created in spite of severe debility.[20] The idea that people with conditions that seemed mysterious in the nineteenth century were malingering is also questionable, as the medical science of the time was unable to diagnose, let alone treat, many conditions effectively. As the era wore on, the widowed Queen Victoria withdrew from public life and female frailty became a gender-defining characteristic; Victorian society increasingly accepted ill or disabled women as a natural occurrence.

Prominent women, such as the campaigning nurse Florence Nightingale and the writer Harriet Martineau, who had been exceptionally robust in their early lives, suddenly succumbed to invalidism and continued their work from their sickbeds. Many different interpretations have been offered for this. For some feminists, invalidism was a choice that removed a woman from patriarchal control.[21]

Martineau herself argued that her period of confinement conferred philosophical and moral advantages:

> If we cannot pursue a trade or a science, or keep house, or help the state, or write books, or earn our own bread or that of others, we can do the work to which all this is only subsidiary, – we can cherish a sweet and holy temper, – we can vindicate the supremacy of mind over body, – we can, in defiance of our liabilities, minister pleasure and hope to the gayest who come prepared to receive pain from the

> spectacle of our pain; we can, here as well as in heaven's courts hereafter, reveal the angel growing into its immortal aspect.[22]

None of these approaches appealed to Anna, although by all accounts she was able to 'cherish a sweet and holy temper' despite being in pain. Since she stopped writing her journal when she started to travel, and since her mother's autobiography skims the periods of life in which her daughter stayed in spa towns, there are no definitive records of her thought process.

She had better models of 'invalid' life closer to home. Her aunt Anne Wright was often bedridden and used these periods to educate herself in natural sciences and theology to a very high level. Elizabeth Fry, who must have been a towering figure in Quaker circles, was the survivor of eleven pregnancies and frequently ill, but never faltered in her campaign for prison and social reform. We can only extrapolate Anna's decisions about the way she managed her disability from the fact that during this period of her life she was seemingly never tempted to take to her bed or confine herself to a sickroom.

As the unknown daughter of a provincial bank manager, a volunteer teacher of no public standing, an active young woman injured in an accident and laid low by periods of weakness, the model of Victorian disability, of idleness, passivity and lassitude, did not attract her. The life of a spa town, on the other hand, full of social amusements and far beyond the reach of her family and their Quaker community, seems to have suited her very well. For three years after this first visit to Marienbad, she spent the majority of her time visiting fashionable spas.

When she came home from Marienbad after her first visit, it was for her brother's wedding. Settled in his profession, with a bright future ahead of him and knowing that his sister now had a life of her own, Philip was ready to get married. His bride was Sarah Woods, whose family lived in Tottenham, in east London, which suggests that the young couple had known each other since childhood, probably again through Quaker connections as the family lived close to the same meeting houses.

It seems that Sarah too had rejected Plain Quaker strictures, because she was an accomplished pianist and singer. Anna often joined her in the evenings to entertain the family, no doubt sharing some of the new

German songs she had learned. Mary Sewell looked back on this period as 'the very brightest in her whole life … when her son and daughter, and her future daughter-in-law, sang together'. She 'looked back on those evenings as something so heavenly, the life of it could never come again'. Sarah was universally described as 'very lovely' and Anna became good friends with her.

Those musical evenings were all the more precious for ending too soon, since Philip's work obliged him to travel frequently. The couple were in Yorkshire when their first child, Mary Grace, was born. The master engineer who had trained him, Charles Vignoles, now called Philip to join a team working in the Basque provinces of northern Spain, where he was building the new railway line connecting the port of Bilbao with the regional capital of Navarre.

Philip and Sarah moved to Spain with their first two daughters and had five more children while living there. Leading the project was Vignoles's son, Henry, who relied on Philip's management style as well as his engineering skills. The original Spanish engineers had abandoned the task and considered it to be impossible:

> A large share, of the merit of the success which was ultimately reached is due to his patient and skilful management of men as well as of material in these formidable operations. Mr. Sewell is to this day (and very properly) proud to remember that it was all accomplished without Sunday labour.[23]

Building this line meant facing the challenge of the Pyrenees and diverting the course of the River Ebro, for which task Charles Vignoles particularly commended him. The chain of the Pyrenees, a relatively young mountain range characterised by sharp limestone peaks and deep ravines and descending to salt marshes and quicksands at the coast, presented far more testing challenges to an engineer than the gentle slopes of the South Downs.

The steepest part of the track is 2,163ft above sea level with an incline of 1 in 70, and a 20ft-long model of the railway was exhibited as a triumph of British engineering in the International Exhibition of 1862 in London.[24] Against the dire warnings of the local newspapers, who predicted that the project would fail and be nothing but 'a memento to the temerity of the English engineers',[25] the line was completed on time.

A branch line was then built to Santander, and when the section from Santander to Ooralles was opened, an embankment collapsed and the engine plunged off the track and overturned. The engineer in charge, Alfred Gee, and his brother, who had been riding in the cab, were both killed but Philip and others who were sitting outside on the engine itself were thrown clear and survived.

The family letters do not record his lucky escape, but Anna and her mother could have learned of it from Gee's obituary in *The Times*.[26] On another occasion, riding as a passenger in a stagecoach, Philip lost his outside corner seat to another passenger who refused to give it up. As the coach thundered through the narrow streets of a town at night, the coachman misjudged a corner, turned too close to an over-hanging roof and killed that passenger in the corner seat.[27]

The station at Bilbao, now known as Bilbao-Abando and constructed by Vignoles close to a former bullring, caught fire a few months after it was opened, perhaps as a result of arson as some citizens objected to its English design.[28] Despite these ill omens, Philip and his family remained in Spain for eleven years.

At home all was calm for a few months and Anna, feeling stronger, could once again take her father to the station every morning and treat her mother to a drive in the country in the afternoon.

Soon, however, her father's restless nature blighted their lives again. Isaac took up brewing, at first as a hobby but soon as a business. For centuries in Britain, beer had been brewed not for its alcoholic content – which was often very weak – but as a means of providing a healthy drink, as the fermenting process killed many of the bacteria in the water. Pasteurisation (sterilising milk by heating) and the anti-bacterial effect of boiling water had yet to be discovered. (The young Louis Pasteur was at this time still working in the French wine industry.) In earlier centuries, the general population simply drank weak beer in preference to dirty water.

Brewers had begun to strengthen the alcohol content of beer and so provide the millions of poor industrial workers a cheap route to oblivion. The beer drunk in Victorian Britain was a strong, adulterated brew that had a similar impact to that of heroin or crack cocaine today, destroying families' lives while creating a criminal underclass.

The temperance movement had focused first on gin, the real opium of the masses in Georgian Britain, but was now turning against beer and the whole culture of drinking. In this, the movement was supported by all the Nonconformist faith groups, including the Quakers. Isaac Sewell concluded that he could no longer benefit from Quaker support and be a brewer, and so in March 1849 confessed to his superiors at the bank and resigned his position.[29]

The family moved again, to a house called Petlands in Haywards Heath, which had been built a little more than fifteen years earlier, part of the suburban development that was swallowing a once-charming village. The house had a large garden and backed on to open fields, but it must have reminded Mary strongly of the dark days of Dalston. She rarely mentioned this period in their lives which suggests that her memories were not pleasant ones.

When someone as determinedly positive as Mary Sewell writes their memoir, the omissions are as important as the inclusions. Mary wrote little about the four years she lived in Haywards Heath, said nothing about her husband's adventure in the brewing trade and also said little about her travels, although, with her son now living in Spain, she and Anna, and other members of their family, took several trips with him.

Sarah Stickney Ellis, who visited the French Pyrenees in 1840 with her husband in the hope of improving his health, was inspired to write a whole book about their experiences, *Summer and Winter in the Pyrenees*, elegantly published by Fisher & Son upon her return, but Mary never wrote a word about her experiences abroad, suggesting that she did not enjoy them. While she had nurtured every kind of courage in her children, and shown considerable fortitude as a young wife and mother, she seems to have become more anxious as she grew older and was markedly much less brave than her daughter, so perhaps travelling itself was too much for her.

Anna, however, enjoyed travelling and soon began to try some English spa towns. Hydrotherapy had now become fashionable in Britain, although the proponents tended to favour the harsher treatments that

Sebastian Kneipp rejected. It was at a spa resort in England that she is said to have met her literary idol and formed a friendship with him.

Her family afterwards believed that Anna met Alfred Tennyson at the spa at Matlock in Derbyshire, a beautiful village in the Peak District where a resort every bit as elegant as Marienbad was developing, complete with ornamental gardens and a humid conservatory full of palm trees and button-back banquettes. However, Anna's most intense period of visiting spas was from 1846 to 1856. At this time, Alfred Tennyson visited spas in Cheltenham, Birmingham and Malvern but no visit to Matlock is recorded until 18 August 1862. By this time, he was the Poet Laureate, famous enough to want to travel incognito, and he did not visit the spa at all.

In his letters, he asks for a book to be sent to 'Miss Sewell'[30] and in 1857 writes of a landscape picture intended to be 'Miss Sewell's gift'. Through her own letters, this Miss Sewell has been identified as Ellen Mary Sewell,[31] a writer and schoolteacher from the Isle of Wight. So, to date, there is no definitive confirmation of the family story.

Certainly Anna and her literary idol were both visiting spas most frequently in the late 1840s. Tennyson was in his late 30s, and considered to be 'one of the finest looking men in the world'.[32] He was in a low mental state, anxious and depressed despite the widespread acclaim for his poetry. Although he had a private income and a small government retainer acknowledging his status as heir apparent to the status of Poet Laureate, he believed himself to be poor.

He was also deep in spiritual doubt and broke off his engagement to Emily Selwood in 1840 for financial and religious reasons. He had no home of his own and divided his life between visiting or travelling with friends and living with his clingy parents in Cheltenham. Suffering from 'nervous stress and irritability', he and his taste for hydrotherapy were the despair of his friends, one of whom wrote:

> Tennyson is emerged, half-cured or half-destroyed from a water establishment: has gone to a new Doctor who gives him iron pills; and altogether this really great man thinks more about his bowels and nerves than about the Laureate wreath he was born to inherit.[33]

The poet himself felt tortured, and explained that:

> The perpetual panic and horror of the last two years has steeped my nerves in poison: now I am left a beggar but I am or shall be shortly somewhat better off in nerves. I am in a Hydropathy Establishment near Cheltenham (the only one in England conducted on pure Priessnitzan principles).[34]

This spa near Cheltenham, run on the principles of Vincenz Priessnitz, the Austrian founder of the movement, would have been attractive to Anna, with her experience of the same therapy at Marienbad. She had fallen in love with Tennyson's poetry there, and Mrs Bayly later observed that 'a good deal of hero-worship' of their favourite poets was indulged in by Anna and also her mother. Meeting him in real life would have been like a No. 1 fan meeting a rock star.

From Tennyson's point of view, he had always been awkward with society women, irritated by his popularity with fashionable hostesses and a grumpy guest at balls,[35] so he could well have found the companionship of a guileless, outspoken young woman with distinct Quaker leanings a refreshing contrast.

His long poem calling for university education for women, *The Princess*, was published in 1847 to a mixed reception and he had been working on *In Memoriam* for some years. Considered one of the finest poems of the century, the work is a tribute to a beloved friend from his days at Cambridge University who had died young, and was published in 1850. Anna Sewell's annotated copy of *In Memoriam* was kept by her family for many years. While there is every possibility that the two met and formed a friendship, there is as yet no hard evidence either way for this.

Isaac Sewell's adventure in the brewing trade was fortunately short-lived. He was once again enfolded in the Quaker business network and appointed as the manager of a bank on a good salary in the gracious and ancient city of Chichester in West Sussex, the final destination of the extended railway line from Brighton. From the family's wills, it is clear that they were all accumulating small amounts of wealth by this time, in shares in the London 7 Counties Bank, and in various railway and other utility companies.

The family were able to continue living in the country and rented a beautiful old farmhouse at Grayling Wells. The memories[36] of local people suggest that it had a crab apple tree and a pond with bulrushes in the garden but no trace of this now remains and the area has been subsumed within the city as a public park.

Early in 1856, Philip came to visit with his wife and family, now three daughters, and a few months later Mary and Anna travelled to Germany for her next spa visit, to the smaller establishment at Marienberg. Marienberg, now Bad Marienberg, is a much smaller resort than Marienbad, with the atmosphere of a mountain village. It seems likely Anna stayed there in the company of friends she had made on her first spa visit, because Mary soon returned home. Anna stayed in Marienberg for a year, and her health improved significantly.

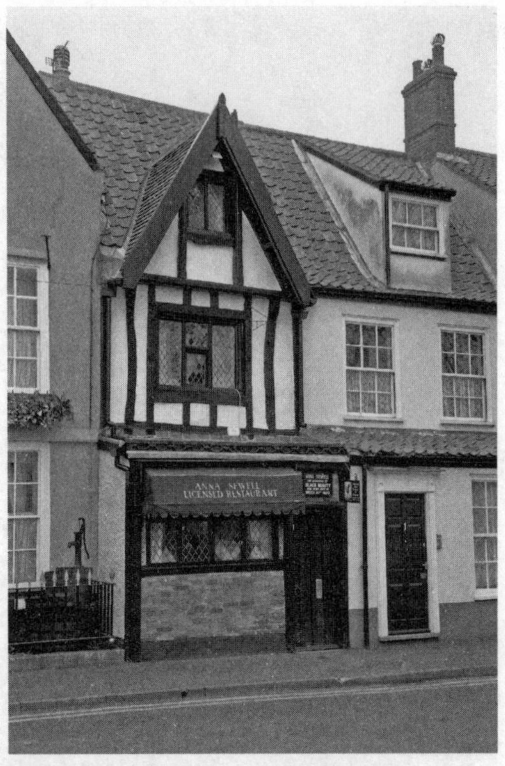

The tiny house in Great Yarmouth where Anna Sewell was born. (David Osborn/ Alamy Stock Photo)

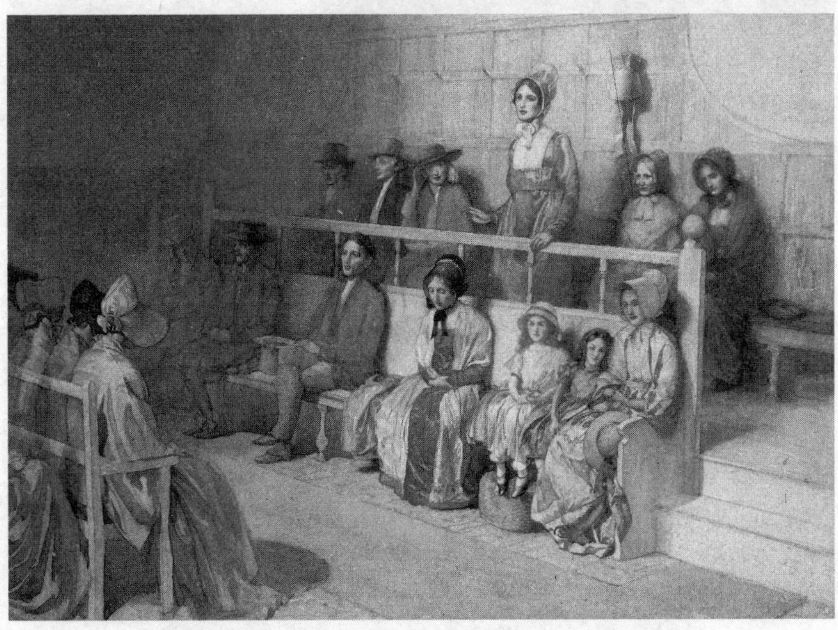

A Quaker meeting pictured by the Suffolk artist J. Walter West. Note the woman speaker and the sleepy children. (© Britain Yearly Meeting)

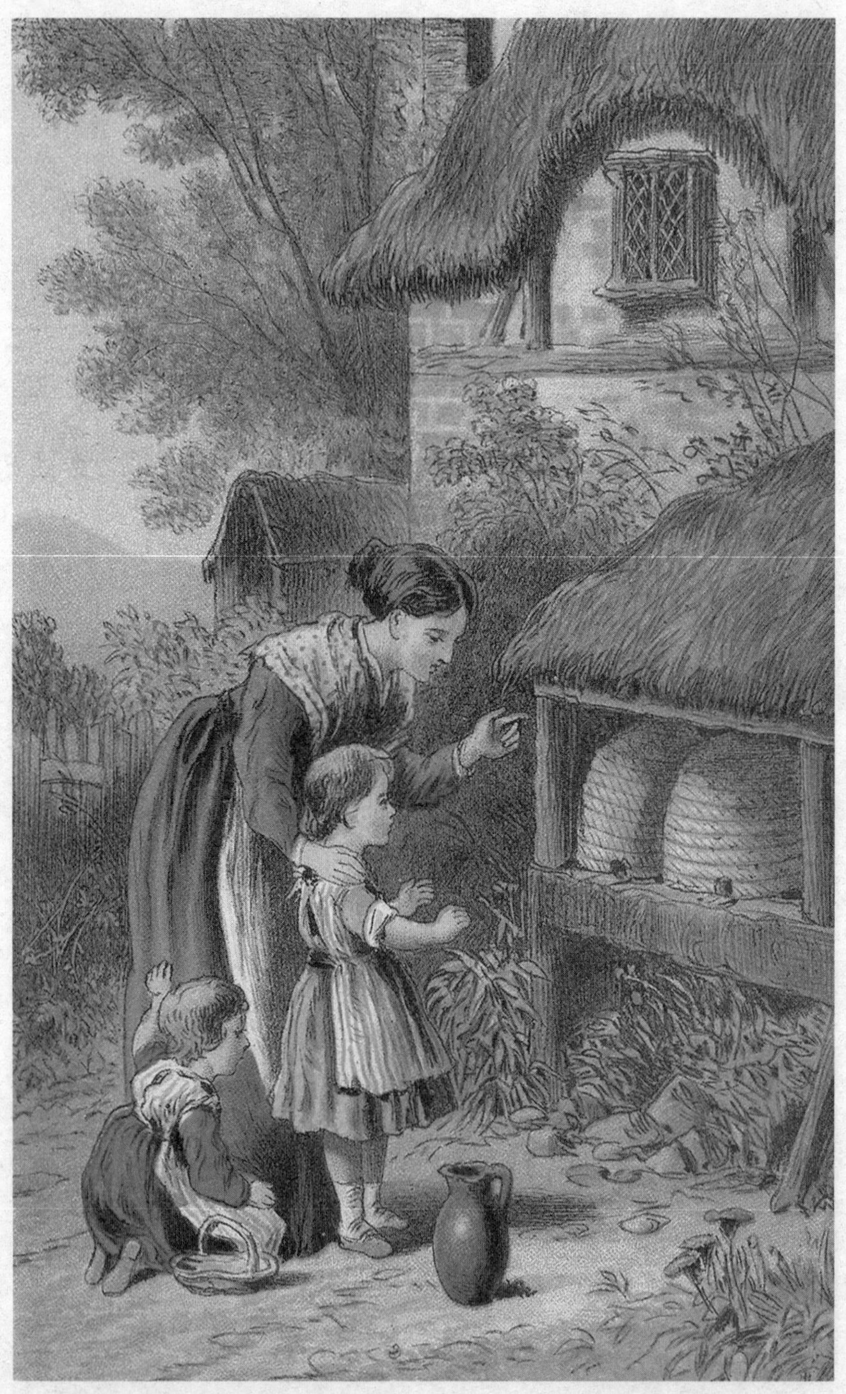

The Victorians encouraged children to admire bees for their hard work. Anna kept bees throughout her life.

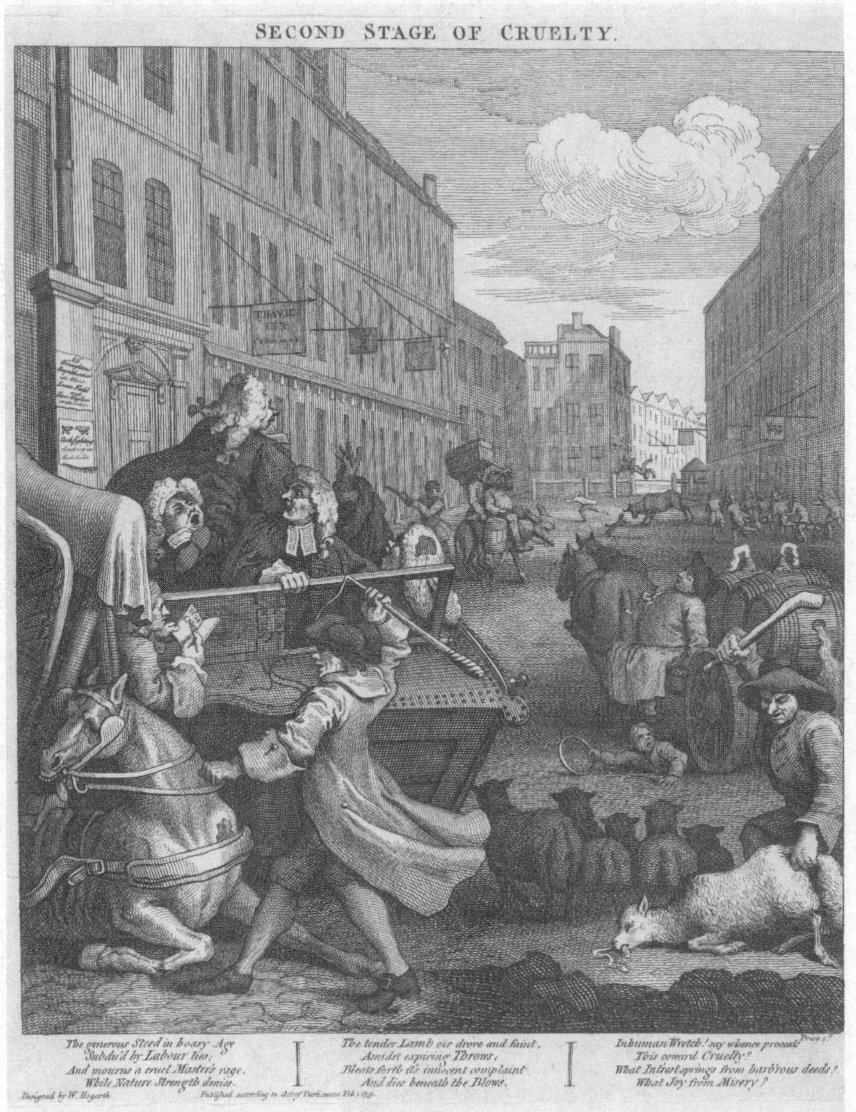

The Second Stage of Cruelty (1751) from a set of engravings by William Hogarth. (Harris Brisbane Dick Fund, 1932)

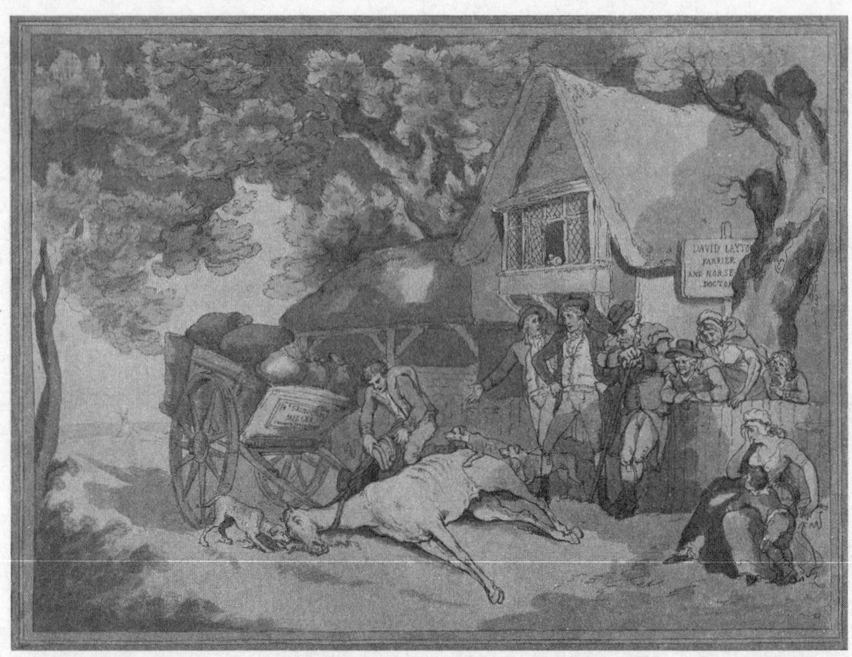

Thomas Rowlandson's 1789 print illustrating 'The High-Mettled Racer', a song from the comic opera *Liberty-Hall* about a racehorse who ends his days as a carthorse and dies in harness. (The Metropolitan Museum of Art, The Elisha Whittelsey Collection, The Elisha Whittelsey Fund, 1959)

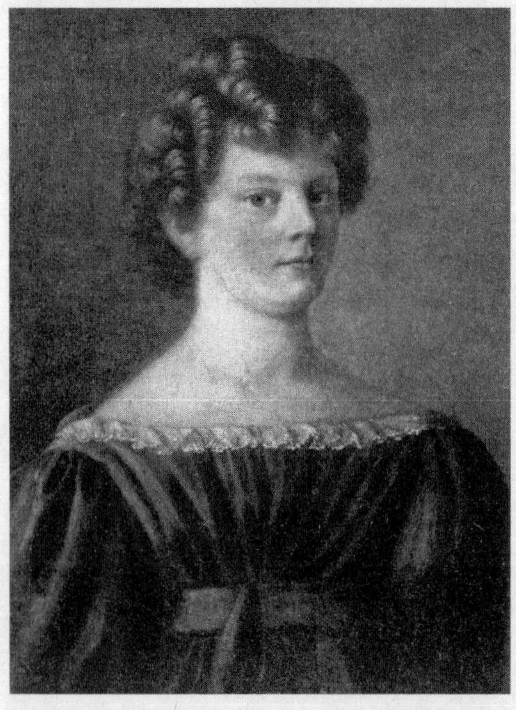

A portrait of Anna Sewell as a young woman in Quaker dress. (Chronicle/Alamy Stock Photo)

Richard Martin, nicknamed 'Humanity Dick' by King George IV, whose Cruel Treatment of Cattle Act of 1822 was the first recorded British animal welfare law. (Chronicle/Alamy Stock Photo)

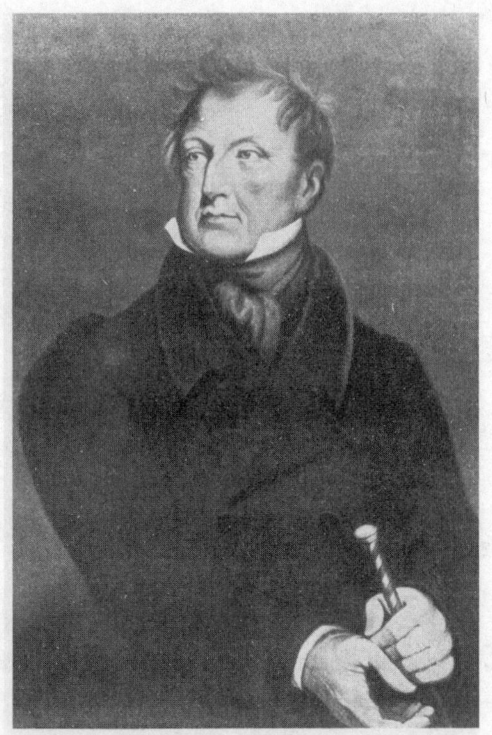

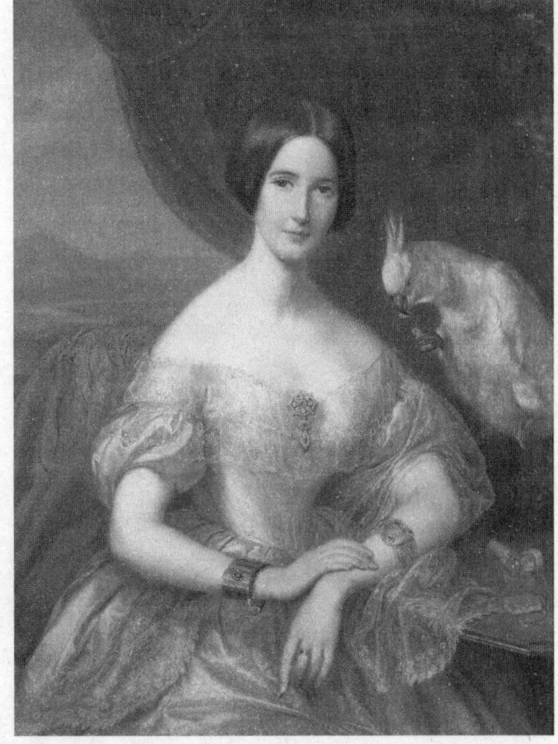

Angela Burdett-Coutts, who donated £5 to the RSPCA before she inherited a fortune at the age of 23. She devoted her life to philanthropy and was the first woman to be ennobled for her achievements when Queen Victoria made her a baroness in 1871. (Bridgeman Images)

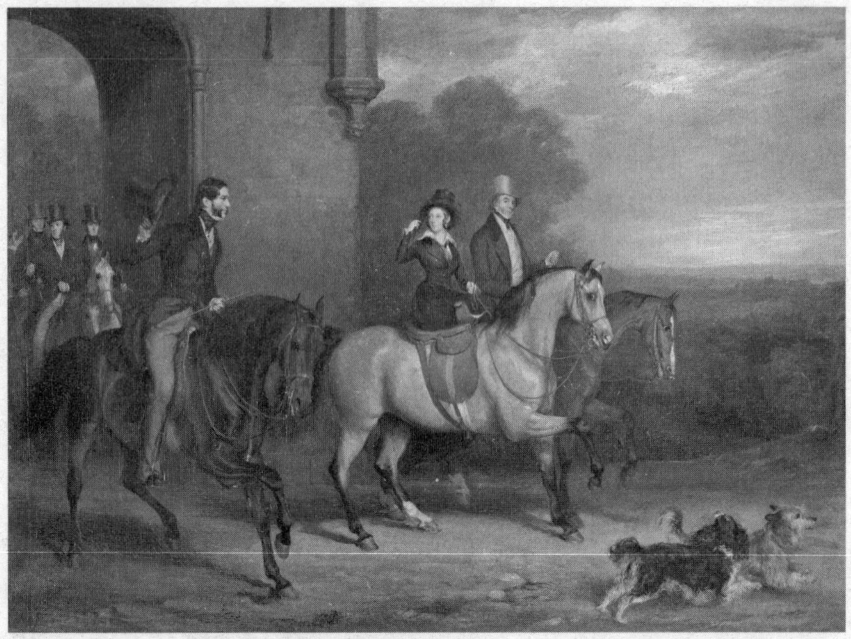

Queen Victoria pictured on her daily ride with her first Prime Minister, Lord Melbourne, and her dogs, Dash and Islay. Painted for the queen by Sir Francis Grant. (Royal Collection Trust)

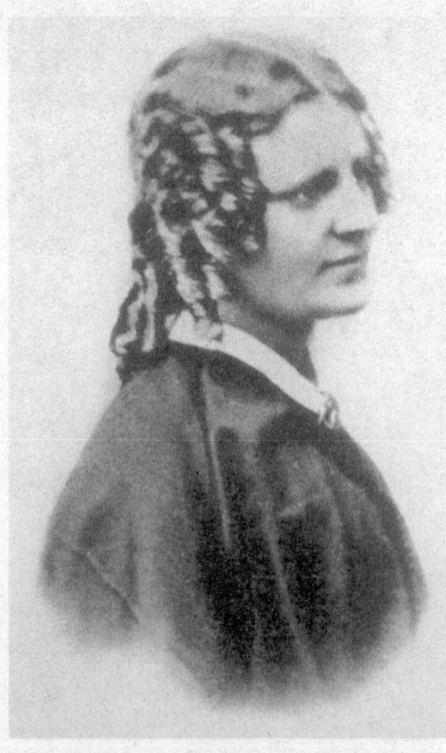

Anna Sewell in later life. (TopFoto)

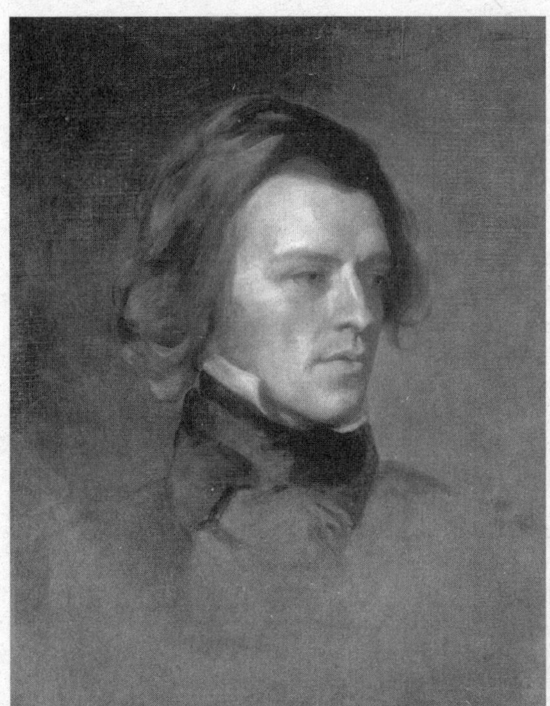

Anna's literary hero Alfred Tennyson around the age they could have met. Painted by Samuel Laurence, *c.* 1840. (National Portrait Gallery, London)

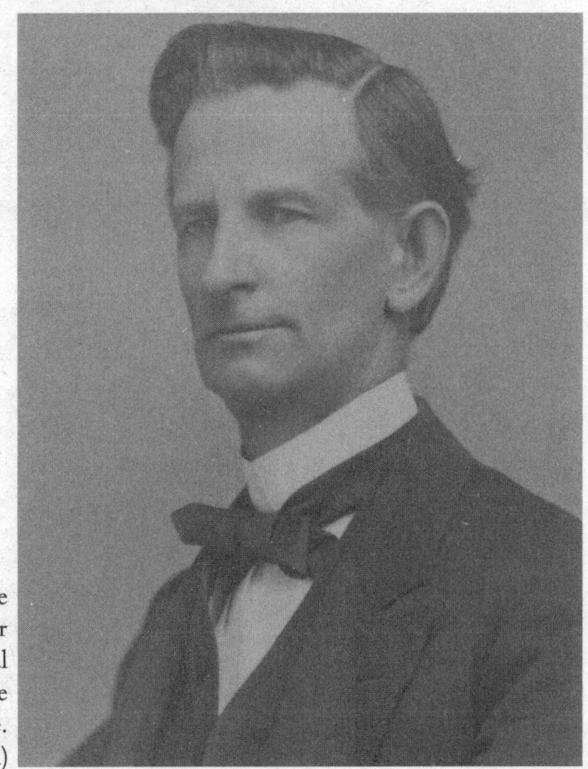

George Thorndike Angell, the Boston lawyer who gave up his legal career to champion the cause of animal welfare. (MSPCA)

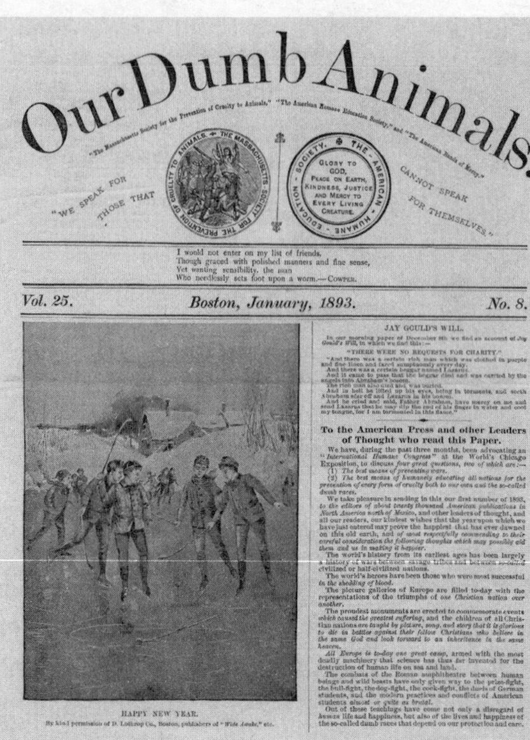

Our Dumb Animals.

"The Massachusetts Society for the Prevention of Cruelty to Animals," "The American Humane Education Society," and "The American Bands of Mercy."

"WE SPEAK FOR THOSE THAT CANNOT SPEAK FOR THEMSELVES."

THE MASSACHUSETTS SOCIETY FOR THE PREVENTION OF CRUELTY TO ANIMALS

THE AMERICAN HUMANE EDUCATION SOCIETY. GLORY TO GOD, PEACE ON EARTH, KINDNESS, JUSTICE AND MERCY TO EVERY LIVING CREATURE.

I would not enter on my list of friends,
Though graced with polished manners and fine sense,
Yet wanting sensibility, the man
Who needlessly sets foot upon a worm.—COWPER.

Vol. 25. *Boston, January, 1893.* *No. 8.*

HAPPY NEW YEAR.

By kind permission of D. Lothrop Co., Boston, publishers of "*Wide Awake*," etc.

JAY GOULD'S WILL.

In our morning paper of December 8th we find an account of *Jay Gould's Will*, in which we find this:—

"THERE WERE NO BEQUESTS FOR CHARITY."

"And there was a certain rich man which was clothed in purple and fine linen and fared sumptuously every day.

And there was a certain beggar named Lazarus.

And it came to pass that the beggar died and was carried by the angels into Abraham's bosom.

The rich man also died and was buried.

And in hell he lifted up his eyes, being in torments, and seeth Abraham afar off and Lazarus in his bosom.

And he cried and said, Father Abraham, have mercy on me and send Lazarus that he may dip the end of his finger in water and cool my tongue, for I am tormented in this flame."

To the American Press and other Leaders of Thought who read this Paper.

We have, during the past three months, been advocating an "*International Humane Congress*" at the World's Chicago Exposition, to discuss *four great questions, two of which are:—*

(1) *The best means of preventing wars.*

(2) *The best means of humanely educating all nations for the prevention of every form of cruelty both to our own and the so-called dumb races.*

We take pleasure in sending in this our first number of 1893, *to the editors of about twenty thousand American publications in North America north of Mexico*, and other leaders of thought, and all our readers, our kindest wishes that the year upon which we have just entered may prove the happiest that has ever dawned on this old earth, and *of most respectfully commending to their careful consideration the following thoughts which may possibly aid them and us in making it happier.*

The world's history from its earliest ages has been largely a history of wars between savage tribes and between so-called civilized or half-civilized nations.

The world's heroes have been those who were most successful *in the shedding of blood.*

The picture galleries of Europe are filled to-day with the representations of the triumphs of *one Christian nation over another.*

The proudest monuments are erected to commemorate events *which caused the greatest suffering*, and the children of all Christian nations *are taught by picture, song, and story that it is glorious to die in battles against their fellow Christians who believe in the same God and look forward to an inheritance in the same heaven.*

All Europe is to-day one great camp, armed with the most deadly machinery that science has thus far invented for the destruction of human life on sea and land.

The combats of the Roman amphitheatre between human beings and wild beasts have only given way to the prize-fight, the bull-fight, the dog-fight, the cock-fight, the duels of German students, and the modern practices and conflicts of American students *almost or quite as brutal.*

Out of these teachings have come not only a disregard of *human* life and happiness, but also of the lives and happiness of the so-called dumb races that depend on our protection and care.

An early edition of *Our Dumb Animals*, the campaigning monthly magazine created by George Thorndike Angell. He used the magazine to crowdfund the US publication of *Black Beauty*. (Library of Congress)

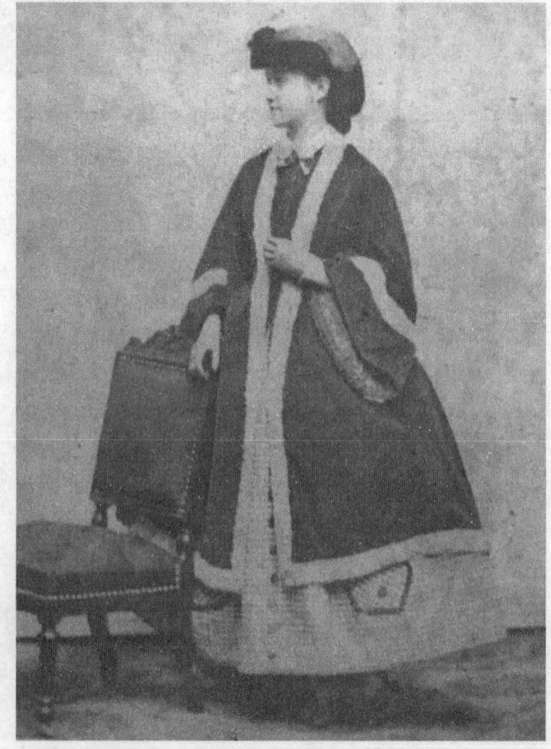

Emily Warren Appleton, who first proposed the Massachusetts Society for the Prevention of Cruelty to Animals.

8

'This Will Do' (1857–67)

Mary Sewell left her daughter at Marienberg and came home to an empty nest. Indeed, she felt that her whole life was empty. When she turned 60 on 6 April 1857, her son was in Spain, her husband was at work all day, the family had moved so often they had left friends behind, she had distanced herself from the comforting circle of the Quaker meeting house and her extended family were mostly still clustered around Norwich in Norfolk. Her own mother had died a few months earlier, three years after her father had passed away.

Her volunteer work was hard to pursue from her new home. While in London and in Brighton she had lived close to areas of deprivation and the workhouses and penitentiaries where her poorest neighbours were housed. She had been naturally drawn into social work by local volunteer groups in towns but she was more isolated in the country at Grayling Wells. Her days were empty and she described herself as feeling 'emptiness' in her life as well.[1]

Perhaps she could write again. It was more than thirty years since she had been a desperate young mother who had earned good money from writing a book, but she had that encouraging memory and now too she had the example of two sisters-in-law to inspire her. Her letters reveal that Sarah Stickney Ellis's series that began with *The Daughters of England* was still the subject of much discussion in 1857.[2] Sarah was prolific and would achieve a career of over thirty books. Inspiring as her four-volume dissertation on the role of women was, however, it was not something that Mary felt she could emulate. The confidence to tell a nation the best way to live was quite beyond her. So too was the sheer scholarship of her brother John's wife, Anne Wright, who was by then an equally successful author of popular textbooks.

The long letters Anne Wright had written to Anna and Philip when they were children, expanding their study of the whole natural world, had become a highly regarded series of volumes under the title of *The Observing Eye*, published individually by Jarrold's from 1850 and finally produced in one volume in 1853. The author seems to have been a compulsive educator who made an advanced but self-directed study of natural history when she was confined to bed by illness. She wrote educational letters to a great many children and, when her health was good, taught at The Red House, the reformatory school founded by her husband near the farm at Buxton.

This institution was to play a major role in the life of Anna Sewell and her family and there can be no doubt that Anna envisaged boys like its pupils among the audience for *Black Beauty*. It was a school created for boys who had committed minor crimes such as stealing food or begging. They had often grown up in a workhouse, separated from their families and, in line with new thinking about youth crime at the time, were kept out of adult prisons and given a basic education and often an apprenticeship, in the hope they would be able to find jobs instead of becoming career criminals or simply dying in the street of malnutrition.[3]

John Wright founded The Red House fifteen years before a young medical student, Thomas Barnardo, set up his school for orphans in the East End of London, vowing never again to close his doors after a child for whom he had not had a place starved to death. Both institutions were modelled on the Ragged Schools set up in the mid-nineteenth century to teach, and often house, feed and clothe, destitute children. These pupils cannot have been the easiest to teach anything, let alone the process of oxygen exchange in a fish's gills or the life cycle of a butterfly.

Nevertheless, the writer of Anne Wright's biography recorded:

> The clear, simple and impressive lectures she was in the habit of giving, were listened to with delight by the hour together. She would

> judiciously throw in questions in the midst of her instructions, which drew out attention and quickened the faculties of the youths ... which gave them an alacrity in their manner, which was more like preparing for some entertainment than the sober business of being taught.[4]

All these varied experiences were gathered into *The Observing Eye*, which unexpectedly earned the praise of highly educated, even expert, critics. In addition:

> The precious little work early reached the Queen, who, wisely on her guard in the selection of works for her family, first examined then placed it in the hands of the royal children, and directed that her thanks should be presented to the author.[5]

Thus one of Anna Sewell's aunts had become a literary celebrity, one of the greatest popularisers of science of her time.

Anne Wright was an educational writer whose philosophy of teaching extended far beyond the simple provision of knowledge. She intended her lessons to create philosophical and spiritual awareness, making her pupils and readers better people by helping them understand the wonders of the natural world. In the introduction to *The Observing Eye*, she wrote:

> The study of natural history is found to possess a great moral influence over children, supplying them with cheerful motives for active employment and intelligent research; whilst the constant displays of wisdom and power which it unfolds, tend to elevate the mind in admiration of the great Creator, and fill the heart with praise.

Like Mary and Anna Sewell, Anne Wright had been brought up as a Quaker. She saw the work of God in all the natural world and interpreted the study of biology as a spiritual quest. She also wanted to promote gentleness and humanity through her teaching. After *The Observing Eye* she wrote an erudite geological textbook, but then followed with a book called *What is a Bird?* Her purpose was to persuade boys not to steal birds' nests, a common game at that time. While some boys had enough knowledge to identify the eggs of rarer species and sell them to collectors, most stole for the fun of it, with no thought of the distress to the parent birds and damage to the ecosystem. (The practice was made illegal in Britain in the Wildlife and Countryside Act of 1981.)

Anne Wright's work influenced the writing of both Anna Sewell and her mother, most obviously in her writing style. She had the phenomenal gift of making her books easy to read. While deliberately avoiding sentimentality or patronising her readers, she achieved an engaging style on which many of her reviewers remarked. One, the editor of the Scottish periodical *Witness*, noted:

> The value lies not so much in the amount of information communicated as in how it is communicated and made attractive to the infant mind, and elevating to the infant heart. The whole of this book is … absolutely delightful and interesting to big people, as well as little.[6]

This opinion was endorsed in a private letter from another reader to Anne Wright, which described staying with friends who entertained themselves in the evening by taking turns to read aloud from *The Observing Eye*. In this precious gift of readability, which rests on real empathy for a book's audience, Anne Wright's sister-in-law, Mary Sewell, and in turn her niece, Anna Sewell, were both to be her direct heirs.

During her years of illness, Anne Wright amassed a substantial library in the process of educating herself, and seems to have been a natural scholar, something that neither Mary nor Anna were. They were both well read and lovers of literature, but Mary's life's work up to now had been giving practical help to people living in poverty and desperation. Her intellectual faculties were much taken up in spiritual discussion, more and more so as she grew older, but her teaching experience was limited to home-schooling her own young children and, once they were grown up, she did not have that delight in the development of young minds that guides many wonderful teachers.

What she had, however, was an impressive dexterity with words and a deep understanding of the harsh lives of ordinary people, the millions who struggled to survive in Victorian Britain, who scrambled for work and lived precariously in fear of starvation, homelessness and the workhouse. She had, as Mrs Bayly put it, 'threescore years of training for [writing] by using her imagination as a power of sympathy'.[7]

It must have been almost natural for Mary to put her ideas into words now that, for the first time in her life, she had the leisure to pick up a pen. She had the inspiration – which stimulated but perhaps overawed her – of two famous authors in her close family, as well as several other women writers among her acquaintance. She could think back to the success of her little book for children, *Walks with Mama*, more than thirty years earlier.

At first she wrote a few simple ballads and eventually found she had a collection. She then began with a book of poems, a work in which her own nostalgia for the country village life of her childhood blended with her memories of the children she had met in her workhouse-visiting days. The verses in *The Children of Summerbrook* depict life in an English village through the adventures of its children.

It is written in bright, deceptively simple rhymes much like the famous poem by the eighteenth-century hymnist Isaac Watts, beginning 'How doth the little busy bee', which Alice tries to recite after she has fallen through the looking glass in Lewis Carroll's famous story. Like Watt's verse, it is blatantly moralistic. Loving, gentle, dutiful children who work hard are rosy-cheeked and destined for happiness, while spiteful, cruel, disobedient children are dirty and unkempt, and destined for misery.

Set in eternal early summer among ever-blossoming orchards, *The Children of Summerbrook* walks a fine line on the edge of sentimental schmaltz but is saved by the writer's gentle but unflinching inclusion of the harshest aspects of the life of the rural poor. It is immediately clear that those dirty, unkempt and naughty children are abused at home and, thanks to their parents' ignorance of basic domestic hygiene, destined to die pretty soon.

One of the most touching poems in the book concerns a seaman's wife who falls ill while her husband is at sea. The doctor tells her that 'were I a lady he had no fear/he'd make me well in less than half a year'. Her two eldest children want to miss school to nurse her and help with the hard work of keeping the home going, but their mother refuses, saying, 'You must not grow up ignorant for me./You'll have to earn your livelihood, you know/and so must learn betimes to read and sew.'

The brother and sister then discuss how they can divide up the chores without missing school, with Mary taking the baking and washing and George drawing their water from the well. It is an optimistic model of a negotiation in which a family faces a crisis and works together to establish priorities, a scene that would not be out of place in a mid-twentieth-century early evening TV drama series.

Mary showed her verses to Anna's old friend from their Brighton days, Henry S. King. King had made his mark in publishing in the intervening years. He had married in 1850, and his wife was a Quaker, Ellen Blakeway, the daughter of a London wine merchant. Four years later, Ellen's sister Elizabeth married another publisher, George Smith, who had, at the family firm of Smith, Elder & Co., recently published *Jane Eyre* by Currer Bell, the pen name of Charlotte Brontë.

In 1853 Henry King became partner in Smith, Elder & Co., so he may have dealt with Charlotte Brontë later in her career, but he was not one of the editors who cancelled lunch appointments and burned candles late into the night, compelled to finish Mr Bell's manuscript.[8] Henry King's sympathies were more with religious and spiritual writing and the partnership was to end in 1868, when King once more struck out on his own.

Mary Sewell recalled that she showed her verses 'in fear and trembling' to their now-successful friend and had to sit by while he turned over the leaves until at last he looked up and said, 'This will do.'[9] Mary hesitated and before she sent the final manuscript to Smith, Elder, she consulted one more alpha reader – her daughter, Anna.

Anna's year at Marienberg had improved her health significantly. While her feet were still weak, she could walk well enough to enjoy it. Her back and chest pains were gone and she felt stronger and more energetic. Her reunion with her mother in May 1857 was a 'gala time for mother and daughter'.[10]

They took a fortnight's holiday at Dorking, then a pretty market town in Surrey close to the Box Hill mentioned by Jane Austen in *Emma* for its 'sweet view – sweet to the eye and the mind. English verdure, English culture, English comfort, seen under a sun bright.' For Mary it was 'ever memorable as a little space of unclouded happiness'.[11]

They did not entirely indulge themselves, as 'in the evenings they were intensely interested in Carlyle's *Past and Present* that they could hardly persuade themselves to go to bed, and drank coffee to drive off sleep and lengthen each delightful day'.

Past and Present, published in 1843, is an odd choice for a binge-reading session, being a highly polemical work in which Thomas Carlyle, responding to the food riots of the early 1840s, contrasts the spiritual focus of medieval society with the worst excesses of capitalism in contemporary Britain. He depicted the working classes as brutalised by greed-driven industrialists. He attacked the aristocracy for lack of leadership and the middle classes for lack of action. There was clearly no danger that Mary and Anna would have 'too much pleasure' in the beauty of the countryside with this sobering volume to entertain them in the evenings.

Carlyle's influence on Mary's writing is hard to trace. Although her experiences with people living in poverty must have prompted political thoughts, she kept them out of her novels. As an author she was always ready to indict the thoughtless and selfish rich, but never went further to propose social change.

In *Black Beauty*, however, there is some overt political content, written in the simple language Anna chose for her readers, which arises naturally during Beauty's days as a London cab horse. A whole chapter is given over to an election. A politician tries to hire his cab for electioneering, but is stoutly refused by Beauty's owner, who declines to engage in the process and rebukes his son for getting into a fight with boys of the 'orange' faction. Although he agrees with some of his would-be customer's policies, the cabman says:

> A man who gets rich by that trade may be all very well in some ways, but he is blind as to what working men want; I could not in my conscience send him up to make the laws. I daresay they'll be angry, but every man must do what he thinks to be the best for his country.

When they returned to Grayling Wells, Mary asked Anna to read and critique some of her writing. Later she told Mrs Bayly:

> I have never made a plan for anything without submitting it to [my daughter's] judgment. Every line I have written has been at her feet before it has gone forth to the world, My Nannie has always been my critic and my counsellor.[12]

From this moment Anna became her mother's first editor and people who witnessed their discussions were surprised at how harsh she could be. Anna was notorious in the family for her outspoken judgement and ruthless honesty; her mother once said that if she asked Anna to arrange fruit in a bowl she would do so without making any effort to turn the most appetising side of the fruit outwards or to disguise any blemishes or rotting bits.

Nevertheless, her mother accepted her notes 'with eagerness'. Mary was something of a perfectionist and happy to continue revising her writing in the hope of improvement. She was to become immensely successful but always doubted herself, while Anna was confident in her judgement, which was generally agreed to be excellent in everything.

As Mrs Bayly described her gift:

> Anna Sewell had the artist instinct for form very strongly developed. Her pencil drawings from nature, full of truth and spirit, are remarkable for excellence of composition; if she did not edit her landscapes, she had a genius for seizing the right point of view, and figures and objects were put exactly in the right spot; this same gift of form made her an admirable critic of manner and arrangement in word-painting.[13]

The working relationship which Anna and Mary developed raises the question of how much of their writing was independently created. At first sight there is no obvious relationship between Mary's brisk, sunny verses and Anna's vividly realistic prose, but there are distinct thematic links and it is beyond doubt that each contributed materially to the other's work.

They were also each other's best friends. One of their circle described Mary's relationship with her daughter as 'the reigning friendship of her life',[14] and described how Anna would often write Mary's letters for her. Later, of course, during the last years of her life, these roles were reversed and several letters attributed to Anna are clearly written in Mary's bold hand. At that time, too, Mary wrote down the text of *Black Beauty* when Anna was too weak to do so.

Many of their friends and neighbours thought of them as a duo and the same writer recalled:

> There was about them a rare distinction … [which] is hard to describe. It was not mere intellect, or mere goodness, or even mere nobility, though it had much of all these in its composition … It was the general effect produced by uncommon intellectual powers, combined with still more uncommon integrity and simplicity, and directed by … charity.[15]

In 1858 Smith, Elder & Co. published Mary's collected verses as *Homely Ballads for the Working Man's Fireside*. This collection of verses – Mary herself would never go so far as to describe her work as poetry – begins with a dramatic ballad describing a shipwreck, from which one orphan child survives and is adopted by a fisherman's wife.

Next is 'The Funeral Bell', in which a village mourns a good citizen. This is generally believed to be a tribute to John Wright, Mary's father. These are written with dynamic passion, but the real energy of the collection soon shifts to an indignant voice of a working-class woman, once a servant in a wealthy home and now married but living in poverty, who is criticised by her former mistress for choosing an independent life:

> Amongst the hard and cutting things
> Poor women have to feel
> When poverty is serving out
> Their lean and hungry meal,
> Is the unthinking ignorance
> Of some we call genteel.

Homely Ballads was extraordinarily successful. By 1888 it had sold over 40,000 copies.[16] Mary Sewell became famous almost overnight. Her publishers began to forward a steady stream of rave reviews and fan letters and were eager for her next book. She seems to have felt uncomfortable with Henry S. King, or with Smith, Elder in general, as her next book went to her former publisher, Jarrold's. Perhaps the nostalgic comfort of the Norwich connection lured her back.

With Jarrold's she would have the weight of the Quaker community in Norfolk behind her, while with Smith, Elder she had only the support of Henry S. King, who seems to have been rather isolated within the firm. Mrs Bayly suggests that she regarded Jarrold's as more sympathetic to her working-class audience than Smith, Elder, whose high reputation with the London elite rested on a stellar list that included John Ruskin, Robert Browning and Alfred, Lord Tennyson.

Her verse novel, *The Children of Summerbrook*, was published the next year, in 1859, and was another immediate success. Despite their very different styles, this and many of Mary's subsequent books share something of the character of *Black Beauty*. There is an emphasis on kindness in every form, including a gentle indictment of the 'mean girls' at the village school.

The verses are suffused with the love of nature and teach care for the natural world as emphatically as they decry lying, stealing or violence. Her next collection included a verse describing birds building a nest, which approaches anthropomorphism in imagining their feelings. In one of the verses in *The Children of Summerbrook*, titled 'The Butterfly', two little girls talk about insects as sentient beings on their way to school:

The dew was sparkling on the grass,
The lark was in the sky;
And dancing on before them went
A yellow butterfly.

'Oh let us catch it, Mary, do
I'll try and beat it down;
See now, 'tis settled on that leaf.
Ah! Silly thing, 'tis gone.'

'Oh Nelly, pray don't beat it down.
You'll hurt the little thing;
Why should you want to catch it, dear?
You'll spoil its pretty wing.'

'I never thought that it would feel,
Or suffer any pain.
But if you really think it will
I won't do so again.'

'But are you sure they can be hurt
As much as you and I;
Such things as beetles, frogs and toads
And little things that fly?'

'I'm very sure they suffer pain,
How much I cannot say.
But I can't bear to have them hurt
Or see them run away.'

Most of the words in these verses are of one or two syllables. Whether Mary was writing for adults or for children, she envisaged that her verses would be read aloud. Educated middle-class households would entertain themselves reading aloud together, as Anne Wright's admirer had described. While this was less common in working-class families, among whom literacy was not widespread and for whom a book was prohibitively expensive, reading aloud was an entertainment that people could enjoy in many different situations: children and adults in school; hospital patients and special interest groups such as mothers' meetings; children in orphanages; people in workhouses or prisons; and even sailors at sea. A book such as *The Children of Summerbrook* had an enormous secondary audience of people who had it read to them.

Mary Bayly recounts the experience of 'a young man, wishing to do good, [who] had undertaken a Sunday class of wild town lads, and could do nothing with them'. When Mary's most successful book, *Mother's Last Words*, came out, telling the story of two orphan boys making their way alone in the world, 'he tried reading it aloud to them and they were spellbound. They begged to hear it another time, and he read it over and over again, Sunday after Sunday, thankful to find anything that would keep them quiet.'[17]

Knowing that their books would be read aloud, writers such as Mary Sewell and her family constructed their work to be vivid, easy to follow and instantly memorable, with robust narratives and strong emotional content that would keep the listeners' attention. They deliberately chose not to use the more complex style of the literary novelists of their day, and avoided long sentences, subtle emotions and nuanced scenarios. Mary's style is comparable to a modern pop song, with bold and simple feelings projected in bouncy rhythms. Of all the poets she admired, she seems to have been most influenced by Sir Walter Scott, in the galloping rhythms of his most popular ballads.

In making the specific choices that created easy readability, she followed the example of the successful writers in her family. Sarah Stickney Ellis, in the preface to *The Women of England*, explained:

> In order to perform my task with candour and faithfulness, I must renounce all idea of what is called fine writing; because the very nature of the duty I have undertaken, restricts me to the consideration of subjects, too minute in themselves to admit of their being expatiated upon with eloquence by the writer – too familiar to produce upon the reader any startling effect.

Mary's rationale was more pragmatic. She described her first book as a collection of 'homely verses' and a 'small contribution to the working man's library'. In the preface to *The Children of Summerbrook*, she wrote:

> The author believes ... that there exists among [our poorer friends and neighbours] generally an instinctive love of simple, descriptive poetry, and that both morally an intellectually it is of more importance to them to have the imagination cultivated and refined by the high sentiment of poetry than it can be to those who have the advantage of a liberal education; to the one it is a luxury – to the other, an

> almost needful relaxation from the severe and irksome drudgery of their daily lot.[18]

Anna and her mother shared a life that was infused with literature. Beyond the 'hero-worship' of their favourite writers and their late-night reading binges, they amused themselves with improvising poetry or playing word games. A favourite was 'capping verses'. This was a popular Victorian game with many ancient derivations including Celtic folk traditions and classical drama. It was also often used by teachers of English literature to strengthen their pupils' memory and language skills. In essence, it is a call-and-response game in which the first player speaks a line of poetry and the second 'caps' it with another line, and any others continue until a group-written poem – which may or may not be nonsense – is created.

According to how difficult the players want the game to be, the lines can rhyme, be in the same metre and begin with the last letter of the preceding line. As described in *Brewer's Dictionary of Phrase and Fable*:

> To cap verses. Having the metre fixed and the last letter of the previous line given, to add a line beginning with that letter, thus:
> The way was long, the wind was cold
> Dogs with their tongues their wounds do heal.
> Like words congealed in northern air,
> Regions Caesar never know
> With all a poet's ecstasy,
> You may deride my awkward pace ...[19]

And so on. Depending on the players' taste, the game can be played in another language or framed as a memory game with quotations from poetry learned by heart, or even stripped of poetic content and played with famous names.[20]

When she critiqued her mother's writing, Anna could be highly specific. Mrs Bayly remembers:

> I was once with Anna when her mother read aloud to us something she was preparing for the press. It was beautiful to witness the intense

> love, admiration and even pride which beamed in the daughter's face, but this in no wise prevented her being, as I thought, a very severe critic. Nature had bestowed on her a remarkable sweet-toned and persuasive voice. I think I hear her now, saying, 'Mother dear, thee must alter that line', or 'Thee must put a fuller word there, that will give out more of thy meaning'.[21]

Isaac Sewell's view of his wife's success is not recorded. Perhaps he was proud to find himself the husband of a bestselling writer; perhaps he felt neglected as mother and daughter threw themselves into the joint enterprise of producing books. Perhaps his habit of over-optimism in financial matters convinced him that she could now be the breadwinner. For whatever reason, he chose the exact moment that his wife made a name for herself to decide that he could afford to retire.

Or almost afford to retire. Mary wrote to a friend in April 1857:

> My good husband has resigned his position in the bank ... we are able to live without his being in much more business than attending to his own, but I am afraid he will find leisure wearisome. We shall have to be more careful, of course, than we have been and that is never very pleasant, is it, dear?[22]

Note that carefully placed 'good'. This is the closest Mary ever came to criticising her husband in writing and there can be no doubt that she did not like his decision. And there was worse to come. Isaac decided that the family should move to a remote and dilapidated old house more than 100 miles away, in a mining area to the north of the city of Bath.

9

The Most Popular Novel of Our Day (1852–65)

While Anna and her mother were enjoying literary success, in London the RSPCA was getting down to business. The greatest progress made in the cause of animal welfare in Britain in the middle years of the nineteenth century was the implementation of long-demanded changes to Smithfield Market in central London. The RSPCA was only one among thousands of individual and organisational voices which had called for this massive vortex of cruelty and abuse to be reformed, and in the event, outside forces, geographical and technological, achieved as much as animal welfare lobbyists.

The campaigners argued on humanitarian grounds but it would be naïve to think that any concern for animal welfare weighed much in the decision. In fact, it was the coming of railways that finally made the difference. The railway lines into London made it possible for fresh meat to reach buyers far more quickly, meaning that live animals for slaughter no longer needed to be driven through the city streets to the market. Animals could be slaughtered outside the city and the fresh carcasses sent by train into the capital.

In 1852 a new livestock market was built near a railway terminus at Copenhagen Fields in Islington and opened by Prince Albert in 1855. Smithfield Market, where live animals had been sold and slaughtered for seven centuries, closed down. Cattle, pigs, sheep and horses were no longer driven through the crowded city streets, and bloody carcasses no longer hauled through narrow alleys around the butchers' market a few blocks away at Newgate. The Smithfield site lay derelict for a short while and then emerged as the imposing ironwork temple it is today, and became a retail meat market.

The Times noted:

> At the opening of the Meat-market by the Prince Consort, Smithfield became waste ground. The arrangements at Copenhagen Fields are about as good for their purpose as any that could have been desired; but since the time the market there was laid out there have been very great changes in respect of the supply of animal food for the population of the metropolis. Then most of the beasts and sheep converted into meat for sale in the shops of London butchers were brought to London alive and slaughtered by the retailers. With the development of our railway system, and the additions to the great main lines by extensions which brought them into the business parts of the metropolis, the dead meat traffic from the provinces exhibited year by year a heavier tonnage.[1]

Tolls were paid on that tonnage, satisfying the investors who had finally been persuaded by the prospect of profit. On other campaign fronts, despite the society's improved financial position and growing network of society contacts, progress was frustratingly slow. They had succeeded in stopping the Stamford Bull Run, despite the violent opposition of the local 'bullards', who threw missiles and yelled death threats at the inspector and the two constables who came with him at the first attempt to enforce the law in 1837. The local magistrate was so intimidated that he gave in to the mob but two years later, when a detachment of dragoons was called in to restore order, this brutal spectacle was seen for the last time.[2]

After the financial debacle, the Education Committee, still chaired by the great philanthropist Angela Burdett-Coutts, had been joined by a campaigner of almost supernatural energy, Catherine Smithies. Smithies was the mother of the founder of Partridge & Co., a house dedicated to what might be termed social publishing. Thomas Bywater

Smithies was to print some of some of Mary Sewell's work and also writing by Sarah Stickney Ellis. His major publication was a periodical, *The British Workman*, dedicated to raising awareness of poverty and promoting temperance.

In 1862 Partridge & Co. also published a book by Catherine Smithies, *Mother's Lessons on Kindness to Animals*. The author was then 71 years old,[3] and presented the book as a collection of anecdotes and verses about people who practised kindness to animals, from various different authors, edited by the mysterious 'C.S.'. This illustrated anthology included several tales about horses who are rescued after being abused or driven too hard.

A paragraph sums up the theme:

> The horse is a beautiful creature. He deserves to be well governed and well fed, for he is one of the most valuable servants that God had given to man. If my little reader should ever become the owner of a *pony*, it will, I hope, do credit to its possessor.[4]

The writers of these stories show a persuasive awareness of the economics of owning a horse at that time, arguing in one case that it was more profitable to feed a horse well and sell it in good condition than to starve it to death. The degree of ignorance assumed in the readership is also striking. After the malnourished carter's horse is bought by a benefactor, fed and cared for, it is let out into a field and starts rolling in the grass for joy. The stable boy is alarmed and assumes the animal is having fits.

Smithies is credited with setting up the Ladies' Committee of the RSPCA in 1870, and while this may have encouraged other women to come forward and join the cause, it also seems to have been a way of separating women activists from the mainstream of the society's work. She seems to have been blocked in her aims by the RSPCA and she finally set up the Band of Mercy movement independently in 1875. This was an educational initiative modelled on the Band of Hope movement set up by temperance campaigners. The Bands of Mercy worked in schools to set up groups of children who took a pledge to be kind to animals and were offered activities and teaching to help them do that.

The movement soon published its own newspaper. Both the organisation and the publication were taken over by the RSPCA in 1888.[5]

The society also campaigned for better treatment of horses, and published *The Horse Book*, by Edward King 'of Lymington', in 1858. Subtitled *Simple Rules for Managing a Horse*, it was intended to teach basic horse-mastership to working people who made their livings as carters or cabmen. It covered feeding, shoeing, grooming, stabling, harness and the ideal care of horses at the end of their lives. Many of the intended readership could not read, so the society began to call meetings at which the book would be read aloud.

These were, however, often organised in smart parts of town, such as Bryanston Square, a few blocks from Mayfair, the most prestigious borough in the city. This was convenient for the gentlemen's clubs where the speakers could relax after the meeting but not at all convenient for the audience of weary cab drivers, who had to drive their exhausted horses home to the outer boroughs over some distance.

The book sold briskly and was revised and reprinted in 1865 with an introduction by a distinguished military veterinarian. The very first lines criticise the 'ignorance' and 'indolence' of horse owners, an approach guaranteed to alienate the reader immediately. Unsurprisingly, this tin-eared insensitivity defeated the whole purpose of this publication. The book listed the patrons and vice patrons of the RSPCA on a page at the front, and a gilded company it is. Beginning with 'Her Most Gracious Majesty The Queen', the list names fourteen patrons, all British or European royalty. The vice patrons list begins with 'Prince Louis Lucien Bonaparte' and names sixteen more aristocrats, meticulously ordered according to diplomatic rules of precedence. London's cab drivers may well have concluded that the promoters of this volume had no real care for their welfare and rejected their advice accordingly.

The abuse of animals in medicine, particularly vivisection, became a major focus of the RSPCA and one which, because it concerned educated middle-class people and institutions susceptible to pressure from the highest levels of society, was easier for the membership to pursue effectively. In 1824, the notorious French surgeon François Magendie, who is estimated to have 'tortured and killed eight thousand dogs'[6] as well as many other animals for the advancement of medical science, came to London to perform a public dissection, an event which horrified and intrigued his audience equally.

Vivisection was regarded in Britain as a foreign technique, but Magendie's work was considered important, particularly for the understanding of physiology, and later in the century the emphasis on this field of study in medical schools in Britain led to its adoption. The impetus against the practice came from another lame, middle-aged woman, Frances Power Cobbe, an Irish writer who witnessed the dissection of live animals when she travelled to the spa town of Aix-les-Bains in France seeking treatment for a broken ankle. She wrote an influential essay, *The Rights of Man and the Claims of Brutes*. After a bruising reception in Europe, she took up the cause in Britain, got up a petition and urged the RSPCA to take action.

Frances Cobbe was a respected thinker, but she was also a lesbian who lived openly with her partner, and a communicator willing to rouse her audience with horrific descriptions of a most unladylike strength. Like Caroline Smithies, she decided to work outside the RSPCA rather than within it, eventually setting up her own Society for the Prevention of Vivisection in 1875.[7]

In 1864 the president of the RSPCA, the Earl of Harrowby, was visited by the retiring head of the American legation in St Petersburg, Henry Bergh. Bergh was a Europhile from New York who, upon inheriting his father's very prosperous shipbuilding company, had left the enterprise to his younger brother and embarked on a grand tour. He was well connected, urbane and diplomatic in manner, and had been appointed to his role in Russia by Abraham Lincoln. A tall man with sloping shoulders, down-turned eyes and a dark, drooping moustache that gave him the air of a disappointed walrus, he cut a memorable figure wherever he was. He also shared Richard Martin's willingness to confront the street drivers who were mistreating their horses.

Legend has it that he was horrified by the brutality which he witnessed in Russia and, when his own carriage drew close to a *droshky*, the Russian equivalent of a cab, whose driver was beating his horse mercilessly, he got out and ordered the man to stop. To his surprise, the man did stop abusing the animal and Bergh became convinced that cruelty to animals could be prevented by direct action. He set up a prototype animal welfare society among his circle in St Petersburg.[8]

When Andrew Johnson succeeded Lincoln as President of the United States, Bergh lost his appointment and returned home by way of London, where he sought out Lord Harrowby, a career politician of 66, who had recently been awarded the Order of the Garter after resigning his position as Lord Privy Seal. Bergh also met the RSPCA's secretary, John Colam, and bought a number of books by animal welfare campaigners, including Catherine Smithies's *Mother's Lessons on Kindness to Animals*. They discussed the need to save carriage horses from ill-treatment and, after he returned to New York, Bergh sent Colam a piece of harness that was in use in that city, which allowed the animal to be released quickly if it fell or if the carriage foundered, saving it from the most severe injuries.

On 8 February 1866, a stormy evening in New York when the weather was so foul he was afraid nobody would attend, Bergh held a meeting at the Clinton Hall, an old opera house that been converted into a library, where he addressed the distinguished audience that included an Astor and two Roosevelts, who he himself had invited personally. He stunned them with statistics, presented his Declaration of the Rights of Animals and announced: 'This is a matter purely of conscience. It has no perplexing side issues. It is a moral question in all its aspects.'

America is a country whose founding fathers had specified kindness to animals in its earliest governing documents. The Body of Liberties adopted by the Massachusetts Bay Colony in 1641 included Passage 92: 'No man shall exercise any Tirranny or Crueltie towards any bruite Creature which are usuallie kept for man's use.'

Importantly, this document was framed as a codification of rights, implying at least comparable status for animals and human beings, whereas the later British legislation did not assume that animals had rights but merely made cruelty to them illegal. The provision of Passage 92 did not make it into the United States Constitution, however, and animal protection in the US became a matter of laws enacted locally by individual states rather than a national issue upon which the federal government ruled. New York already had an animal cruelty statute, passed in 1828, as had several other states, including Massachusetts (1835), Connecticut (1838) and Wisconsin (1838), but these laws, like Martin's Law in Britain, were not framed so as to be easily enforceable.

Bergh followed the example of the RSPCA in Britain and created an animal protection society chartered by the state as well as an animal cruelty law that gave his organisation the power to enforce it. On 10 April 1866, the charter was approved, and on 19 April a statute was enacted that granted the newly minted American Society for the Protection of Cruelty to Animals (ASPCA) the right to enforce the law 'throughout the United States'. Bergh was so active himself in carrying out the new law's provisions, and indeed exceed them, that he won the nickname of 'The Great Meddler'.[9]

Although the implication of animal rights was significant, Bergh had already handicapped his enterprise in the wording of his Declaration. He had deliberately paraphrased the United States Declaration of Independence in its title and expected his document to be equally venerated.[10] However, it was clearly not written in any great egalitarian spirit and began with the same judgemental tone as *The Horse Book*. Its author saw nothing inappropriate in patrolling the streets of New York in a top hat and tails to accost offending horse owners.

The year after the ASPCA was founded, Bergh received a letter in an oversized but graceful hand from Emily Warren Appleton. He would have recognised her names immediately – her father-in-law, William Appleton, had been one of the wealthiest men in Boston and the US Representative from Massachusetts First District. Her grandfather had founded Harvard Medical School and her father, its first dean, was a prominent surgeon involved in the first use of anaesthesia in the US. Like many others among his correspondents, Emily Appleton wanted to set up a society equivalent to the ASPCA in her own city, Boston. Bergh replied to her suggesting that work with children would be more appropriate and sending a copy of 'a little story book which we have just published',[11] which may well have been *Mother's Lessons on Kindness to Animals*.

Emily Appleton no doubt thanked him but persisted with her desire to set up an organisation. She travelled to New York to meet him and came away with the draft of his legislation. Bergh seems to have had a vexed relationship with women and had failed to engage the support of the most influential society hostesses in his city, something which readers of Edith Wharton will appreciate would have been a check on his ambitions.

He seems to have warmed to Mrs Appleton, however. Her photographs show her as a soft-faced and luxuriously dressed young woman but at the time she met Bergh she was almost 50, with an intense gaze and somewhat chiselled features. Bergh was to describe her in glowing terms as 'most distinguished' and 'most excellent'[12] and compared her favourably to the 'hard-hearted' socialites of his home town.

When Emily had married his son, William Appleton Sr noted in his diary, 'Our son … married to Emily; J Warren; we are fully satisfied with his choice; she is a fine woman with excellent principles and good disposition. I think his opportunities for happiness are as good as almost any young Man.'[13] Everyone seemed to like and, more importantly, trust Emily, and now that she was no longer a young bride but a junior matriarch with an impressive record as a philanthropist and a powerful family behind her, it was hard for most people to deny her anything.

She gathered the signatures of ninety equally distinguished supporters in Boston. She used the New York legislation as a template and drafted an act for incorporation for the society, which her husband sent to the Speaker of the House of Representatives. There the matter would have rested forever, until the following year, when she opened a copy of the *Boston Advertiser* and saw a letter from George Thorndike Angell, a successful lawyer of radical tendencies, who had decided to abandon his legal career and devote the rest of his life to campaigning for animal welfare.

The story of *Black Beauty* is not only the story of one woman and one book. As I hope this study has demonstrated, it is in fact the story of several women and a number of books. It is also the story of one man of extraordinary vision and talents who, after decades of hoping to find a book like *Black Beauty*, was to discover it years after Anna Sewell's death and transform it into a worldwide publishing phenomenon. That man was George Thorndike Angell.

Unlike Henry Bergh and Emily Appleton, Angell's background was one of well-connected disadvantage. 'His paternal and maternal ancestries read like a who's who of Great Migration families',[14] meaning that both his parents were from the highest social class in Boston, but neither of them had personal wealth and what little money they had they lost to a swindler shortly after they married.

His father was a Baptist minister, the Reverend George Angell, for many years the pastor of the Baptist church at Southbridge, Worcester County in Massachusetts, where George Junior was born on 5 June 1823. His mother was Rebekah Thorndike, the youngest of the eleven children of Lieutenant Paul Thorndike and a schoolteacher for most of her life.[15]

Angell can hardly have remembered his father, who died when his son was 4 years old. Contemporary reports describe the reverend as:

> Elegant in person and manners. He was tall and well proportioned, and his whole address was easy and prepossessing. Without any extraordinary strength of mind, he had talents which that qualified him for usefulness in any situation in which he was placed.[16]

The portrait photographs of Angell from early in his career show a good-looking, open-faced young man, suggesting that he inherited some of his father's qualities. The Reverend George Angell was a charismatic preacher who grew his congregation successfully, and his son's later career as an animal rights activist also suggests that he inherited some talent for evangelical oratory as well.

Through his mother in particular, Angell had many relatives among the First Families of Boston, the dominant social group who could trace their ancestry to the very earliest settlers of New England who had arrived there in the seventeenth century. This ruling elite also became known as the Boston Brahmins after the writer Oliver Wendell Holmes called them the 'Brahmin Caste of New England' in an 1860 story in *The Atlantic Monthly*. His description began:

> There is, however, in New England, an aristocracy, if you choose to call it so, which has a greater character of permanence. It has grown

> to be a caste – not in any odious sense – but, by the repetition of the same influences, generation after generation, it has acquired a distinct organization and physiognomy …[17]

Holmes's use of the term 'brahmin', which denotes the priestly caste in Hindu society, suggests not only their elite status but also, perhaps ironically, a way of life dedicated to voluntary poverty.

In nineteenth-century Boston, the caste identified by Holmes was variously noted for wealth, philanthropy, public service, elitism and snobbery, and included the Thorndike, Warren and Appleton families. Rebekah Thorndike seems to have married out of this golden circle, and to have had a great many siblings and cousins, with the result that, as her son recalled, she was a poor widow who kept working as a teacher and, as he also wrote, 'otherwise exerted herself to maintain us both, and to educate me'.[18]

By the age of 14, George was working in a grocery store to pay his way in high school. He went to Dartmouth College and then to live with his mother in Vermont. Determined to make his own way in the legal profession, he spent a year writing job applications to law firms in many different states without success.

He finally despaired and took the night stagecoach to Boston, where a cousin of his mother, Judge Patrick Fletcher, agreed to train him and gave him the run of his library. He was called to the bar on 17 December 1851[19] and was then offered was a partnership with the Hon. Samuel E. Sewall, 'a very learned and eminent member of the same bar'. (The name Sewall is only coincidentally similar to Sewell and there is no connection between the two families.)

Mr Sewall was a prominent opponent of slavery, had been for several years the abolition candidate for governor and was unpopular with those who supported the Southern slave owners with whom they did business. Boston at that time was becoming bitterly polarised between the abolitionists and the slavery lobby. Angell wrote:

> I was told that if I became [Sewall's] partner, my prospects as a lawyer would be ruined, as Boston merchants would never employ

> an abolitionist. I concluded to try it, and, as I am now satisfied, was more successful than I should have been if I had chosen the other partnership.[20]

As a lawyer, Angell was ever ready to go extra miles on behalf of the underdog or the unjustly accused, and proud of his success in doing so. One can imagine a judge, seeing his name on the day's schedule, torn between weary anticipation of a long and volatile hearing and the promise of some entertaining speeches. Angell was clearly a gifted speaker but had a propensity for thinking so far outside the box that some of his moves were barely legal.

A typical anecdote from later in his career illustrates his eager zeal for justice. During a strike of railway engineers, who were facing severe pay cuts, he discovered that the railway company had been bribing judges and jurymen with free travel passes. He immediately drafted a bill proposing that it should be illegal for anyone who had received such a bribe to adjudicate in a dispute with the railwaymen's union. He did nothing more than put the bill before the state legislature, which was enough to expose the corruption.

Angell was a lifelong animal lover who was deeply affected by the horrors he saw all around him. He wrote a memorandum detailing some of them:

> Calves taken from their mothers when too young to eat hay were carted through our streets, and lain heaps at the cattle-markets, tied, and piled on each other like sticks of wood; and they were bled several times before they were killed, to make their flesh look white and more delicate. Sheep, from which their fleeces had been taken, stood, in cold weather, about the slaughter-yards shivering for days before they were killed. Nothing had been done to lessen the horrors of cattle transportation. Old horses, long past service, were whipped up and down the streets … and sold sometimes for thirty seven and a half cents each. Worn-out and aged horses, dogs, and other animals were ignorantly and thoughtlessly killed, in ways most brutal. A man in my town near Boston, who had mortgaged his stock of cattle to

> another, quarreled with him, locked the stable doors, and starved them all to death in their stalls to prevent his getting his pay. There was no law in Massachusetts to punish him![21]

Even to a committed activist such as Angell, the welfare of animals in America was of less concern than the welfare of human beings. While the Civil War consumed the country from 1861 to 1865, the cause of animal welfare in the United States found few supporters. All Angell could do was act as a private individual, which he did on 22 August 1864 by adding a clause to his will to pay for teaching kindness to animals in schools, writing:

> It has long been my opinion, that there is much wrong in the treatment of domestic animals; that they are too often overworked, overpunished, and, particularly in winter and in times of scarcity, underfed. All these I think great wrongs, particularly the last; and it is my earnest wish to do something towards awakening public sentiment on this subject; the more so, because these animals have no power of complaint, or adequate human protection, against those who are disposed to do them injury.[22]

With the war over, and Bergh's initiative in New York pointing the way, Angell was finally moved to take action on 23 February 1868, the day after two men raced their horses over 40 miles of rough roads from Brighton to Worcester. Both horses were whipped brutally and driven to death. Angell read a report of the race in the *Boston Daily Advertiser*.

Resolving that somebody needed to take action and it might as well be him, he wrote a letter to the same newspaper which appeared in its columns in the next edition, on 25 February 1868, under the heading 'Cruelty to Animals'. He referred to their report of the fatal race, then wrote:

> It seems to me that it is high time for somebody to take hold of this matter in earnest, and see if we cannot do something in Boston, as others have in New York, to stop this cruelty to animals. And I wish further to say through your columns, that I, for one, am ready to

> contribute both time and money; and if there is any society or person in Boston, with whom I can unite, or who will unite with me, in this matter, I shall be glad personally or by letter to be informed.

The very same morning Emily Warren Appleton rushed out to call upon George Thorndike Angell, at his home at 46 Washington Street, and told him, no doubt with due politeness and charm, that she was way ahead of him and had already drafted the documents necessary to set up an animal protection society in Massachusetts, with ninety signatures of support from the most prominent citizens of Boston. So a great partnership was born between a society matron lapped in privilege from birth and a street-fighting lawyer from the school of hard knocks.

Angell sped down to the office of the Speaker, who first claimed he could not find Mrs Appleton's act and then told Angell that 'if I expected the Legislature would pass a law to prevent cruelty to animals, he thought I was mistaken, as he thought the Legislature would not enact such a law'. Naturally this did not deter Thomas Angell in the slightest.

Generously, he observed that 'prevention of cruelty to animals was then a very new thing in this country, and neither [the Speaker] nor the Legislature knew quite so much about it as they [would soon do] afterwards'. He then drafted a new act of incorporation and added the names of the many other supporters who had also answered his letter in the *Boston Daily Advertiser*.

The only name that was missing was that of Emily Warren Appleton, because:

> public opinion had not then reached the point when it was deemed judicious to make this use of a lady's name. Indeed, Mrs. Appleton did not think it proper to even attend the meeting at which our society was organized ; and at our first election of directors, it was deemed (singular as it now seems) improper to elect her as a director, and so we elected her husband, Mr. William Appleton, and conferred upon her all the honor we thought we could by electing her our first honorary member.[23]

Angell, however, never omitted to acknowledge her initiative and her support, and in 1871 Emily Appleton was elected as a director of the Massachusetts Society for the Prevention of Cruelty to Animals (MSPCA), which was incorporated on 23 March 1868.

Angell also wrote to Henry Bergh in New York, who sent him a personally dedicated copy of *A Mother's Lessons in Kindness to Animals*, which carries the imprint of Partridge & Co. in London, suggesting that Bergh's claim that the ASPCA was also printing and publishing was exaggerated.

Forty people then came to the first meeting of the society and approved the constitution and by-laws which Angell had written 'with, I believe, the alteration of only one word'. The MSPCA then found itself in the same position as the RSPCA in London and the ASPCA in New York, with a glittering roll of supporters and no immediate route to the hearts and minds of ordinary people. Angell's next move was to start a magazine, and rather than rely on his wealthy patrons, he set out to raise money.

He also looked for help in kind, reasoning that every dollar saved was another dollar added to the funds of his cause. Thinking about launching an appeal to the widest number of possible supporters, he asked a random acquaintance he met on the street for advice and: 'He said at once that there were most excellent men on the police force, who could be spared as well as not, if permission could only be obtained to use them.'

As Angell knew the chief of police, the chairman of the Police Committee of Aldermen and the city attorney, he swiftly got the permission he needed and 'seventeen policemen, picked from the whole force, clothed in their best uniforms, were put under my orders on April 15, 1868, for three weeks, reporting to me daily, to canvass the entire city, at the city's expense, to raise funds for our society'.[24] They raised $13,000 in three weeks, much to the annoyance of an alderman with ambitions on the mayoral office, who immediately moved to censure the mayor and have the police banned from supporting charities in the city.

Angell, to whom all obstacles were merely challenges and whose address book had golden pages, called on a supporter who intervened with the hostile alderman with the result that, once the magazine had been printed, police officers then delivered 30,000 copies of it throughout Boston. The magazine, *Our Dumb Animals*, was soon distributed all over the eastern United States. Every issue contained an editorial by Angell and plenty of news items, anecdotes and illustrations which grateful newspaper editors seized upon and reprinted.

Eager to learn what he could from the British experience, Angell travelled to London and met the secretary of the RSPCA, John Colam. He no doubt appeared to be a typical brash American, announcing that the MSPCA had got more done in its first year than the RSPCA had in about fifty, 'because we believed, through and through, in the power of humane education, and in spending our money instead of hoarding it'.[25]

Colam was, in effect, the hard-working CEO of the society. In the near future, both he and Henry Bergh would extend their humanitarian care to children; both men were involved in the establishment of societies for the prevention of cruelty to children.

On this occasion, Colam met Angell again, and introduced him to Catherine Smithies, who shared her experience with the Bands of Mercy. Angell also addressed a three-hour meeting of the RSPCA, chaired by the Bishop of Gloucester, with 'a fine-looking body of elderly gentlemen around the great table, which would, I should think, accommodate some forty or more persons'.[26]

He moved their mood from 'cool' to 'genial' and was then invited to visit Angela Burdett-Coutts at her country estate. By then, he felt too ill to eat or socialise, and so, much to her secretary's surprise, asked to call on her one afternoon in London instead.

He consequently arrived at her sumptuous London home, Holly Lodge in Hampstead Heath, and did not feel up to a walk in the garden or a viewing of his hostess's Pompeiian antiquities, but talked to the distinguished company for over five hours. They seem to have been at cross purposes, with the other guests believing that he was there to raise money, while he was unprepared to answer questions such as 'Do you intend to call on the Empress [Eugenie] while you are in Paris?'

Angell finally addressed his hostess, saying:

> I think it in her power to accomplish more good than any woman has ever accomplished in all history, by entering upon this grand movement to carry humane education into the schools of all nations. I think she can enlist the best women of Great Britain, and then perhaps at the courts of France, Italy, Germany, Holland, and possibly other countries, to form similar organizations, and so bring an immense power to bear, not only in preventing cruelty to God's lower creatures, but also to even prevent or mitigate the severity of wars.[27]

The meeting then seems to have grown quite heated. Lord Harrowby remonstrated that nothing could possibly be done at that time, as the social season was about to end, and Angell pointed out that there was nothing to stop any of them doing anything while they were still alive.

Duly impressed, Burdett-Coutts wrote a letter to *The Times* in the same words, published on 14 September 1869. She was subsequently described as Angell's 'most distinguished and efficient ally'.[28] In the end, the RSPCA borrowed his idea of a magazine and Angell took away their innovation of Bands of Mercy. He also went on to Paris and decided he might indeed call upon the empress while he was in town.

Back on his home turf, Angell was indefatigable in lecture tours, which took him all over the country. *Our Dumb Animals* was widely distributed, the Bands of Mercy proliferated in schools, but he still longed to find a way of rousing public support for his cause, and specifically hoped someone would write a popular book to do it.

Looking back on the progress of the abolitionist cause, he wrote:

> For more than twenty years this thought has been upon my mind. Somebody must write a book which will be as widely read as *Uncle Tom's Cabin*, and shall have as widespread and powerful influence in abolishing cruelty to horses as *Uncle Tom's Cabin* had on the abolition of human slavery.[29]

Today, *Uncle Tom's Cabin*, an overtly polemical popular novel by Harriet Beecher Stowe that was first published in 1851 and tells the story of a family of enslaved Americans, has been criticised for its racist perspective and stereotypical Black characters. It has been derided by many, including James Baldwin, for its sentimentality. It has also been described as the first bestselling novel and an iconic work, and its influence on public opinion in the decade before the Civil War is widely acknowledged.[30] Angell, as he shuttled from city to city, week after week, lecturing to audiences ranging from society ladies to reformatory boys, longed for a book that would seize public imagination on the same scale in the cause of animal welfare.

10

'The Very Spot for Authorship' (1858–66)

Blue Lodge, near the village of Wick, was not an ideal home for Anna and her mother but it was here that her mother's reputation as an author reached its zenith and here too that Anna had many of the experiences that led directly to the writing of *Black Beauty*.

The house was isolated, on a high, windy hill north-west of the city of Bath, 'a long way from everything',[1] and they were decisively cut off from all their former friends: 'Everyone who came to see us had to climb up a long steep hill so that they had to be very much in earnest to do it.'[2] Isaac had been welcomed back into the Quaker movement but it was a long journey to the nearest meeting house.

Blue Lodge, now Blue Lodge Farm, still stands and today is surrounded by rolling hills, lush green fields and pockets of woodland where oak trees flourish. There is now an award-winning nature reserve nearby, with a picturesque blue lake filling what was once a stone quarry. In Anna's time, the area had famous beauty spots such as Wick Rocks, a wild craggy outcrop unexpected in a gentle West Country landscape and a favourite picnic destination in *Northanger Abbey*. It is in the area of South Gloucestershire, at the south-western edge of the Cotswolds region which is now designated an Area of Outstanding Natural Beauty.

Two miles away from the Sewells' new home, down Lodge Road, was the village of Wick, where the historic centre of grey stone cottages gives some idea of how Anna would have seen it. The Cotswolds region is now noted for its picturesque villages and the dry stone walls that mark out fields on the rolling hillsides, the legacy of centuries of prosperity generated by the sheep who grazed there and whose wool was a profitable export. Wick is not a settlement in this mould and owed its existence to heavy industry rather than the wool trade. While there are grand manor houses in the area, most of the village's historic homes are small, grim and uniform workers' cottages, while new-built housing has sprung up on derelict industrial sites.

When the Sewells were at Blue Lodge, there was a far harsher aspect to the region, which was as notorious for its unsparing industries as it was famous for its natural beauty. For centuries, this had been a mining and ironworking area and now industrialisation was moving fast. Hundreds of men were employed in the mills and foundries. The picturesque little River Boyd, which runs in a rocky gorge, had been dammed to power the ironworks, and blasts of dynamite from the quarries regularly scared the birds from the trees.

The area was known as the Golden Valley, perhaps from the autumn colour of the elm trees but more likely because there were also ochre mines in the area. Ochre is a red or yellow rock, tinted by oxides of iron, which is ground to powder and used as a colourant. It has been used in paints since prehistoric times, but was also part of many other industrial processes; the red sails of fishing boats in old paintings, for example, were achieved by painting the canvas with a mixture of fish oil, red ochre and oak bark which protected it against rot and wear. Ochre from Wick was used to colour the tarmac outside Buckingham Palace.[3]

At the time of the Sewell family's arrival, the large-scale exploitation of the ochre deposits was beginning. A small army of men were employed as miners, quarrymen and foundry workers. Pit ponies hauled the ore and coal out of the mines and massive working horses pulled carts laden with coal, iron and building stone to the railway station at Keynsham, near Bristol.

The ochre works were shallow trenches but extraction was a filthy process which stained the men's bodies and their clothes, and blanketed the trees in red dust.[4] When spoil was cleaned from the works, the river ran red. The working conditions were hellish. A contract from 1803 with the Wick Iron Company was signed by a man who worked as a 'furnace man, roller, slitter, cutter, bundler and labourer' and specified twelve hours of work every day of the week, for wages of 12 shillings a week.[5]

In Anna Sewell's lifetime, in the succeeding century, and in the teeth of opposition from employers, laws were passed in Britain to get the working day down to ten hours and give most workers a day off on Sunday, to prevent children working and to introduce basic industrial safety, but these battles were continuing in the 1860s. The man who signed the contract could not write, and so signed it with a cross.

Anna's health was still good when she moved to Blue Lodge. She could ride as well as drive, which was just as well as the house was so far from the nearest villages, Wick and Liston, that going to post a letter took 'two good hours'. 'Neither postman, carrier, omnibus, nor rail, neither shop, needlewoman or charwoman to be had, so that everything has to be done and obtained with the greatest difficulty,' her mother complained.

They were two and a half hours from a school where Anna's teaching skills were soon used, and the roads were often impassable for their pony chaise or on foot in the winter months. This was a voluntary establishment; Wick did not have a village school until 1874, after the Sewells had left the area.[6]

When one of her friends asked Mary why on earth they had settled there, she evaded a direct answer and declined to indict her husband's cockeyed judgement, but conceded that 'humanly speaking it was a great mistake, a mistake through and through' before hoping that 'in time some divinely ordained benefit would become apparent'.

They soon discovered that Wick itself was a miserable village. The population had increased to 700 people, most employed at the mine works, but in those days of laissez-faire government, the infrastructure and facilities the community needed were not there. Mary remembered:

> We have settled in a thoroughly neglected parish, where there have been many changes and quarrels, and now for some time everybody has given it up, not being able to pull together. There is one sermon from the curate on Sunday, and that is all he does for the souls of seven hundred

> parishioners. There is a Sunday and a day-school, but which no one but the poor discouraged master ever entered. This broke our hearts, and we determined to put forth our strength, with the Lord's help, to do something for them. There was not a tract or a book for anyone to read ... This we felt must be mended also ... We are rather afraid that we have engaged with too much for our strength, but the cry seemed to loud, 'Come and help us,' that we were anxious to try.[7]

The first thing Anna and Mary did was set up a lending library full of 'beautiful books'. This proved tricky in an area that actually covered three parishes, each with a suspicious Anglican clergyman in charge of it who wanted to vet the books to make sure that they did not promote Nonconformist views. They rejected *The Anxious Inquirer After Salvation Directed and Encouraged*, a popular introduction to Christian belief by a Congregationalist, John Angell James, 'from the name of the writer'.

Anna volunteered at the school and rode there alone at least twice a week, but it was clear to her that the adults in the community needed education almost as much as the children. In 1863 she decided to rent a one-room building in the village, 14ft square, christened it the Working Men's Hall and set up a free school where she taught literacy, numeracy and natural sciences to anyone who wanted to learn.[8]

Following Anne Wright's model of learning from nature, she would teach biology from the plant and animal specimens around her. She would pull up a stray wheat plant from the edge of a field and demonstrate its root system, or even go so far as to ask the village butcher for a bullock's or sheep's eye to dissect in front of the class.[9] Her mother joined her in making full use of their tiny schoolroom for a Sunday school, mothers' meetings – which were effectively parenting classes – and later for temperance meetings too.

In the twenty-first century it is easy to be cynical about a middle-aged, middle-class woman and her elderly mother behaving like stereotypical Victorian do-gooders in trying to patch up the human damage done by deprivation and unregulated capitalism with a few literacy lessons, some patronising poetry and a homily from the Bible. This would be to overlook the despairing and hopeless lives of the people for whom they worked. Mary well understood how the illiterate labourers that Anna was teaching existed. In 1860 Jarrold's published a collection of her essays, under the title *Thy Poor Brother: Letters to a Friend on Helping the Poor*, in which she described the life of a mine worker who lived about 4 miles from the pit:

> At about three o-clock in the morning his wife creeps downstairs and makes him a cup of tea that he may set out warm. She goes to bed again and away he goes – rain, wind, snow all the same – plunging into the dark of winter through miry roads and over ill-trodden tenacious field paths till, in the dark or early dawn, he arrives at his post of labour. He is then lowered down into the close atmosphere of the pit, and makes his way along the subterranean path to his place of work, and there lies down, half naked – in some – often wet – seam of coal, to pick it out – his eyes, nose and mouth exposed to the dust, and his skin covered with it. Here, hour after hour, he lies in his black sepulchre quarrying out our comfortable fires. The allotted hours of toil finished, he walks his four miles home again. He is not a young man, and I have often noticed his weary steps as he ascends the hill to his own house. Then he must wash all over, to avoid the injurious effect of coal dust on the skin ... After a supper of potatoes and a scrap of bacon to relish it, my friend goes early to bed, that he may gain sufficient rest for the next day's toil.[10]

This description was written around 1862, decades before D.H. Lawrence, in *Sons and Lovers* (1913), and then George Orwell, in *The Road to Wigan Pier* (1929), portrayed the same cruel reality of a miner's life. It is astonishing that anyone who had endured such an arduous working day would have the energy to take literacy lessons in what little leisure time they had, and a tribute to the quality of the teaching that many apparently did so.

Mary and Anna also went out into the community as freelance social workers, a role in which they came into conflict with the local landlords who shamelessly rented barely habitable properties to working people. In this remote village there was no sewage system nor piped water. Lucky villagers lived near a pump but the unlucky had to fetch water from a stream, often struggling over muddy fields with a bucket to reach it.

Both Mary and Isaac gained a reputation for their personal generosity, which was applied in very practical ways. After visiting one family who lived in a house with a defective chimney, Mary took up their cause with their landlord, with no success, then paid for the chimney to be rebuilt herself.

When Anna and Mary moved from Blue Lodge in 1864, many people wrote to thank them for their work in the community. One of them expressed his feelings ardently:

> Dear Lady, I felt I could not let you go off without sending you these few lines. But I feel much Contrition in writing to you – my heart is full while I write. I feel like the Disciples did when Jesus was going to leave them, but I hope the Lord will still Bless us all and Bless you wherever you go. When I think how Benificial [*sic*] you have been to the inhabitants of wick how they will all miss you and Miss Sewell when you are gone away.
>
> I hope dear Miss Sewell got home safe – when I met her in the rood to wick [*sic*], I was so overjoyed I felt like one lifted out of the Body. I couldn't help my tears after we parted.[11]

That writer might well have been concerned that Anna got home safely, as teaching and visiting people in Wick meant she did more driving than ever before, going out almost every day over rough roads and steep hills, and often at night, leaving at eight o'clock in almost total darkness, with only moonlight or starlight to see by. She was fearless, unlike her mother, who could not drive and freely admitted that she lacked physical courage.

The pony chaise was an open carriage, so if it was raining the passengers needed an umbrella but the driver got wet. A friend who visited them in 1858 wrote that:

> These drives often fell on cold and wet winter nights, and I remember Anna's gentle triumph in having falsified her friends' predictions of physical harm to herself from the exposure, her mother gaily adding,

> 'In fact, we've come to regard night drives in an open carriage in bad weather as a positive cure for delicacy.'

Their friend noted that at this point Anna was 'unable to stand for more than a few seconds at a time, although she moved freely about the house'.[12]

Driving even a small pony requires some physical effort as the reins themselves, made of leather, are long and weighty, the more so when wet, but great strength is not needed as a good driver communicates orders to the horse with a gentle touch. Hauling on the reins and dragging the horses about, seen too often in old Western films, is plain bad driving.

Anna had a remarkable rapport with her horses and talked to them all though their drives. Mrs Bayly recorded a typical conversation:

> Anna seemed simply to hold the reins in her hand, trusting to her voice to give all needed directions to her horse. She evidently believed in a horse having a moral nature, if we may judge by her mode of remonstrance. 'Now thee shouldn't walk up this hill – don't thee see how it rains?' 'Now thee must go a little faster – thee would be sorry for us to be late at the station.'[13]

Mary Bayly also records mentioning an essay by the American theologian Horace Bushnell about the treatment of animals to Anna during one drive the station, and paraphrases its content. She says that Anna afterwards wrote to her to tell her that she had never forgotten her words and that they had formed her own ideas for *Black Beauty*.

Mrs Bayly honestly admits that she tried to identify this essay but failed to do so. A search of Bushnell's considerable output suggests that he in fact wrote less about humans' responsibility for animals than many other commentators of the time. Mrs Bayly named another of Bushnell's works, *Inner Life*, as something the Sewells were reading when she visited in 1863, but this author's search for that essay in the records of Bushnell's work has also been unsuccessful, so it seems likely that Mrs Bayly's own admiration for Bushnell has played tricks with her memory, and that her own interpretation of Christian duty towards animals was in fact what Anna noted down.

Several friends who visited at that time recorded the writing days. They had breakfast in the sunny parlour, and fed the dogs and cats, before Mary began her day by walking up and down a long avenue of trees in the garden, letting her ideas develop. She preferred a straight walk while she was thinking, complaining that a 'crinkle-crankle' path jumbled her thoughts. Anna might limp to the door of the house to watch her mother return. Anna and their guest then found quiet places for letter-writing and reading and Mary Sewell disappeared into her study, to re-emerge at midday with some writing to share with her daughter and their visitor before lunch.

Anna lay on the sofa and her mother massaged her painful foot while she read aloud from her new pages. They broke for tea on the lawn and talked about their work. After supper they recited Wordsworth's Ode on *Intimations of Immortality* and discussed poetry, or took a moonlight walk in the garden, before bedtime.[14] At about this time, Mary Bayly records a change in Anna's attitude to her disability, which she describes as 'having come into the light'. She frames this as a spiritual shift towards resignation to the will of God. Finding a community in which she could play a useful part, and participating in her mother's literary success, must also have contributed to a Anna's new sense of validation and purpose.

Despite her full programme of teaching and social work, these were Mary Sewell's most productive years as a writer. She produced *Thy Poor Brother* in 1860, an epistolary book which is in fact an account of her own experiences in social work, couched in advice to a friend. Next was *The Rose of Cheriton* (1867), the story of woman whose life is ruined by alcoholism. She continued in letter form for *Patience Hart's First Experience in Service* (1862), about a country girl who works as a servant (and is called snobby by another of the maids in the household because she can read and write). In between peeling vegetables and darning clothes, she tells of nursery politics, moral lectures from the housekeeper and fending off sexual advances from a guest. Mary then returned to ballad form for *Mother's Last Words* (1865). Subtitled *A Ballad for Boys*, it tells the story of young brothers who become orphans when their mother dies in a dingy London basement, not unlike that of the Sewells' first home in the city. They scrape a living as street children, begging for tips for sweeping a crossing and getting handouts of food and clothes. Only one of the young brothers survives to be taken in by a Sunday school teacher and found an apprenticeship.

While all Mary's books sold well, this one was exceptionally successful, both in Britain and America, and by the time they reissued the text in a combined volume with two others, Jarrold's claimed sales of 1,088,000 copies – a bestseller even by twenty-first-century standards and nothing less than phenomenal in the mid-nineteenth century.

Winsome as her rhymes are, and unfailingly observant in the passages of nature writing, Mary did not shrink from the darker side of lives lived in poverty. Soon afterwards, she wrote *The Lost Child* (1867), set in a village very similar to Wick where a country girl is seduced and abandoned by a casual worker at the mill. She conceals her pregnancy, gives birth alone in a wood, smothers and buries the child, survives in the city as a homeless alcoholic and returns to her widowed mother to die – a scenario as bleak as any devised by Thomas Hardy.

While the reading public clearly adored Mary Sewell's stories, she met with criticism from other quarters. Her brother, John Wright, was shocked by her vivid portrayal of working-class life and exclaimed, 'Why Mary, what company has thee kept?'[15] This is an odd observation from someone who had known the author well and who must have been fully aware that she spent much of her life in social work with the most deprived people in her community. It seems that what really shocked him was Mary's empathy with her subjects, who he felt should have been held at a distance. Sarah Stickney Ellis was disturbed by *Patience Hart*, and declared, 'I don't know that I should have liked it, if I had been her mistress, to have a servant with such a gift for writing long letters about all that went on in the house.'[16]

The entire genre of what William Makepeace Thackeray described as 'low-church verses' was roundly despised by the literary lions of the time. Anthony Trollope singled out *The Rose of Cheriton* as 'one of the worst poems ever written' and attacked Mary for political naïvety which will 'hardly do much to stem the tide of drunkenness'. He acknowledged, however, that 'it must be put in a very different category from that in which we would class the general writers of such little books'.[17]

To be reviewed at all was an achievement, however, let alone to attract the attention of an illustrious literary grandee such as Trollope. Mary found an unexpected champion in the poet and critic Matthew Arnold, who also acknowledged her modest literary ambitions but wrote:

> Even over works which cannot take this high rank, but which are yet freshened, as they pursue their aim of edification, with airs from the true poetical sky – such as *Mother's Last Words* of Mrs Sewell – literary criticism will be tempted to linger; it will, at least, salute them in passing and say, 'There, too, is a breath of Arcadia!'[18]

Her fame meant that she made many new friends and had many approaches from magazines and from other publishers. She found it impossible to write a single poem for a magazine, but was very willing to use her new celebrity to attract support for good causes. She wrote political pamphlets which Jarrold's and a new publisher, Partridge & Co., were also happy to bring out. *An Appeal to the British Working Man on Behalf of the Lancashire Weavers* appeared in 1862, and *An Appeal to Englishwomen* in 1863 called for a boycott of American cotton as it was the product of slavery.

While their old allegiance to the abolitionist cause was not forgotten, Mary and Anna had a new mission. Mary never forgot the sight of the desperate fruit-seller calming her baby with gin who she had observed on Camomile Street when Anna was a baby. In her decades of work with people living in poverty, she had met many who had started drinking to numb the misery of their lives and lost their health, their homes and their families as a result. In Wick she saw many more lives lost to alcohol among the shifting population of migrant workers.

In defiance of Trollope's contempt, they started a temperance group in the neighbourhood, and the men who attended very quickly asked Mary, as a famous author, to lead them, at which she was embarrassed: 'I don't know what to do. I feel so utterly unqualified ... I ... told them that we must meet to edify and strengthen one another, and to keep together those who may sign the pledge and join the Society.'[19]

Wick had one poorly managed church and three predatory pubs. It also had a substantial population of casual workers at the mill, miserably housed in rented rooms. On cold, wet winter evenings the large number of single men had nowhere else to gather except in the pubs, where unregulated and adulterated alcohol was freely available. Landlords exploited every vulnerability in their customers, even the need to water their horses.

The constant traffic between the industrial complex and the railway at Keynsham meant that many carters also passed through the village, often in need of somewhere to stay. One publican refused to provide water for a carter's horses unless the man came into the pub and spent money on drinks for himself – even though the carter offered to pay for the water.

As was the case all over the country, many men and women spent almost all their day's wages on drink just to forget the hopeless misery of their lives. The only significant difference between alcohol in nineteenth-century Britain and the use of Class A drugs today is that the drugs trade is illegal whereas alcohol production was a legal and profitable industry. Alcohol abuse was acknowledged as a major social problem, destroying lives and families.

In *Black Beauty*, Beauty himself is 'ruined' by a drunken rider who forces him over stony ground on a night ride and causes him to fall and cut his knees. The rider is killed, leaving a widow and six children who have to seek help at the workhouse. Another horse has to be put down after a drunken drayman drives into the cab he is pulling.

Mary and Anna opened up their schoolroom for temperance meetings, offering 'coffee, cocoa and currant cake'[20] to all comers. The meetings were run as a discussion group in which the men could share experiences and support each other, with the addition of prayers and a hymn, although the religious content was deliberately non-denominational. They welcomed Quaker and Methodist speakers and even persuaded the local Anglicans to join. In a few months, they had about 120 regular attenders and threw a garden party at Blue Lodge, with more cake and bread and butter.[21]

If this combination of writing and social work was meat and drink to Anna and her mother, it did not appeal to her father. From the outset of their time in Wick, Mary fretted about her husband, 'with only the ploughmen to talk to', and, with a dilapidated house to manage, she wished that he had at least some DIY skills to practise.

Yet again Isaac's Quaker connections saved him. He returned to the movement and attended the Friends meetings at Frenchay near Bristol.[22] In 1864, at the age of 71, he was offered a job managing a branch in Bath of the London and Southwestern Bank, which was later amalgamated with Barclays. The family once more packed up their belongings and moved, this time to a rented apartment in the southern hillside of Bath, at Combe Down.

Anna was physically and mentally exhausted by the move, and even Mary's inextinguishable good cheer wavered. 'When cut off from the occupations and circumstances that to a great degree build up our personality, we almost lose ourselves and hardly know where to find up the I and me,' she wrote to a friend, adding that she felt like 'a poor, empty, barren, hard-hearted, pitiful wretch'.[23]

Before long, however, she made a new friend, Mrs Williamson, another philanthropic matron who lived close by and had founded two small orphanages. They became close friends for the rest of their lives, and Mary's letters to her, detailed and unsparing, give a good picture of Anna's last years.

Although she had 'lost a good deal of her walking power', Anna had only a short distance to cover to get to the church, chapel, schools and shops – these being the most necessary local amenities in her mother's eyes. Like Brighton, Bath was a smart spa town just settling down after some decades as a fashionable destination for London society.

The fact that Anna was still a good-looking woman did not go unnoticed. A friend who was also a poet wrote to Mary, 'My husband, chancing once to meet her in a shop in Bath, came home, saying, "I've just seen Anna Sewell's beautiful face".'[24] Other friends remarked that even when Anna must have been in great pain, she never showed it and 'the calm radiance of her expressive face was remarkable'. Even her mother found this unsettling, and once asked, 'Does thee never break down or fret about it darling?'

'Sometimes when I am alone in my room, I do say, "Poor Nannie",' her daughter answered.[25]

Mary herself was ill after they moved to Combe Down and their optimistic plans to keep driving over to Wick for the night school had to be abandoned. Once she had recovered, she and Anna started to explore the glorious countryside around them in the pony chaise. Anna was driving a sturdy grey pony in Bath, the prototype of Beauty's stable companion Merrylegs. In the city itself, Anna had the opportunity to watch the fashionable carriages that crowded the cobbled streets and notice how the horses were suffering.

Carriage drivers often used a device called a bearing rein to make their horses pull in their heads and curve their necks, giving them the showy look of the horses painted on Greek vases. When a horse was ridden, the rein prevented it from carrying its head low, which was more dangerous for a bad or inexperienced rider, and also made it less likely that the horse would bolt. Used when driving, however, the bearing rein was painful and inflicted injuries on the horse.

Several different types of rein were used, of varying severity, and the worst of them could cut the horse's mouth. George Angell wrote of discovering a horse with cuts 2in long in its mouth, inflicted by bearing reins. These reins, known as check reins in America, exerted considerable pressure on the horse's jaw and were at best uncomfortable and at worst painful for the animal. Prolonged use led to problems in the horse's neck, breathing and spine.

This painful piece of harness is introduced in the eighth chapter of *Black Beauty* as part of the abuse that has been inflicted on Beauty's stablemate, Ginger, the chestnut mare. Unlike Beauty, who is a complete paragon of equine good temper, Ginger is inclined to kick and bite, the result of ill-treatment. She was previously owned by a fashion-conscious London gentleman, whose carriage drove about in the park or took his wife to smart parties and entertainments. He used the bearing rein on his horses because 'he cared only to have a stylish turnout, as they call it'.

Ginger describes how:

> You have two bits instead of one, and mine was a sharp one. It hurt my tongue and my jaw, and the blood from my tongue coloured the froth that kept flying from my lips as I chafed and fretted … Besides

> the soreness in my mouth, and the pain in my neck, the bearing rein always made my windpipe feel bad and if I had stopped there long, I know it would have spoiled my breathing.

In Bath, the horses had to contend not only with cruel owners but also with steep hills. The bearing rein made it painful and difficult for horses going uphill. The city lies in a steep-sided river valley and many of the streets are precipitous, with gradients around 9 per cent – a severe challenge to a horse in any circumstances and nothing better than torture if the harness included a bearing rein.

11

'You Have Been Doing Angels' Work' (1867–77)

Anna was delighted when her brother Philip decided to return to England with his wife and family in 1864. By now, Philip and Sarah had seven children aged between 1 and 14 years old. He had become a wealthy and successful man and his engineering project, the Bilbao to Tudela railway line, had been finished on time in 1863.

Afterwards, the branch line to Santander was added and repaired after its ill-fated opening. The line seems to have been cursed after the station in Bilbao burned down, which must have seemed like a divine hint that his future in Spain would not be rosy. The railway company, undercapitalised from the outset, declared bankruptcy in 1866 and was bailed out by the Bank of Bilbao. Spain was then engulfed in civil war which closed the line between 1873 and 1875, damaging its facilities and material. The line was then taken over by the Compañía del Norte. It has since been extended and improved, and remains a spectacular ride through the mountains, but Philip made a characteristically good decision to leave the project before it ran into trouble.

He was a man who valued family connection very highly, and his uncle John, approaching 70 and a widower since Anne Wright had died in 1861, was anxious to have him closer. Philip was John's heir and would soon inherit the beautiful family home, Dudwick House, an imposing manor mostly built in the eighteenth century, with four wings ending in Dutch gables at front and rear and a magnificent park of sweeping grassland dotted with specimen trees.[1]

One of his unmarried aunts, Mary Sewell's sister Maria, was now living with John on the farm at Buxton, and two others lived together not far away. By this time John Wright, through the Quaker community in Norfolk, had become very closely involved with the wealthy Gurney family. When he set up The Red House Reformatory School in 1853, John Henry Gurney was listed as its treasurer.[2] (John Henry Gurney, Elizabeth Fry's nephew, was a banker and elected an MP the following year, but he won his place in history as an ornithologist and soon retired to dedicate his life to the study of birds – a passion he shared with Anne Wright.)

Philip was offered the job of managing a branch of Gurney's bank in Norwich, and when Gurney's was eventually merged with Barclays, now one of Britain's big five high-street banks, he would become a director of that group. In deciding to abandon his engineering career, for which he had studied so hard and in which he had been so successful, he was also thinking about the education of his children, which would have been restricted abroad.

His wife's health was also on his mind. She seemed to be ill more and more often and the Basque region, far from enjoying Mediterranean heat, has one of the highest rainfall volumes in Europe. So Philip, Sarah and their children returned to England, at first to live at Clare House in Norwich. He also assumed a position as a governor of The Red House School.

This was now something of a model farm, where about forty boys who would otherwise have been in prison were taught mostly agricultural skills. Many would otherwise have struggled after the workhouse and, with no marketable skills, have continued to live by theft or begging, becoming part of the criminal underworld. Perhaps as a result of Philip's involvement with these vulnerable children, he and Sarah adopted seven orphans to add to their own brood. Anna's brother was by now a wealthy man, having been considerably more astute in his investments than his father. In their wills, Anna, Mary and Isaac had shares, particularly railway shares, to leave, indicating the extent to which he had taken care of his family.

They had hardly been in Norwich two years when tragedy struck and Sarah died suddenly in the depths of the winter of 1866. Philip was distraught and became ill himself. Without hesitation, Mary, Isaac and Anna Sewell resolved to move to live near him and do what they could to support the family.

There was nothing to detain them in Bath, now that Isaac had finally, and ignominiously, retired. In his last position, a cashier had been found guilty of 'defalcations', which is described as the misappropriation of funds or, in plain language, stealing. Isaac was not implicated in the theft, but equally he had not noticed it, which a more rigorous manager would certainly have done.[3]

For the first time since Anna's infancy, the Sewells bought a house. Her parents, who were now in their 70s, expected in all probability that it would be their last home. In contrast to the rambling, dilapidated piles they had rented throughout the earlier years, The White House in the village of Old Catton,[4] to the north of the city of Norwich, was a neat, red-brick dwelling with Georgian sash windows.

The house still stands at 125 Spixworth Road but the village has been swallowed by sprawling urbanisation. Norwich Airport is nearby and the long, straight road carries heavy traffic, so there is now no sense of the rural tranquillity the Sewells enjoyed. From the late eighteenth century, the area had been popular with wealthy Norwich citizens wanting to build country homes and attracted by the rich farmland, meandering rivers and lush water meadows fringed with willows. Like most of the county of Norfolk, the area is low-lying, with clear light and the sense of a big sky, which had inspired the Norwich school of painting earlier in the century.[5]

Modest as it was, The White House was close to several grand manors whose owners were mostly associates of John Wright and Philip Sewell.[6] For example, the front of the house overlooked 'Mr Buxton's Park where the deer would come to lie in the cool shade'[7] of the beech trees. Mr Buxton was Samuel Gurney Buxton, a Justice of the Peace, son of a local MP and a co-founder of The Red House. As his names suggest, he was connected through his mother to the Gurney family. After years of isolation on a windswept hilltop where their nearest neighbours were miners and mill workers, Anna's family found themselves nestled in a valley of benevolent privilege.

Anna was still in relatively good health and became governess to her brother's fourteen children. Of these, her niece Margaret, Philip's second daughter, born in Brighton, who would have been about 14 when the family was reunited in Norwich, became a remarkable figure. From 1884 she studied at Newnham College, Cambridge, leaving in 1887 with a second-class degree in the Natural Science Tripos Part I. (Women were allowed to study but not to graduate at this time. She was later awarded an MA.)[8]

Margaret Sewell went on to found the Women's University Settlement in London, effectively a training college for social workers that offered women students free accommodation and lectures in exchange for voluntary social work. After her father's death, she returned to Norfolk to take charge of The Red House.

Margaret wrote a personal memoir of Anna which was used as an introduction in a 1935 edition of *Black Beauty*. It included many of the family stories about her which have been explored in this work. She remembered her as 'practical, critical, far-seeing and fundamentally as much of an idealist as her mother, but possessed of much larger fund of common sense and balanced judgment'.

Anna reciting poem after poem by Tennyson was another memory that stayed with her. She was also impressed with Anna's courage:

> Physically weak, she had a very strong character and was quite fearless; many instances of her courage were told to us. She always had a pony or a horse and was a very good whip, and drove herself everywhere. [Her lameness] no doubt led to a much closer acquaintance with horses than she would otherwise have had.[9]

Forthright and brutally honest as she was, Anna also had a good sense of irony and a dry wit. However much she suffered, she was always aware that she was fortunate compared to many and felt specially blessed in her relationships with her mother and brother. And she could be impatient with sympathy. When news of her final illness began to spread, and her friends wrote to her offering condolences, Anna read one letter aloud to her family, and then said, 'I don't think I can appropriate all this pity. No one needs to be pitied who has mother and Philip.'[10]

It is from this final chapter of her life that the clearest inspiration for *Black Beauty* can be traced. She brought her pony from Bath, the chunky grey, who hated the narrow old streets of Norwich, many of which were surfaced with pebbles rather than cobbles. This surface 'gave great offence' to the pony, who very quickly learned his way around the city centre and refused to take any route that led over the pebbles.

'Neither coaxing nor scolding would move him', so Anna had to agree to take a detour, but she remembered this rare argument with her pony and used it in creating the character of Merrylegs in *Black Beauty*. Merrylegs looks like a cute little pony but in fact has an iron will, and if children riding him do not behave he has no hesitation in throwing them.

Philip's carriage horse, named Bessie, was also a strong character who became well known in the local area. As Philip told a good story himself, the eccentricities of Bessie became an entertainment for the whole family. She was a particularly impatient creature, who would willingly convey her master to his destination but within a quarter of an hour would be whinnying and stamping, wanting to be on the road again. Mrs Bayly fancied that the horse embodied the spirit of the whole family, and described her as:

> a splendid creature, holding rank with the fastest trotters in the country, with any amount of go, courage and spirit in her; yet when, in the fading light of the short winter afternoon, she is brought to the door, and the master takes her reins in his hands, then, as if she divined the responsibility of her task, she seems to be made up of caution and care. How in the pitch darkness and narrow lanes, where guiding must be impossible, she manages never to let a wheel get entangled, is known [only] to Him.[11]

Several times a week Philip drove out to The Red House from his home in Norwich. In winter, this meant driving in the dark on icy roads or snow. Bessie sometimes found herself pulling a sleigh rather than a carriage. The east of England has a severe winter climate, being exposed to polar air flows from the north of Europe,[12] and in one winter when the roads had been partly cleared, she kept up her pace through snowdrifts high enough to reach Philip's knees.

While Anna was fully occupied with her pupils, her mother found that being a celebrity came with responsibilities. While she kept working with Anna in her constant quest for perfection, the tranquil days of writing together were fewer. Writer friends came to visit and they were well received both within and outside the Quaker community. The postman delivered a steady stream of fan letters and persistent requests for more writing from her publishers.

Mary wrote less at Old Catton than she had done at Wick, citing the fact that people were always coming to see her and her life was 'cut up', but she was, by any standards, a prolific author and Jarrold's busily capitalised on her popularity by producing anthology volumes, the equivalent of modern box-sets, in which they republished her most popular work.

The White House, small as it was, was admired by many of those visiting friends, who recalled it as a welcoming haven. At last the family were financially stable and Anna described her parents as 'wonderfully well and active'.[13] Anna and Mary entertained many friends, who admired their style, which was evocative of Plain Quaker interiors but certainly more decorative:

> An old-world look, a low, subdued harmony of colour, and a scent of pot-pourri, in keeping with the quaint speech, the silver hair, and antique, old-world courtliness of the lord and lady of the home. An exquisite perception of the effect of colour was seen in every part of the house – or rather, felt: all was too simple and harmonious to have any striking effect. The paper on the walls was of the quietist tone – no showy patterns, no one piece of grand furniture to spoil the look of the rest, but plants at the windows and flowers in vases arranged lightly, never in solid clumps; at meals, no profusion of dishes but simple delicacies daintily served.[14]

Around the house was a large garden, now sadly built over. There was a summer parlour, or conservatory, which overlooked the garden, and beside the house a special walk and a flower bed planted close to the house so that Anna could enjoy it even when her health was poor. In time, after her final illness took hold, Mary planted climbers in pots on the balcony outside her room and hung up a bird-feeder so she could watch the blue tits peck at it.

The garden was planted with wildflowers as well as cultivated species, including primroses, wood sorrel, speedwell, wild geraniums and lily of the valley. Two large beech trees shaded the lawns. The front of the house had a view of the deer park and its majestic specimen trees, while at the back the garden looked out to the village church, which Mary and Anna attended. They also had a piano at home and enjoyed singing together, suggesting that they had never sought readmission to the Quaker faith, even though they lived by so many of its precepts.

For both Anna and her mother these first years at The White House were a precious interlude of almost perfect happiness. In August 1870 Mary wrote to her friend Mrs Williamson in Bath, saying, 'I think we have done little but be happy ... We have allowed ourselves to enjoy the sunshine all day long, and no harm of any kind has come near us.' This relaxation was unusual, as Anna and her mother still passed most of their time trying to make the world a better place by whatever means possible. Mary wrote more books when she could and tirelessly sent off campaigning letters in support of Poor Law reform.[15]

Anna's diary reveals that her mother also taught in local schools and took private pupils at home.[16] Once the garden was established they began to invite local schoolchildren, as well as the boys from The Red House, to garden parties in the summer months. The tradition of inviting children for sweet treats in a well-kept garden had grown up in Britain, possibly the most garden-proud country in the world, in this period and lasted well into the late twentieth century. It meant simply that those with pleasant gardens shared them with children who came from homes with little or no outside space, providing sandwiches and cake as well as games on the lawns. Anna's diary records that these events happened once or twice a month:

> August 9 – Miss Riches' class of thirty girls come to tea.
> Sept. 1 – We gave tea and frolic to thirty-four children, Miss H's Band of Hope ...
> Sept. 13 – Mother's Sun Lane Infants (50) had tea and play.[17]

Fifty frolicking children must have been quite exhausting for the 70-plus-year-old mother and her disabled daughter. In their spare time, they still read voraciously, eagerly consuming essays, pamphlets and newspapers, and read poetry aloud. They also made toys for local children and collected clothing for gifts to people in need.

While they themselves lived surrounded by much grander homes, there was also a much poorer area nearby, known as New Catton, which housed industrial workers from the city, and here Mary set up a community organisation to support widows and their families. Much of this was funded by Mary herself, in the Quaker tradition of giving away surplus goods and using herself only what was necessary.[18]

In 1870 Philip, a man of 'very strong domestic affections', married again. His bride was Charlotte Sole, a 44-year-old single woman from Devon, who took charge of his household and the children still remaining at home. At around the same time Anna was taken ill. In November 1870, she had attacks of fainting and giddiness, which the doctor thought might indicate 'something serious'.[19]

A few months later, in March 1871, she noted in her diary, 'I have not been well. Dr R thinks it is a troublesome case.' This time she was feeling pain of new intensity. 'I am quite poorly with pain,' she wrote a few months later, and this was a rare admission from someone who had been in perpetual pain for most of her life. For the first time she did not add that she had prayed for courage and been answered, as if she sensed that God now had other plans. She had a few months of respite after the initial onset of her illness but then began to decline unmistakably. The doctor suggested that she would hardly live more than a year.

The same year brought more blows for the Sewell family. Anna noticed that her father was becoming forgetful and prone to strange imaginings. Soon he could no longer conduct the family reading. Many middle-class homes maintained the tradition of family prayers or Bible reading when the whole household, servants included, came together. In Philip's home he read from the Bible every morning before breakfast, but surprisingly, when Mary Sewell took over from her husband the leadership of their little gathering around 9.30 in the evening, she read from a wide range of texts, essays, newspapers or sermons as well, and was as likely to end the little ceremony with a poetry reading as a hymn.

The early morning she always reserved for her solitary walk, and at this time chose Mr Buxton's deer park as her destination.

With the benefit of twenty-first-century medical knowledge, it seems likely that Isaac was succumbing to dementia. Then John Wright, Mary's uncle, died and Philip inherited Dudwick House. The following year, Sarah Stickney Ellis and her husband also passed away, within a week of each other. In October, Philip's youngest daughter died unexpectedly. Anna wrote a poem about the family's year of grief which, apart from *Black Beauty*, is the only composition of hers to have survived:

Seven young trees grew close together,
All fresh and green in the summer weather,
A little one, beautiful, tender and tall,
Grew in the middle, the joy of them all;
And lovingly twining their branches together,
They circled it round, in the fine summer weather.
On the Sabbath eve of an autumn day
The beautiful plant was taken away,
And left a lonely and leafless space,
And nothing was found to fill the place –
Nothing of rich, nothing of rare,
Could fill the spot that was left so bare;
Nothing below, nothing above,
Could fill this empty spot but love.
Then closer the young trees grew together,
In the chilly days of that autumn weather;
And every branch put forth a shoot,
And new life quickened at the root.
They grew in the winter, in the spring they grew,
Silently nourished by heavenly dew,
And when they came back to the summer weather,
One beautiful group they stood together;
And their greenest leaves hung over the place
Where the youngest had stood in its tender grace;
Nothing below, nothing above,
Nothing can heal the hurt but love.[20]

Anna lived for six more years after the doctor's fatal diagnosis and did not decline steadily but had periods of remission lasting months at a time. After each, though, she relapsed a little further, and neither she nor her mother ever allowed themselves false hope.

As soon as she was told that her life would soon end, Anna began to write what would become *Black Beauty*, noting in her diary in 1871, 'I am writing the life of a horse'. At first the work was disconnected scenes and sketches, experimenting with what was then a radical innovation: using the horse's own point of view as narrator.

Stories with an animal protagonist had been told for centuries, since before the time of the enslaved Greek storyteller Aesop, living in the sixth century BC, whose fables, including *The Tortoise and the Hare* and *The Town Mouse and the Country Mouse*, were widely read to British children in the nineteenth century. The evidence of ancient artefacts from Egypt, India and Mesoamerica suggests that endowing animals with human characteristics, and vice versa, was a common feature of spiritual belief in ancient times.

In Anna's own century, Hans Christian Andersen had published stories that attributed human qualities to animals and to objects, famously including *The Ugly Duckling*, but there is no evidence that Anna had read these stories. What she undoubtedly had done, as her paintings proved before they were lost, was study the paintings of Landseer, showcasing his gift for endowing animal subjects with human qualities.

In *Black Beauty* the great difference is that, instead of attributing human characteristics to the horse, Anna Sewell created a horse who walked and talked like a horse. It was her specific intention to give her readers an insight into the horse's mind. Her subtitle for the book, 'translated from the original equine', suggests that the horse was quite definitely of a distinct species.

Throughout the book she is dedicated to evoking the horse's feelings and actions, although Beauty can understand human speech and reports the conversations he hears, which means that the human characters are equally important in the text, and their relationship to their horses clearly shown as the product of their own characters and circumstances. All this was done with the deliberate aim to improve the way horses were treated, which places *Black Beauty* in the didactic tradition of popular fiction to which her mother's books also belonged, even though they were very different in form and style. Anna's decision to create the horse's point of view, and the empathy for both people and animals which she brought to the whole task, moved her book decisively away from the preaching tone of her mother's writing and made it a revolutionary work.

Five years later, when she was confident she was producing a book, she defined her intentions:

> I have for six years now been confined to the house and to my sofa, and have from time to time, as I was able, been writing what I think will turn out a little book, its special aim being to induce kindness, sympathy and an understanding treatment of horses. In thinking of Cab-horses, I have been led to think of Cabmen, and I am anxious, if I can, to present their true condition, and their great difficulties, in a correct and telling manner.[21]

In 1873 a book was published by yet another of Anna's close relatives, her aunt Maria. Mary's sister had cared for their brother John in his last years and after his death moved in with her other two unmarried sisters, the three of them living together in Dudwick Cottage, a handsome brick-and-flint house.

Maria's first book, *The Happy Village and How It Became So*, was dedicated to Mary:

> To my sister, Mrs Sewell, I dedicate this tale of country life, in loving admiration of the talent which has enabled her by her works, both in prose and verse, to contribute so much to the pleasure and improvement of the cottagers of England.[22]

The book is a lively blend of a moral tale, a family mystery and a romantic novel, with occasional cookery tips worthy of Martha Stewart, a sharp but brief dig at uncomprehending upper-class temperance campaigners and plentiful moralising with biblical references.

While Maria's first novel badly needed an editor, it did contain some acute characterisation. The introductory scenes feature a sweet-voiced

Sunday school teacher, of whom one of the villagers says, 'I and my wife call her the angel of the place; for she is always just the same, Sundays and working days, always teaching in one way or another.'[23] The description of her mixed-age classes fits exactly the work that Anna had done in Brighton and Wick.

This passage moves on to the observation that the teacher taught better for having learned her own life-lessons, and concludes with 'Thy will be done'. The parallels with Anna and the state of resignation she had achieved are clear. Mary Sewell loyally recommended her sister's work to her friends, describing it as 'pretty writing and reading'[24] but quite missing the presence of her daughter in it.

It is often particularly difficult for a good editor, whose approach is analytic and critical, to become a good writer. Creativity and criticism are different mental processes and one does not lead to the other. So it is not surprising that Anna kept her writing to herself for the first few years. After a while, however, she felt confident enough to share her book with her mother, and also with Philip, who visited them at least once a week and whose advice on horsemanship from a man's point of view she particularly valued. She also consulted other riders and drivers, including the carters and cabmen who passed their house:

> Some weeks ago I had a conversation at my open window with an intelligent Cabman who was waiting at our door, which has deeply impressed me. He led the conversation to the Sunday question, after telling me that he never plied on the Sabbath. I found there was a sore, even a bitter feeling against the religious people, who by their use of cabs on Sunday, practically deny the Sabbath to the drivers. 'Even ministers do it, Ma'am,' he said, 'and I say it's a shame upon religion.' Then he told me of one of the London drivers who had driven a lady to church – as she stepped from the cab, she handed the driver a tract on the observance of the Sabbath. This naturally thoroughly disgusted the man. 'Now, Ma'am,' said my friend, 'I call that hypocrisy – don't you?' I suppose most of us agree with him, and yet it might not have been done hypocritically – so few Christians apparently realise the responsibility of taking a cab on Sunday.[25]

In 1875 Anna rallied significantly. 'My darling maintains a slight improvement,' Mrs Sewell wrote to a friend:

> [She] has been really better the last few months; it is a comfort and pleasure to see her. My heart is filled with thankfulness, and I think with wonder of all the manifold mercies showered upon us, until I remember the Lord is so very pitiful to all His weak things, made of such poor clay that they cannot take any very high polish.[26]

Having been at her daughter's side almost constantly since the onset of this illness, Mary took the opportunity to go to a religious convention in Brighton. This was probably a large-scale meeting of the Higher Life movement, an evangelical Protestant conference in which American former Quakers, Anglican reformers and various other Nonconformist groups played a part. The larger of the conferences held that year in Brighton was attended by 8,000 people from twenty-three countries.[27]

Anna's mother returned almost transfigured with enthusiasm and laden with books and papers to share. After many years of feeling spiritually adrift, she felt she had found a kind of abundant paradise where she could live in plenty and perfect peace.[28]

After a few more months of happiness, Anna relapsed again. Her father's health was also failing fast, and Mary employed a nurse to help her care for them both. Mary Bayly hints that Mary was 'liable to turns of severe but seldom disabling suffering, brought on by the constant strain upon her. Everyone who has had experience in such things knows the tendency to depression when two in a household of three are chronic invalids.'[29]

Her mother described Anna's daily routine.

> At present I dare not myself look fully into the future. I endeavor with all thankfulness to live only in the day, either as to home or fear about my darling. It is a year and a half since she left the house, except occasionally for a few steps in the garden … The disease which the doctors expected would have worn her out by this time from extreme suffering, is not manifestly worse, but by little and little the strength keeps wasting and her capacity for any effort decreases. She is usually in bed

> till midday, and then dresses, resting between whiles. She lies on the sofa for the remainder of the day, sometimes sitting down to meals with us only for a very short time. She requires almost complete quiet; conversation and reading are usually too fatiguing for her.
>
> Internally there is perfect peace – the sweetest, most cheerful patient – the most unselfish sufferer I have ever seen – the expression of her dear face combines it all, and sometimes she has such a lovely colour, and looks so animated and beaming, that no one would think she ailed much … The doctor attributes the very slow progress of the disease to her tranquillity and her courage, and the exceptional advantages she enjoys in the way of nursing.[30]

Soon, however, the doctor was no longer called upon and there was another brief improvement in Anna's health:

> My sweet one is so cheerful – so charmingly patient, that the days are not wearisome, and just now she is not suffering so much – indeed her general health is better now than it was some months ago. Sometimes she really looks well and always uses what little power she has; never hopelessly giving up because she can do no more, never wishing or complaining but cheerfully submissive.[31]

Anna was often too weak to do more than write a few sentences at a time in pencil on a slip of paper, and these her mother faithfully transcribed. In time, the story was finished and the complete book assembled.

There is very little similarity between Mary Sewell's writing and that of her daughter. In particular, the lack of religious references in *Black Beauty* is nothing like the constant references to God in Mary's books and so it seems that, just as Anna had edited Mary's work with due respect for her voice, so the vivacious Mary now took the same objective care with her daughter's story. If she did in any way influence its development it is difficult for a reader to work out how, as the work is completely coherent in tone and the narrative seamless in construction.

Mary then took the book to her own publishers, Jarrold's, and asked their manager, Mr Tillyard, for his opinion on 'this little thing of my daughter's'.[32] Mr Tillyard was not used to publishing revolutionary novels. He wrote to her a few days later offering £20 for the copyright. While it was common, at that time, for publishers to buy copyright completely in this way, the offer of £20 can easily be understood to be reasonable in comparison with the £3 made by Mary for *Walks with Mama*.

The £20 – the only profit that Anna and her estate were to see for many years from one of the all-time greatest bestsellers – represented the least sum the firm felt able to offer to the daughter of one of their star authors without seeming insensitive, given that the author was known to be terminally ill. Mary advised Anna to accept the offer and the last entry in her diary, dated 21 August 1877, reads, 'My first proofs of *Black Beauty* are come – very nice type'.[33]

The book was published at the beginning of winter in the same year. Anna sent a few copies to friends, relatives and acquaintances who she knew were interested in animal welfare. Often she relied on her mother to write the letters or cards that accompanied the books.

The first printing was very small and so this first edition is now rare. Maria Wright's own copy, with another that is not dedicated, is kept at Norwich Library. There is only one illustration in the book, and on the cover is an image of a horse's head, looking to the right – in later editions the horse looks to the left. The book sold for 2 shillings. Everything about the design of this first printing suggests that Jarrold's regarded this weird little fantasy as the next-worst thing to a vanity project.

The full title of the book was *Black Beauty: His Grooms and Companions. The Autobiography of a Horse Translated from the Original Equine.* The dedication was to Mary: 'To my dear and honoured mother, whose life, no less than her pen, has been devoted to the welfare of others, this little book is affectionately dedicated.' Anna also chose a passage from a biography of the novelist, historian, poet and Anglican priest Charles Kingsley, who had died in 1875, for the opening page:

> He was a perfect horseman, and never lost his temper with his horse, talking to and reasoning with it if it shied or bolted, as if it had been a rational being; knowing that from the fine organisation of the animal, a horse, like a child, will get confused by panic fear, which is only increased by punishment.

Immediately a flood of letters of praise began to arrive at The White House. On 18 January 1878, a friend wrote with the reaction that millions of readers would soon share:

> As an imaginary entrance into and mastery of horse nature, it is extremely clever, – as a story it is thoroughly well planned and told; and last, not least, it must do good among all, high and low, who have the care of these noble creatures ... It has made me cry more than twice or thrice. Poor Ginger! ... My dear Anna, you have been doing angels' work in writing this book.[34]

On 29 January 1878, one of Mary's friends wrote of meeting a 'Mr Flower' – probably Edward Fordham Flower, a prosperous brewer and politician based in Stratford-upon-Avon, who was also a campaigner against cruelty to animals and the author of several books on humane harness design for horses. He was, she wrote:

> In a complete state of enthusiasm over *Black Beauty*. 'It is written by a veterinary surgeon,' he exclaimed. 'By a coachman, by a groom; there is not a mistake in the whole of it ... I must make the lady's acquaintance; she must come to London.' Are we right in supposing that the book is written (translated, by-the-bye) by your daughter? Is it being actively circulated? That was a point Mr Flower was very anxious about. Will you forgive so many questions, but Mr Flower could talk of nothing else. Now and then, when the conversation strayed away to the war, or anything else, he would exclaim 'How could a lady know so much about horses!'

Mary took the letter up to Anna's bedroom and told her she had:

> come to put her crown on. I assure you it was a triumphant moment. She had ventured to send a copy of her book to Mr Flower but had thought, if he noticed it at all, it would be chiefly to point out inaccuracies; but when his entire approbation came, it brought indeed a full measure of gladness and confidence.

Jarrold's had already decided to print a school edition of the book, prompted by Anna and Mary, who 'have both a great desire that it should become a reading-book in Boy's Schools', certainly thinking of the boys at The Red House, most of whom were learning to work with horses.

One of Anna's cousins wrote:

> I am so delighted, so proud of my cousin, that I can never thank you enough for my Christmas present. Read it! I should think I did … I do like the book exceedingly, it is so good; an, forgive me, so unlady-like that but for 'Anna Sewell' on the title page, and a certain gentle kindliness all through the story, no one, I think, would believe it to be written by a lady.

Like many millions of readers in the future, she was most deeply moved by the friendship between Black Beauty and his tragic stablemate, Ginger: 'The Story of poor Black Beauty and Ginger is most touching and the different characters of the horses admirably carried out.'[35]

By the time this shower of praise began Anna was already bedridden and too weak to reply herself, so she asked her mother to write for her.[36] Mary also suggested that the sheer strain of this unexpected admiration was exhausting.

The cruel East Anglian winter also took its toll on Anna's frail health. She tried a milk diet, evidently having trouble keeping food down, but felt no better. Then she developed a chest infection and Mary wrote to a friend that:

> rapid decline set in. Step by step, day by day, the dear life seems to be slipping away, gently just now, comparatively little pain, quiet and praiseful, taking medicine, food; – but the life goes. She can scarcely be moved without faintness … We do not talk of the future – the parting; it might unnerve us both, and we each know what the other thinks and feels.

Mary wrote of the relief Anna got from lying on a 'water bed', but as she lost weight and passed more and more immobile days she developed pressure sores. When she was awake she never gave any sign of suffering; it was only when she was asleep that her face contorted in pain.[37]

By April 1878, Mary was writing:

> What shall I say? A little weaker, and a little weaker – two or three words at a time is all she can say, and all she can bear to hear. I dare not say a word that would touch her tender feelings. 'My dearest Jewel,' I say and her response is, 'My dearest Mother' – neither of us dare venture further.

On 23 April, she wrote, 'Day by day, the precious life is longing for its home.' A few days later came a note beginning, 'We are going through the valley in tender sunshine.'

A few days later, Mary heard her daughter coughing incessantly in the night and went into her room at about four in the morning. Anna said, 'Go back to bed, darling; I really have had some nice sleep.' At six, her mother went in again to put something soft under her back. The nurse called Mary about an hour later, saying Anna was faint and struggling to breathe, but she said, 'I am not going yet, I am so strong.'

Evidently Philip was sent for. After four more hours of painful, laboured breathing, when she did not speak but seemed to be praying, she turned to her brother and said, 'Pray.' He 'commended her into the Redeemer's hands, giving thanks for her full salvation, for all He had revealed to her and for her perfect peace'. 'Amen. It is all quite true,' she responded, then saying in a clear voice, 'I am quite ready.' She looked towards her mother and Mary laid her cheek next to her daughter's. 'A few more long-drawn breaths and she had left me behind. The angel had gone out of the house, and left a void never to be filled until we meet again.'[38]

Anna was laid to rest in the burial ground by the Quaker meeting house in Lamas, the next village, where her parents had been married and where many of her ancestors had also been interred. This was done despite her equivocal feelings about the movement, probably on the initiative of Philip, who was now the head of the family and prominent in the movement. Mary described the place as 'a sequestered spot, surrounded by trees and a high hawthorn hedge, where the birds are never disturbed'.

Traditionally there are no headstones in a Quaker burial ground. More than a century later, the meeting house building was converted to a private home and the burial ground illegally bulldozed.[39] Three headstones bearing the names of Anna, Mary and Isaac are now set in the brick-and-flint garden wall of the house, but it seems unlikely that these were original.

Mary wrote a poem, which is significantly different in tone and complexity from the bouncing verses of her usual style. As ever, she filtered her responses through the lens of her spiritual belief:

I had a treasure – so dear – so dear –
So strong for comfort, so fair to see;
A whisper came from the heavenly shore,
'Wilt thou give the light of thine eyes to me?'

My jewel! My jewel! But I only cried,
'He must not take thee by force away.'
I gave thee, I gave thee, with joy and pride,
Such a gem at His feet to lay.

And I thought of the glow that would light His eyes,
As He turned from angels to welcome thee.
But ah! My Lord, if with Thee I joy,
Thou wilt not forget to weep with me.[40]

The stream of visitors to the house ceased and she withdrew from the world for a while, not least because her husband's health was declining. For the first time for many years, her joy in living deserted her and she could not even enjoy time with nature in her morning walk. 'Now, when I wake in the morning – it is a burden,' she said. In November of the same year Isaac died. 'His passing away was as gentle as a child falling asleep in its mother's arms', and she was briefly alone until one of her granddaughters came to live with her. From Mary Bayly's description of her, 'fully in sympathy with [Mary's] philanthropic ardour, very executive … a first class reporter', it may well have been Margaret Sewell.[41]

Mary's buoyant nature was almost defeated by her grief and she was bewildered by well-meaning messages of support from friends, saying, 'In my own experience I do not know what is meant by getting over a deep heart-loss.'[42] She missed her daughter in every day-to-day activity and going to church brought no relief, as when the congregation was singing, 'I could fancy I heard my Nannie's sweet voice ... and I strained my hoarse little pipe to join with her'. When there were flowers in the garden, she picked some to put in a vase in Anna's room.

To turn the knife in this new wound, in the same year that *Black Beauty* was published, Partridge & Co. brought out a historical novel by Anna's aunt Maria, *Jennett Cragg, the Quakeress: A Story of the Plague*. Set in the reign of Charles II, a time when Quakers were persecuted as heretics, it imagines the story of an intrepid woman of 45, who rode her fine black horse, Midnight, to London and back from her home in Lancashire to rescue her two grandsons from the plague-stricken city.

Midnight and Jennett are called the 'best horse and ... the best rider in this country side'.[43] Jennett talks to Midnight all the time and 'horse and rider seemed to understand each other'. The novel offers a poignant fantasy of Anna Sewell as she might have been, an intrepid and courageous horsewoman, if she had not fallen on her way home from school that rainy day in London.

Eventually Mary was able to pick up her writing again and once more welcome visitors to The White House. Energised by grief, she demanded that the publishers make more effort to sell her daughter's book, a suggestion they accepted readily as the sales were telling their own story. As the year continued, more and more rave reviews were printed across a great range of publications, educational, religious and commercial.

The reviews were not all positive, however, and reveal the attitudes that animal welfare campaigners needed to defeat. In the *Ipswich Journal*, one critic wrote:

> The authoress of this book writes to inculcate a love of gentleness with animals. It must be confessed that she has the courage of her convictions when we find her in the second chapter of the book

> condemning, by implication, the practice of hare-hunting as cruel. Many a lover of horses reading so far will throw down the book as the work of some mealy-mouthed humanitarian, not worth reading. The authoress would no doubt submit that it was not for the horsey men that she had written, but for young people, who, if unchecked are only too apt to become habitually cruel to animals more from want of thought than from innate propensity to be cruel.[44]

Most of the reviews kept in Jarrold's scrap book were rapturously enthusiastic. 'We have rarely read a book with so much genuine pleasure as this,' said the *Daily Press*. 'We most cordially commend the book,' wrote the *Literary World*. 'Most attractively written,' opined the *Norwich Mercury*, which noted that it had only recently carried the author's death notice and that the book would be 'a memorial of the most enduring kind'.

'This promises to be the autobiography of a horse and very ably it is written,' exclaimed the *Mothers' Treasury*. The *Essex Standard* announced that:

> While it may be read with pleasure and profit by educated people, it is an excellent book to put into the hands of stable boys or any who have to do with horses. We expect to hear that it meets with a large sale.

It was 'very pleasant reading', according to *The Freeman*. A Norfolk farmer is quoted as declaring it was 'the very best book I have ever read. It ought to be in every family, especially where dumb animals are kept.' Another publication also noted that the author's mother was 'well known to the world by her pathetic ballads for the poor'. Another reviewer, however, named the author as Mr A. Sewell, and considered that 'No landowner or farmer, we think, would be the loser if he took care that the little book should be read by or read to every man on his property, who has charge of dumb animals'.

Most of these reviews are dated 1878 and many note that a fifth edition of the book was then in preparation. Jarrold's did not archive their day-to-day management documents, so we have no idea how many copies were printed in each edition, nor could the author authenticate the sales figures claimed in subsequent editions. It is clear that many different editions were produced, from budget versions selling for a shilling to luxury illustrated volumes with gold-edged pages. Some also have poignant, if somewhat exploitative, introductions giving versions of Anna's last days of life.

The press coverage makes it clear that the reviewers' advice was widely accepted and many welfare organisations as well as private employers bought the book to give to working men. The *Eastern Daily Press* of 7 February 1880 reported that a meeting of cabmen had been called in Norwich at the Free Library and noted:

> A very pleasing feature of the evening was the distribution to the men of copies of that charming volume, *Black Beauty*, written and published in Norwich. The city ought to be proud of this exquisite book. It is full of genuine touches and feeling. Nothing ever written is better calculated to encourage and develop kindness and gentleness and true human grace towards the brute creation. I hope the cabmen may make good use of it.

The writer swiftly added that he would not accuse the Norwich cabmen of ill-treating their animals. A similar meeting was held for cab drivers in London, and Emma Saunders, an urban missionary who was based at Bristol Temple Meads Station and looked after the railwaymen, carters and draymen employed there, also circulated many copies.[45] A Somerset landowner, Lady Theodora Guest of Henstridge, ordered fifty copies for her estate workers and naïvely asked for the author's address so she could write to her.

Many of the reviewers specifically noted that the RSPCA ought to take an interest in the book. Finally the RSPCA itself agreed, and endorsed several special editions. By then, John Colson had noted that the book was having a marked effect on the society's work with horses, which by now included campaigns to improve roads and to protect pit ponies (horses that worked in the mines) of which there were an estimated 200,000 when the initiative was launched in 1876.[46]

Black Beauty includes two scenes in which ordinary people make the kind of interventions for which Richard Martin and Henry Bergh had been ridiculed. They saw people maltreating horses, intervened to stop them, cited the law and in effect made citizen's arrests. Evidently, Anna was aware of the struggle to popularise the cause of animal welfare and of the fact that early activists had resorted to personal action. Given the book's popularity, this alone normalised the enforcement of legislation that had long languished without grass roots support among the public.

In 1885 Angela Burdett-Coutts started a tradition that endured for a century, the London Cart-Horse Parade, for which many of the draught animals in London were groomed to the maximum, decorated with ribbons and horse brasses, and displayed in a long parade through the streets before their drivers enjoyed entertainment and prize-giving in one of the parks. The aim was to approach the welfare of working animals positively, encouraging good practice and disseminating information about caring for the horses almost by stealth in the process.[47]

The effect was to shine a spotlight on the horses whose hard work was taken for granted and bring them into the public consciousness. While the legislation that was introduced to Parliament still took decades to be passed, the processes that protected pit ponies and outlawed the bearing rein were begun at this time.

Perhaps the most decisive influence of the novel was on the fate of horses at the end of their lives. Beauty narrowly escapes being classed with the 'aged, lame, diseased and worn-out' horses destined for slaughter at a London horse fair. The treatment of horses at the end of their working lives was much improved and live export of decrepit horses was banned. The RSPCA's historian wrote:

> The Society's stand on the decrepit horse traffic was much assisted by *Black Beauty* written by Miss Anna Sewell ... [which] ranks with *Uncle Tom's Cabin* as a classic in humane propaganda with its epic appeal for justice and mercy for the weak and the helpless.[48]

Six years after losing her daughter, Mary herself died, peacefully and prayerfully at home, surrounded by her family. By that time, *Black*

Beauty had enjoyed so much success that sales had reached 90,000 and a new law had been introduced to ban the bearing rein, the cruel piece of harness Anna had damned in the book.

Jarrold's had allowed a French edition, but when, on 2 October 1889, an Englishwoman who had become an Italian princess by marriage and was then resident in Naples wrote to enquire about an Italian edition to be published by the Naples Anti-Cruelty Society, she was disdainfully informed that 'a good round sum' would be required for this privilege.[49] Anna's little book had become, by the standards of the day, a bestseller. But that was only the beginning of *Black Beauty*'s story. The best was yet to come.

12

'At Last the Book Has Come to Me' (1884–85)

In Boston, the Massachusetts Society for the Prevention of Cruelty to Animals grew rapidly after it was founded by George Thorndike Angell and Emily Warren Appleton on 1 June 1867. Angell's vision was of kindness as an enormous popular movement and so, in contrast to the RSPCA, the MSPCA set out to penetrate every level of American society, by every possible means. His principal weapon was the MSPCA's monthly newspaper *Our Dumb Animals*, which he edited and used to popularise the cause of animal welfare in myriad initiatives.

The earliest editions carried no illustration on page 1, merely the title, a ribbon banner proclaiming, 'We speak for those who cannot speak for themselves', and the MSPCA's seal, which showed an angel hovering over a fallen cab horse. Later the design changed to incorporate an engaging masthead collage of different animals, from perky lapdogs to avuncular dray horses. The content was lively and eclectic and included short stories, poems, news reports, tips on caring for animals, anecdotes of heroic or amusing animal behaviour and editorial opinion, all interspersed with large illustrations.

Much of this material was reprinted from newspapers all over the world, so the publication worked similarly to a news aggregation site online. The issue of June 1872 contained a story about a child saved from drowning by a flock of geese in Florida, an ingenious weasel observed dragging a rat that had become its prey out of a pit in Springfield,

Illinois, and a macabre short story, translated from Spanish, about a little black dog who haunts the spot on a mountain road where his mistress was murdered.

Each issue contained a Children's Corner, with advice on caring for pets, and a section called Scholar's Compositions, offering nuggets of factual information which might usefully embroider an essay. Between these colourful items are hints on rubbing down a horse, a report of the illegal clipping of dogs' ears, a careful rendering of a speech by Henry Bergh in New York which also reported on sister organisations in other American states, and a summary of the MSPCA's activities in the past twelve months.

They had certainly been busy. In the past year:

> [The] Society has prosecuted 365 cases of cruelty to animals, 9 other cases are awaiting trial by jury, 336 lame and disabled horses have been turned out of harness and their owners warned; 136 disabled horses which have fallen in the streets have been removed by the ambulance of the society, and 443 condemned animals have been humanely destroyed by the officers of the Society. Day and night raids have been made frequently on the different care and stage routes. Horse-stables, cow-sheds, poultry-dealers stores, dog fanciers dens and hundreds of the private stables of the store-keeper, the peddler, charcoal dealer and other vendors, have been overhauled and the proprietors compelled to cleanse and ventilate the dark and loathsome holes, many of them being underground cellars, in which the animals were found.[1]

News reports also brought the readership up to date with the progress of national legislation to protect animals – which was very slow – and with the activities of animal welfare groups in other countries, which seemed impressive.

Angell could not have known it at this time, but his international focus in reporting on the activities of humane societies all over the world was building a sales network for *Black Beauty*. Germany had followed Britain and founded a society for the protection of animals in Stuttgart, and it is described as growing faster than any of the societies in the English-speaking world. 'About forty' regional societies in Britain were noted, as well as others in Russia, Prussia, Italy, Switzerland, Algiers and Calcutta. These groups came together in international congresses in Dresden in 1861, Hamburg in 1863, Venice in 1865, Paris in 1867 and Zürich in 1869, the last of which was attended by Angell himself.

Buried halfway down a page of the June 1878 edition is a disclaimer: 'What we write here is without his knowledge and Mr Angell claims to exercise no control over these columns.' This may have been so – the use of the word 'claims' suggests otherwise – but his characteristic combination of fearless verbal combat married to quirky humour is carried through the entire publication. A report of $100 reward for finding a lost horse is indignantly followed by the tart observation that the owner would do well to contribute another $100 to save the livestock on farms surrounding him from brutal treatment.

The factual content of *Our Dumb Animals* reported the progress of the animal welfare movement in America and throughout the world. Angell had an instinctive understanding of confirmation bias – the impulse to search for agreement and favour information that supports existing values or beliefs. His publication constantly sang its own praises, praised the good work done by others and demonstrated that everyone, from royalty to blacksmiths, was jumping on the animal welfare bandwagon.

It reprinted the names of the MSPCA's original patrons, constantly acknowledged similar societies in other American cities and reported in detail on the MSPCA's own work. In 1872, an editorial declared:

> Mrs Appleton and Mr Angell may well congratulate themselves upon the success of their work, both having given almost daily attention to it – Mrs A. by constant personal investigation into cases of cruelty, by exciting the interest of her many friends, and by freely giving 'material aid,' and Mr Angell … by correspondence, by interviews with public authorities and individuals, by public addresses in various places, by essays on this subject and by his effective labor in Europe and Chicago.[2]

It is also noteworthy that Angell was scrupulous in sharing the glory of the MSPCA with Emily Appleton and always acknowledged Henry Bergh as the first standard-bearer of the cause in America.

By 1884 the MSPCA had 234,000 members and in schools all over America 3,403 children's groups, the Bands of Mercy, had been set up to inspire the next generation. The groups took their inspiration from the English temperance movement, which also aimed to reach children before they had fully absorbed the values of their parents. Angell had marshalled his army of supporters into directors, officers, inspectors, foreign correspondents, field workers and organisers, and had diversified into a sister enterprise, the American Humane Education Society, which enabled him to operate nationally while Henry Bergh's New York organisation remained only modestly effective.

This was not enough for him. As a diligent student of human nature, he knew that the grudging compliance of adults who had made a lifelong habit of brutalising animals and now resented legislation to prevent them would never achieve the universal value of kindness that was his ambition, as indeed it had been Anna Sewell's. Kindness could not be imposed from the top down.

Angell believed passionately that the key to success in his cause lay in capturing hearts, particularly the hearts of children. The child-friendly content of *Our Dumb Animals* was always substantial and promoted by large pictures. When a school held an essay competition on a humanitarian theme, page after page was devoted to quoting from all the entries – while many publications would merely have named the winner.

In 1872, at the age of almost 50, George T. Angell got married to a widow, Eliza Martin of Nahant, and 'thereby secured a good wife and a happy home to help in future labours'.[3] This seems to have been the literal truth as Eliza is mentioned subsequently in dealing with his copious correspondence and the avalanche of work that came after *Black Beauty* entered their lives. His personal activities expanded to writing essays and textbooks – his essay on the check rein, as the bearing rein is known in America, was internationally distributed.

Black Beauty was to become a decisive weapon in Angell's war against cruelty to animals, not only in America but in the whole of the rest of the world. He learned of the book because one of the society's officers, Miss Georgiana Kendall of New York, visited London and bought a copy of *Black Beauty*, which she immediately sent to Angell with no recommendation other than that he should read it. He read 'each of its two hundred and thirty-eight beautifully printed pages, from its cheerful beginning to its happy end, and then called in the printers'.[4] With his astonishing vision, he immediately saw what could be achieved and how.

The ever-willing Emily Warren Appleton and another lady immediately chipped in with donations that enabled him to get the book typeset and the first 10,000 copies printed. Angell negotiated with Jarrold's for rights to publish *Black Beauty* outside Britain and paid them £1,000. In an appeal in *Our Dumb Animals* on 12 February 1890, he explained that:

> For more than twenty years this thought has been upon my mind. Somebody must write a book which shall be as widely read as *Uncle Tom's Cabin*, and shall have as widespread and powerful influence in abolishing cruelty to horses as *Uncle Tom's Cabin* had on the abolition of human slavery. Many times, by letter and word of mouth, I have called the attention of American writers to this matter and asked them to undertake it. At last the book has come to me – not from America, but from England, where already over ninety thousand copies have been sold. It was written by a woman – Anna Sewell. It is the autobiography of an English horse, telling of kind masters and cruel – of happiness and of suffering. I am glad to say that happiness predominates and finally triumphs.

He stated his aims in detail at that point:

> I want to print immediately a hundred thousand copies here. I want the power to give away thousands of these to drivers of horses – and in public schools – and elsewhere. I want to send a copy, post-paid to the editors of each of about thirteen thousand American newspapers and magazines ... I would be glad, if I had the means, to put a copy of it in every home in America, for I am sure there has never been a book printed in any language the reading of which will be more likely to inspire love and kind care for these dumb servants and friends who toil and die in our service. I hope to live long enough to print and distribute a million copies.

He appealed to 'each reader who has ever loved or cared for horses' to send him money to subsidise this edition, promising an acknowledgement in *Our Dumb Animals*. Within a few months he was able to fund not only the publication of the first American edition but also its sale at a discounted price because 'it must attract the attention and approval of the American people … To do this it must under sell – even at a loss of thousands of dollars.'

Two years later, he had achieved his ambition in America and was also giving news of *Black Beauty*'s publication in 'Mexico, Brazil, Europe, Persia, Japan, China and Syria', as well as New Zealand. He was attacked, however, for depriving the author of her earnings and wrote this comprehensive rebuttal of the accusation which also set out his ambitions for the book in some detail:

> We have received from a leading Boston paper a long attack on *Black Beauty*. The attack is that our 'American Humane Education Society' sells this beautifully printed book of 260 pages for one quarter of the price it ought to bring, and that the English author gets nothing.[5]

He notes that Anna Sewell was unmarried, and her mother a widow, and both had passed away, implying that there were no heirs to profit from the book. He then confirmed that the English publisher paid £20 for the copyright 'and no one but the English publisher gets a sixpence from the profits'. At that point 103,000 copies had been sold in England, and Angell noted that his deal with Jarrold's provided for them to receive 'thousands of dollars' from the book's sales in Britain, Canada and 'other British provinces'. But he could not sell his cheap edition in Britain and undercut Jarrold's.

With some passion, he then continued to explain that the American Humane Education Society was constituted to be able to hold half a million dollars tax free by the Massachusetts Legislature, and the funds it raised would underwrite its work:

> I want to send missionaries into every State and Territory. It wants to form powerful 'Humane Societies' in every State and Territory. It wants to form half a million of its 'Bands of Mercy' in American

> schools and Sunday schools, and supply them gratuitously, or at bare cost, with the choicest humane literature. To do this it must attract the attention and approval of the American people. To do this it wants to flood this whole country (1st) with 'Black Beauty,' and (2nd) with other publications of a similar kind. To do this it must undersell – even at a loss of thousands of dollars.

He continued with a litany of animal victims of cruelty and noted that these 'can be effectively reached by no law or power … except by the power of humane education'. In conclusion, he wrote:

> Under Divine Providence, the sending of this book, '*Black Beauty*' into every American home may be – as was the publication of '*Uncle Tom's Cabin*' – an important step in the progress, not only of American, but the World's, humanity and civilisation.

That year, according to Angell, *Black Beauty* was the bestselling book in America after the Bible, with copies bought both individually and in bulk by institutions to distribute for free. This claim is impossible to authenticate. Angell reported a jump in growth in the number of Bands of Mercy in the following year, 1891, and also noted that, as there was no American copyright in the work, other publishers were now producing *Black Beauty*. He estimated his own sales at around 600,000 and the others' at 400,000, saying that his target of a million had been reached.

By February 1892, he had made the novel his manifesto and his advertising campaign, and as the MSPCA continued to grow almost exponentially he continued to cite the novel as the agent of his success. Writing to a clergyman, he made the point that *Black Beauty* reached people who would never attend church or read a tract. In an essay, *Humane Literature: Not a Golden Dream but a Golden Prospect*, he described the book as the AHES's million and a half missionaries and described how he was now offering prizes for more writing in 'this new field of literature, almost unworked before'. He had publicised these prizes by writing to the presidents of all American universities and colleges, and arguing that they should establish animal welfare as a new field of study in addition. Like many of his wilder ideas, this has become a reality, with the establishment of academic journals in the1970s and early 1980s, and an international Animal Welfare Research Network in 2016.

Emily Warren Appleton died in 1905 and left almost all her remaining fortune to charities, with the leading bequest of $20,000 to the MSPCA. George Thorndike Angell died in 1909, an honoured and respected citizen whose name lives on in a memorial park and plaza in Boston. On Angell's memorial, a horse drinking fountain, is a plaque bearing a quotation from the 30th President of the United States, Calvin Coolidge: 'However much the Society for the Prevention of Cruelty to Animals has done for animals, it has vastly more for mankind through the reaction upon them of the spirit of justice and kindness shown to the creatures below them.'

Epilogue

Black Beauty became one of the bestselling novels of all time. The actual figures are impossible to establish, as many publishers did not keep records of their sales and the book was popular all over the world by the end of the nineteenth century, many decades before electronic point-of-sale figures introduced some accuracy into bestseller lists.

Margaret Sewell, not a woman given to exaggeration, spoke of it as the sixth most popular book in the English language, and the sales at the time of Anna Sewell's 1971 biography by Susan Chitty were estimated at 30 million. An article in *The Times* of 29 February 2008 announced that 50 million copies of the book had been sold.

Black Beauty himself has become an iconic figure, a horse with a great cultural presence, as important to us as a symbol of the relationship between animals and humans as the white horses carved in chalk hillsides by our prehistoric ancestors were to them. Anna Sewell's animal-centred anthropomorphism has 1,000 heirs in popular culture, including Disney's *The Lion King* and even *Paddington Bear*.

The novel soon became much more than a book and has inspired artists in many different fields. Jarrold's began to produce illustrated editions soon after the first publication, and in 1915 Lucy Kemp Welsh, the president of the Society of Animal Painters, produced a definitive series of twenty paintings for a luxury edition. This was reissued in

1950 by Dent. The original paintings fetched £179,190 when they were sold in 1915.

One of George T. Angell's wackier ideas was to offer a prize of $1,000 for the best equestrian drama of *Black Beauty*. His memoir does not record the production of such a play, but the afterlife of this novel very quickly included other dramatic adaptations. Britain has seen two plays adapted from the book.

The first, by James Stone, premiered in 2011 and toured outdoor venues including Epsom Racecourse with great success. The second, produced at the Traverse Theatre, the premier new writing venue in Edinburgh, was a rave-reviewed surreal comedy, a collaboration between Shona Reppe, Andy Manley and Andy Cannon, described as 'not so much an adaptation of as a free-associating theatrical gymkhana'.[1] Two actors play brothers famous in the pantomime horse business but now unemployed, who discover a volume of *Black Beauty* in their late mother's belongings and proceed to perform the story. Staged in front of a full-size horsebox, the production creates horses out of shadow images, boots, handbags and My Little Pony figures.

Film and TV were easier media for the story. In 1917 a silent film was made, *Your Obedient Servant*, directed by Edward H. Griffith, who made another silent version in 1921. In 1946 it was filmed by Max Nosseck, a German director who had previously worked on *The Return of Rin Tin Tin*, and in 1971 by James Hill who also directed *Born Free* and the children's TV series based on the character of the scarecrow Worzel Gummidge.

From 1972 to 1974 a British TV series, produced by London Weekend Television, *The Adventures of Black Beauty*, shifted the story away from Sewell's original in the guise of a sequel, and extrapolated a series of adventures about a black horse and a young woman, played by Judy Bowker. While this had only a tangential relationship to the novel, it was accompanied by award-winning theme music by Denis King. The series continued in repeats all over the world for some decades.

The best film adaptation appeared in 1994, written and directed by Caroline Thompson, whose writing credits include *Edward Scissorhands* and *The Addams Family*. Beauty is voiced by Alan Cumming, with Sean Bean, David Thewlis, Peter Davidson and Rupert Penry-Jones in the cast.

This seems to be the only film not to attempt to introduce an element of romance into the story or to at least insert a woman character. To many interpreters, the emotional appeal of the story, and the fact that horse riding as an amateur sport attracts more women than men, posed a dilemma in that Anna Sewell's story is almost entirely peopled by men and horses, with very few significant women characters. The solution, adopted by the London Weekend Television series, as well as the 2015 film directed by Daniel Zilli, was to abandon the original story.

The Disney film of 2021 went one step further and made *Black Beauty* the story of a mare, voiced by Kate Winslet, and a girl, played by Mackenzie Foy. This was a controversial course to take, especially in an age of social media, and the film significantly failed to win the approval of the many potential viewers indicated by the novel's 259,074 Goodreads ratings.

In reviewing this production in *The Times*, the newspaper's leading art critic Rachel Campbell-Johnston pointed to the real significance of *Black Beauty*:

> In the end, Sewell was delivering a fundamentally tough lecture about the enslavement of living beings; imbalance of power and the brutality that it can bring; and the moral imperative to show more compassion. This is a message that we still need to hear.[2]

It is extraordinary that a woman who lived, as the introduction to my own edition of *Black Beauty* describes, 'an uneventful but beautiful life' should have left such a decisive mark on the world. The one book that Anna Sewell wrote was the product of continuous acts of empathy, with both horse and people, throughout a life that was physically limited by her disability. The act of creation, sustained over the years of her final illness, seems almost spiritual, although, as this book is intended to show, it was the product of innovative education, personal experience and lifelong study. Her ambition for the book was to 'induce kindness', but the story of Anna Sewell's life shows us how kindness itself can be created.

ACKNOWLEDGEMENTS

A woman who wants to win a place in history should ideally be a worthless entitled airhead from a royal, or at least aristocratic, family. Whatever letters she scrawls on monogrammed paper between love affairs will be lovingly preserved by the heirs she abandoned to nursemaids at birth. In contrast, a woman like Anna Sewell, brought up in poverty, whose major ambition was to do good in the world while living with her disability, who never married, had no children and unfortunately died before her only book became one of the greatest international bestsellers of all time, is almost invisible to history.

Although Anna wrote almost every day, a few letters and ephemera are all that survive, some of them now lovingly preserved but many scattered in twos and threes with the descendants of people connected to her nieces and nephews. In her lifetime, the famous writer in Anna's life was her mother, Mary. Much of what we know of Anna comes to us through Mary's words, and the determined optimism which buoyed up her and her family through many challenges means that she was the most unreliable of narrators. The story of Anna's life has been pieced together from many different sources and I had a great deal of help in doing so.

Although I had been collecting material for this book since 2013, and Lady Susan Chitty's biography of 1971 provided a solid foundation on which to build, the bulk of the research was done in Britain during the Covid-19 crisis, when all the essential archives were closed during lockdowns and consulting archival material meant planning guerrilla raids in the brief periods in which government restrictions were lifted.

I am very grateful to the intrepid librarians who found alternative and accessible sources for me, including Katie Rickard at Bath Spa University and Melissa Atkinson, the Special Collections Curator, and Lucy Saint Smith, Library Assistant for The Society of Friends. At the Norfolk Record Office, Jenny Watts, Theresa Palfrey and Tom Townsend were extremely helpful. For help in diagnosing Anna Sewell's disabling injury almost two centuries after the event, I am grateful to Tom Treasure, MD MS FRCS FRCP, and to Cleo Kenington, Consultant in Emergency General Surgery & Major Trauma.

Black Beauty's most benevolent owner, George Thorndike Angell, is a character in complete contrast to Anna Sewell. Robustly healthy, awesomely energetic, socially well connected and with bountiful self-belief, his written legacy runs to reams of correspondence and many volumes of publications. Just as the key archives were closed in Britain, so international travel was also halted by Covid-19 regulations and so, above all, I am grateful to Kylie Nelson, then a postgraduate student at the University of Massachusetts, who spent many hours in archival research on my behalf.

For excellent advice on reading cross-written letters, I am grateful to my colleagues at Bath Spa University, Professor Robert Morrison and Professor Ian Gadd, and I have also appreciated the enthusiasm and support of my colleague Richard Kerridge.

As early readers who advised me on specific aspects of the book, I would like to thank Professor Philip Gross for his help with my portrayal of The Society of Friends, Amelia Bennett for her advice on riding and horse-mastership, and Dr Toni Chappell, Kylie Nelson and Dr Carrie Etter for casting American eyes over the Boston and New York passages.

My agent, Eleanor Birne at PEW Literary, has been most helpful in guiding me through a new literary field, and the wonderful team at The History Press, particularly Claire Hopkins, Alex Boulton and Graham Robson, who have worked with great vision and expertise to send this book out into the world.

One of the nicest things about writing this book has been the instant enthusiasm of almost everyone I have talked to about it. First and best of this cheering crowd has been my daughter, Chloe, in her turn the light of her mother's life.

Celia Brayfield
Dorset, 2023

Notes

Introduction

1. Bayly, Mary. 1888. *The Life and Letters of Mrs Sewell*. 2nd ed. London: James Nisbet & Co., p. 272.
2. Bayly, *Life and Letters of Mrs Sewell*, p. 272.
3. Bayly, *Life and Letters of Mrs Sewell*, p. 280.
4. Bayly, *Life and Letters of Mrs Sewell*, p. 285.

Chapter 1: My Little Darling (1820–22)

1. Bayly, *Life and Letters of Mrs Sewell*, p. 52.
2. Bayly, *Life and Letters of Mrs Sewell*, p. 53.
3. Bayly, *Life and Letters of Mrs Sewell*, p. 53.
4. Bayly, *Life and Letters of Mrs Sewell*, p. 42.
5. Bayly, *Life and Letters of Mrs Sewell*, p. 53.
6. Bayly, *Life and Letters of Mrs Sewell*, p. 51.
7. Bayly, *Life and Letters of Mrs Sewell*, p. 122.
8. Bayly, *Life and Letters of Mrs Sewell*, p. 48.
9. Glendinning, Victoria. 1995. *A Suppressed Cry*. 1st ed. London: Virago, p. 10.
10. Rose, June. 1980. *Elizabeth Fry: A Biography*. 2nd ed. London: Macmillan, p. 42.
11. Chitty, Susan. 1971. *Anna Sewell: The Woman Who Wrote Black Beauty*. 2nd ed. London: Hodder & Stoughton/Stroud: Tempus Publishing (2007), p. 33.
12. Bayly, *Life and Letters of Mrs Sewell*, p. 48.
13. Bayly, *Life and Letters of Mrs Sewell*, p. 51.
14. Sewell, Mary. 1883. *Autobiography*. Norwich: Jarrold & Son.
15. Bayly, *Life and Letters of Mrs Sewell*, p. 45.

16. Bayly, *Life and Letters of Mrs Sewell*, p. 51.
17. Sewell, M., *Autobiography*.
18. Chitty, *Anna Sewell*, p. 44.
19. Chitty, *Anna Sewell*, p. 44.
20. Sewell, M., quoted in Chitty, *Anna Sewell*, p. 42.
21. Bayly, Mary. 1859. *Ragged Homes and How to Mend Them*. Echo Library (2018), p. 28.
22. Glendinning, *Suppressed Cry*, p. 10.
23. Bayly, *Life and Letters of Mrs Sewell*, p. 116.
24. Bayly, *Life and Letters of Mrs Sewell*, p. 80.
25. Bayly, *Life and Letters of Mrs Sewell*, p. 54.
26. Bayly, *Life and Letters of Mrs Sewell*, p. 55.

Chapter 2: Hell for Animals (1822–24)

1. Almeroth-Williams, Thomas. 2020. *City of Beasts*. Manchester: Manchester University Press.
2. Almeroth-Williams, *City of Beasts*, location 849.
3. Almeroth-Williams, *City of Beasts*, location 1507.
4. Lloyd, Marie. 'Don't Dilly Dally on the Way' (monologues.co.uk/musichall/Songs-D/Dont-Dilly-Dally.htm).
5. Thomas Rowlandson. 1811. *A Bird's Eye View of Smithfield Market taken from the Bear & Ragged Staff*. British Museum.
6. *The Farmers Magazine*. 1849. London: Rogerson & Tuxford, p. 142.
7. Almeroth-Williams, *City of Beasts*, location 507.
8. Dibdin, Charles. 1789. *Liberty-Hall: or, a Test of Good Fellowship*. Graphic Arts Collection. London: Samuel Fores (graphicarts.princeton.edu/2014/03/10/the-high-mettled-racer/).
9. Almeroth-Williams, *City of Beasts*, location 7.
10. Almeroth-Williams, *City of Beasts*, location 3806.
11. Peacock, Mabel. 1904. 'Notes on the Stamford Bull Running'. *Folklore*: 15:2, pp.199–202. *Lincolnshire Life*. 2019. 'Bull Running in Stamford' (www.lincolnshirelife.co.uk/heritage/bull-running-in-stamford/).
12. 'Bull Running in Stamford'.
13. Quoted in Ritvo, Harriet. 2005. *The Animal Estate: The English and Other Creatures in the Victorian Age*. Cambridge, MA: Harvard University Press, p. 126.
14. Ritvo, *The Animal Estate*, p. 125.
15. Hogarth, William. 1 February 1751. 'The Second Stage of Cruelty', from *The Four Stages of Cruelty* (Etching and Engraving). London.
16. Shevelow, Kathryn. 2008. *For the Love of Animals: The Rise of the Animal Protection Movement*. 1st ed. New York: Henry Holt & Co., p. 8.

17. Quoted in Shevelow, *For the Love of Animals*, p. 219.
18. Shevelow, *For the Love of Animals*, p. 216.
19. Shevelow, *For the Love of Animals*, p. 234.
20. Lynam, Shevawn. 1989. *Humanity Dick Martin 'King Of Connemara' 1754–1834*. Dublin: The Lilliput Press, p. 203.
21. Shevelow, *For the Love of Animals*, p. 247.
22. Lynam, *Humanity Dick Martin*, p. 223.
23. Engraving after the painting by P. Matthews, *The Trial of Bill Burns*, 1838.
24. Lynam, *Humanity Dick Martin*, p. 234.
25. Quoted in Lynam, *Humanity Dick Martin*, p. 253.
26. Shevelow, *For the Love of Animals*, p. 268.
27. 17 February 1821. 'Clerus', *Morning Post*, p. 3.
28. Heyrick, Elizabeth. 1823. *Cursory Remarks on the Evil Tendency of Unrestrained Cruelty; Particularly that Practised in Smithfield Market*. London: Harvey & Darton.
29. Shevelow, *For the Love of Animals*, p. 274.

Chapter 3: 'I Think We Were Exceedingly Happy' (1824–32)

1. Bayly, *Life and Letters of Mrs Sewell*, p. 55.
2. Bayly, *Life and Letters of Mrs Sewell*, p. 55.
3. Bayly, *Life and Letters of Mrs Sewell*, p. 59.
4. Bayly, *Life and Letters of Mrs Sewell*, p. 56.
5. Bayly, *Life and Letters of Mrs Sewell*, p. 56.
6. Montessori, Maria, and Annette Haines. 2018. *The 1946 London Lectures*. Amsterdam: Montessori-Pierson Publishing Company, p. 98.
7. Bayly, *Life and Letters of Mrs Sewell*, p. 57.
8. Dickens, Charles. 1861. *The Life and Adventures of Nicholas Nickleby*. New York, NY: W.A. Townsend & Company, p. 140.
9. Bayly, *Life and Letters of Mrs Sewell*, p. 57.
10. Bayly, *Life and Letters of Mrs Sewell*, p. 46.
11. Bayly, *Life and Letters of Mrs Sewell*, p. 60.
12. Bayly, *Life and Letters of Mrs Sewell*, p. 59.
13. Bayly, *Life and Letters of Mrs Sewell*, p. 60.
14. Bagster, Samuel. 1834. *The Management of Bees. With a Description of the 'Ladies' Safety Hive'. With Forty Illustrative Wood Engravings*. London: Saunders & Otley, p. 109.
15. Bayly, *Life and Letters of Mrs Sewell*, p. 57.
16. Bayly, *Life and Letters of Mrs Sewell*, pp. 113, 116.
17. Bayly, *Life and Letters of Mrs Sewell*, pp. 109–10.
18. Butler, Marilyn. 1972. *Maria Edgeworth*. Oxford: Clarendon Press.
19. Edgeworth, Maria. 1802. *Moral Tales For Young People*. London: Blackie. Preface, p. ii.

20. Bayly, *Life and Letters of Mrs Sewell*, pp. 85–6.
21. Bayly, *Life and Letters of Mrs Sewell*, p. 86.
22. Bayly, *Life and Letters of Mrs Sewell*, p. 72.
23. Daniels, Peter. 2022. 'Quakers in Stoke Newington: The 19th and 20th Centuries'. *Hackney History*: 14.
24. Heyrick, Elizabeth Coltman. 1824. *Immediate, Not Gradual, Abolition*. 4th ed. London: Forgotten Books.
25. Farrant, Ann. 2014. *Amelia Opie: The Quaker Celebrity*. 1st ed. Hindringham, Norfolk: JJG Publishing, p. 251.
26. Marwick, William H. 1960. *Quaker Biographies*. London: Friends House Service Committee, p. 566.
27. Bayly, *Life and Letters of Mrs Sewell*, p. 61.
28. Mayhew, Henry, and Robert Douglas-Fairhurst. 2012. *London Labour and the London Poor*. Oxford: Oxford University Press.
29. Dickens, Charles. 1839. *Oliver Twist*. London: Richard Bentley, p. 25.
30. *Old Bailey Online*, quoted in layersoflondon.org/map/records/homerton-children-starve-on-christmas-eve.

Chapter 4: Troubled Waters (1832–36)

1. Sewell, Philip Edward. 1912. *Philip Edward Sewell. A Sketch. January 14th, 1822–February 6th, 1906*. London: Jarrold & Sons, p. 2.
2. Bayly, *Life and Letters of Mrs Sewell*, p. 69.
3. Bayly, *Life and Letters of Mrs Sewell*, p. 126.
4. Sewell, P., *Philip Edward Sewell*, p. 18.
5. Sewell, M., *Autobiography*, p. 2.
6. 'The Proceedings of the Old Bailey', *Old Bailey Online: The Proceedings of the Old Bailey, 1674–1913* (www.oldbaileyonline.org/browse.jsp?foo=bar&path=sessionsPapers/18560107.xml&div=t18560107-185&xml=yes).
7. Bayly, *Life and Letters of Mrs Sewell*, pp. 61–2.
8. Bayly, *Life and Letters of Mrs Sewell*, p. 62.
9. Anna Sewell: Two Autograph Letters Signed, with Four Related Family Letters, 1832–63 (www.sothebys.com/en/buy/auction/2021/books-and-manuscripts-19th-and-20th-century-2/anna-sewell-two-autograph-letters-signed-with-four).
10. Valenze, Deborah. 1991. 'The Art of Women and the Business of Men: Women's Work and the Dairy Industry c. 1740–1840'. *Past and Present*: 130:1, pp. 142–69. Doi: 10.1093/past/130.1.142.
11. Hearfield, Marion. 2009. 'Cowkeepers – Introduction' (www.johnhearfield.com/Cowkeeping/Cowkpr_Intro.htm).
12. Bayly, *Life and Letters of Mrs Sewell*, p. 62.

13. Burke, Lois Margaret. 2019. 'Nineteenth-Century Girls and Authorship: Adolescent Writing, Appropriation, and Their Representation in Literature, c. 1860–1900'. Dissertation, Edinburgh Napier.
14. Farrant, *Amelia Opie*, p. 252.
15. Hearfield, 'Cowkeepers'.
16. Bayly, *Life and Letters of Mrs Sewell*, pp. 69–70.
17. Bayly, *Life and Letters of Mrs Sewell*, p. 71.
18. Bayly, *Life and Letters of Mrs Sewell*, p. 70.
19. Bayly, *Life and Letters of Mrs Sewell*, p. 61.
20. Chitty, *Anna Sewell*, pp. 95–6.
21. Chitty, *Anna Sewell*, pp. 95–6.
22. Garrett, Jan. 2015. 'W.E. Channing, "Unitarian Christianity" (Abridged Version)' (people.wku.edu/jan.garrett/channsht.htm).
23. Bayly, *Life and Letters of Mrs Sewell*, p. 66.
24. Bayly, *Life and Letters of Mrs Sewell*, p. 71.
25. Bayly, *Life and Letters of Mrs Sewell*, p. 70.
26. Ross, Elizabeth Kubler. 1969. *On Death and Dying*. 1st ed. New York: Macmillan.
27. Bayly, *Life and Letters of Mrs Sewell*, p. 68.
28. Bayly, *Life and Letters of Mrs Sewell*, p. 68.
29. Bayly, *Life and Letters of Mrs Sewell*, p. 68.
30. Sewell, P., *Philip Edward Sewell*, p. 18.

Chapter 5: 'I Am Very Miserable' (1836–46)

1. Glendinning, *Suppressed Cry*, p. 10.
2. Bayly, *Life and Letters of Mrs Sewell*, p. 28.
3. Cobbett, William, and Margaret Cole. 1930. *Rural Rides*. Vol. 2. P. Davies, p. 690.
4. Glendinning, *Suppressed Cry*, p. 10.
5. Berry, Sue. 2000. 'Pleasure Gardens in Georgian and Regency Seaside Resorts: Brighton, 1750–1840'. *Garden History*: 2:28, pp. 222–30.
6. Bruin, Mary. 2005. 'The Transcription and Notation of Elizabeth Fry's Journal 1780–1845'. Dissertation, Brunel University London.
7. Austen, Jane. 1813. *Pride and Prejudice*. London: Military Library, Ch. 41.
8. Sewell, M., *Autobiography*, p. 3.
9. Douglas, Averil. 2015. *While It Is Yet Day: A Biography of Elizabeth Fry*. Leominster: Orphans Publishing, location 572.
10. Brighton Quakers. 2022. 'History of Brighton Meeting' (www.brightonquakers.co.uk/content/history-brighton-meeting).
11. Bayly, *Life and Letters of Mrs Sewell*, p. 77.
12. Lloyd, Amy J. 2007. *Education, Literacy and the Reading Public*. Detroit: British Library Newspapers.
13. Lloyd, *Education*.

14. Bayly, *Life and Letters of Mrs Sewell*, p. 248.
15. Bayly, *Life and Letters of Mrs Sewell*, p. 86.
16. Thomas, D.P. 2014. 'The Demise of Bloodletting'. Dissertation, Royal College of Physicians, Edinburgh.
17. Bayly, *Life and Letters of Mrs Sewell*, p. 245.
18. *Dictionary of National Biography*. 2022. 'Dictionary of National Biography, 1885–1900/Maitland, Charles (1815–1866)' (en.wikisource.org/wiki/Dictionary_of_National_Biography,_1885-1900/Maitland,_Charles_(1815-1866)).
19. Berry, Sue. 2011. 'Places of Worship in Georgian and Regency Brighton and Hove'. *The Georgian Group Journal*: XIX, pp. 157–72.
20. Tidrick, Kathryn. 2007. *Gandhi: A Political and Spiritual Life*. London: I.B. Tauris.
21. Bayly, *Life and Letters of Mrs Sewell*, p. 92.
22. Bayly, *Life and Letters of Mrs Sewell*, p. 248.
23. Bayly, *Life and Letters of Mrs Sewell*, pp. 246–7.
24. Boyce, Charlotte. 2012. 'Representing the "Hungry Forties" in Image and Verse: The Politics of Hunger in Early-Victorian Illustrated Periodicals'. *Victorian Literature & Culture*: 40, pp. 421–49.
25. Boyce, 'Representing the "Hungry Forties"'.
26. Bayly, *Life and Letters of Mrs Sewell*, p. 95.
27. Bayly, *Life and Letters of Mrs Sewell*, p. 96.
28. Bayly, *Life and Letters of Mrs Sewell*, p. 88.
29. Quoted in Bayly, *Life and Letters of Mrs Sewell*, pp. 88–9.

Chapter 6: No Idle Passing Patronage (1837–61)

1. Lytton, Judith Anne Dorothea Blunt. 1911. *Toy Dogs and Their Ancestors. Including the History and Management of Toy Spaniels, Pekingese, Japanese and Pomeranians. With … Illustrations [Including Portraits]*. New York: D. Appleton & Company.
2. Croft, Christina. 2016. *Queen Victoria's Creatures: Royalty & Animals 1800–1918*. London: Hilliard & Croft, p. 20.
3. Kemble, Fanny. 1879. *Records of a Girlhood*. 2nd ed. Project Gutenberg, p. 475.
4. Weber, Caroline. 2005. *Queen of Fashion*. London: Picador Press, p. 87.
5. Forrest, Susanna. 2022. 'A (Not So) Short History of Women Riding Astride' (susannaforrest.blog/2012/06/15/a-not-so-short-history-of-women-riding-astride/).
6. Gurney, Mrs Gerald. 'The Childhood of Queen Victoria', quoted in Croft, *Queen Victoria's Creatures*, p. 73.
7. Shevelow, *For the Love of Animals*, p. 277.
8. Moss, Arthur W. 1961. *Valiant Crusade*. London: Cassell, p. 27.

9. Fairholme, Edward. 1924. *A Century of Work for Animals: The History of the RSPCA*. 2nd ed. London: John Murray, p. 71.
10. Animal Legal & Historical Center. 1972. 'The History of the RSPCA' (animallaw.info/article/history-rspca).
11. Fairholme, *Century of Work for Animals*, p. 43.
12. Hibbert, Christopher. 2000. *Queen Victoria: A Personal History*. 2nd ed. London: HarperCollins, p. 63.
13. Hibbert, *Queen Victoria*, p. 88.
14. Hibbert, *Queen Victoria*, p. 75.
15. Croft, *Queen Victoria's Creatures*, pp. 18–19.
16. Croft, *Queen Victoria's Creatures*, p. 23.
17. Croft, *Queen Victoria's Creatures*, p. 34.
18. Ormond, Richard, Joseph Rishel and Robin Hamlyn. 1981. *Sir Edwin Landseer*. London: Thames & Hudson, p. 5.
19. Chitty, *Anna Sewell*, p. 106.
20. Fowle, Frances. 2000. 'Dignity and Impudence'. Tate, London. (www.tate.org.uk/art/artworks/landseer-dignity-and-impudence-n00604).
21. Martin, Theodore. 1880. *The Life of the Prince Consort*. Vol. 1, pp. 194–5, quoted in Croft, *Queen Victoria's Creatures*, p. 194.
22. Croft, *Queen Victoria's Creatures*, p. 33.
23. Croft, *Queen Victoria's Creatures*, p. 34.
24. Walford, Edward. *The Life of the Prince Consort*, p. 55, quoted in Croft, *Queen Victoria's Creatures*, p. 36.
25. Chitty, *Anna Sewell*, p. 75.
26. Ellis, Sarah Stickney. 1839. *The Women of England*. 1st ed. London: Fisher, Son & Co.
27. Carlson, Ashley Lynn. 2011. 'Influence, Agency and the Women of England: Victorian Ideology and the Works of Sarah Stickney Ellis'. Dissertation, University of New Mexico, p. 8.
28. Ellis, Sarah Stickney. 1842. *The Daughters Of England*. London: Fisher, Son & Co., p. 65.
29. Bayly, *Life and Letters of Mrs Sewell*, p. 128.

Chapter 7: 'She Consciously Studied for *Black Beauty*' (1846–56)

1. UK Parliament. 2022. 'Railways in Early Nineteenth Century Britain' (www.parliament.uk/about/living-heritage/transformingsociety/transportcomms/roadsrail/kent-case-study/introduction/railways-in-early-nineteenth-century-britain).
2. Wright, E.H. and Anne. 1861. *A Brief Memorial of Mrs. Wright, Late of Buxton, Norfolk. [Signed: E.H. With A Portrait.]*. London: Jarrold & Sons.

3. Wilson, Cindy C., J.C. Fitzpatrick and J.M. Tebay. 2001. 'Essay' in *Companion Animals in Human Health*. Thousand Oaks, CA: Sage, p. 42.
4. Lieber, Mark. 2018. 'Equine Therapy May Help Autism, PTSD and Pain: Why Isn't It Used More?' CNN, 10 July, sec. Health.
5. 'Lis Hartel Biography and Olympic Results'. 2012. *Olympics* at Sports-Football-Reference.com. USA Today Sports Media Group (web.archive.org/web/20120131132041/http://www.sports-reference.com/olympics/athletes/ha/lis-hartel-1.html).
6. Sheidhacker (1994) quoted in Wilson et al., 'Essay', p. 42.
7. Bayly, *Life and Letters of Mrs Sewell*, p. 98.
8. Treasure, Tom. 2021. *Dr Samways Writes to the Editor: The Life and Times of an Exceptional Physician*. Cambridge: Cambridge Scholars Publishing, pp. 167–72.
9. Bayly, *Life and Letters of Mrs Sewell*, p. 145.
10. 'Brighton Works' (brightonlocoworks.co.uk).
11. Chitty, *Anna Sewell*, p. 110.
12. Sewell, Anna, and Margaret Baker. 1935. 'Introduction' in *Black Beauty … With Recollections of Anna Sewell by Margaret Sewell*. London: G.G. Harrap & Co.
13. Sewell, P., *Philip Edward Sewell*, p. 5.
14. Sewell and Baker, 'Introduction' in *Black Beauty*, p. 49
15. Sewell, P., *Philip Edward Sewell*, p. 2.
16. Sewell, P., *Philip Edward Sewell*, p. 7.
17. Sewell, P., *Philip Edward Sewell*, p. 5.
18. UNESCO. 2022. 'The Great Spa Towns of Europe' (whc.unesco.org/en/list/1613).
19. Chitty, *Anna Sewell*, p. 122.
20. Winter, Alison. 1995. 'Harriet Martineu and the Reform of the Invalid in Victorian England'. *The Historical Journal*: 3, pp. 597–616.
21. Cicoria, Rachel. 2021. 'The Ability System and Decolonial Resistance: The Case of the Victorian Invalid'. *Journal of World Philosophies* 6(2): pp. 45–60.
22. Martineau, Harriet. 1844. *Life in the Sickroom*. 2nd ed. London: Bradbury & Evans, p. 162.
23. Vignoles, Olinthus John. 1889. *Life of Charles Blacker Vignoles*. London: Longmans, p. 377.
24. Shaffner, T.P., and W. Owen. 1862. *The Illustrated Record of the International Exhibition of the Industrial Arts and Manufactures, and the Fine Arts … 1862*. Google Books. (www.google.co.uk/books/edition/The_illustrated_record_of_the_Internatio/WycBAAAAQAAJ?hl=en&gbpv=1&dq=Tudela+to+Bilbao+railway+history&pg=PA46&printsec=frontcover).
25. Vignoles, *Life of Charles Blacker Vignoles*, p. 377.
26. Vignoles, *Life of Charles Blacker Vignoles*, p. 400.
27. Chitty, *Anna Sewell*, p. 126.

28. Olaizola, Juanjo. 2019. 'ABUAF – Ferrocarril Tudela De Navarra – Bilbao' (www.abuaf.com/bilbao/index.htm).
29. Chitty, *Anna Sewell*, p. 124.
30. Tennyson, Hallam. 2012. 'Derbyshire and Yorkshire. Letters. 1862–1864', in *Alfred, Lord Tennyson: A Memoir*. Cambridge: Cambridge University Press, pp. 487–96.
31. Tennyson, Alfred, and Cecil Y. Lang. 1981. *The Letters of Alfred Lord Tennyson: Vol. 2: 1851–1870*. Cambridge, MA: The Belknap Press of Harvard University Press, p. 170.
32. Ricks, Christopher. 2006. 'Tennyson, Alfred, First Baron Tennyson'. *Oxford Dictionary of National Biography*. OUP (doi.org/10.1093/ref:odnb/27137).
33. Batchelor, John. 2014. *Tennyson*. London: Vintage Books, p. 151.
34. Ricks, 'Tennyson'.
35. Batchelor, *Tennyson*, p. 152.
36. Chitty, *Anna Sewell*, p. 127.

Chapter 8: 'This Will Do' (1857–67)

1. Bayly, *Life and Letters of Mrs Sewell*, p. 151.
2. Bayly, *Life and Letters of Mrs Sewell*, p. 128.
3. Godfrey, B., et al. 2017. *Young Criminal Lives: Life Courses and Life Chances from 1850*. Oxford: Oxford University Press.
4. Wright, *A Brief Memorial of Mrs. Wright*.
5. Wright, *A Brief Memorial of Mrs. Wright*.
6. Wright, *A Brief Memorial of Mrs. Wright*.
7. Bayly, *Life and Letters of Mrs Sewell*, p. 131.
8. Howsam, Leslie. 1998. *Kegan Paul: A Victorian Imprint*. 2nd ed. Abingdon: Routledge, p. 236.
9. Bayly, *Life and Letters of Mrs Sewell*, p. 132.
10. Bayly, *Life and Letters of Mrs Sewell*, p. 128.
11. Bayly, *Life and Letters of Mrs Sewell*, p. 132.
12. Bayly, *Life and Letters of Mrs Sewell*, p. 133.
13. Bayly, *Life and Letters of Mrs Sewell*, p. 133.
14. Bayly, *Life and Letters of Mrs Sewell*, p. 172.
15. Bayly, *Life and Letters of Mrs Sewell*, p. 167.
16. Bayly, *Life and Letters of Mrs Sewell*, p. 147.
17. Bayly, *Life and Letters of Mrs Sewell*, p. 149.
18. Bayly, *Life and Letters of Mrs Sewell*, p. 131.
19. Brewer, E. Cobham. 1912. *A Dictionary of Phrase and Fable*. London: Cassell & Co., p. 211.
20. 'Capping' has many different meanings, not all related. If people compete to tell jokes or anecdotes, one can try to 'cap' another with a better idea. The principle

of capping is used in Buddhist practice. In a social media context, with the 'I'd cap that' app, 'cap' refers to 'caption'.

21. Bayly, *Life and Letters of Mrs Sewell*, p. 248.
22. Bayly, *Life and Letters of Mrs Sewell*, p. 129.

Chapter 9: The Most Popular Novel of Our Day (1852–65)

1. Walter Thornbury. 1878. 'The Metropolitan Meat-Market', in *Old and New London*. Vol.2. London, pp. 491–6. *British History Online*: www.british-history.ac.uk/old-new-london/vol2/pp491-496.
2. O'Kane, John. 2015. *Portillo's State Secrets*. BBC Two (www.bbc.co.uk/programmes/p02mw8j5).
3. Murray, Frank. 2004. *Oxford Dictionary of National Biography*. Oxford: OUP.
4. Smithies, Catherine. 1862. *A Mother's Lessons on Kindness to Animals*. London: Partridge & Co., p. 80.
5. Cronin, J. Keri. 2018. *Art for Animals: Visual Culture and Animal Advocacy, 1870–1914*. Harrisburg, PA: Penn State University Press, p. 58.
6. Phelps, Norm. 2007. *The Longest Struggle: Animal Advocacy from Pythagoras to PETA*. New York: Lantern Books, p. 117.
7. Phelps, *The Longest Struggle*, pp. 129–38.
8. Nelson, Kylie (n.d.). 'A Lawyer, a Diplomat, and a Socialite: Origin Stories and Gender Constructs in the Infancy of the MSPCA and ASPCA'. Dissertation, University of Massachusetts Boston, p. 1.
9. Phelps, *The Longest Struggle*, p. 106.
10. Nash, Roderick Frazier. 1989. *The Rights of Nature: A History of Environmental Ethics*. Madison, WI: University of Wisconsin Press, p. 43.
11. ASPCA Letter Book. 1867.
12. Letter, Henry Bergh to George Angell, 26 February 1868. ASPCA Letter Book 1867, pp. 318–19.
13. Appleton, William. 1926. *Selections from the Diaries of William Appleton, 1786–1862*. Boston: privately printed, p. 141.
14. McGuiggan, Amy. 'Christmas for the Horses', *Vita Brevis* (vitabrevis.americanancestors.org/2019/12/christmas-for-the-horses/).
15. Angell, George Thorndike, and American Humane Education Society. 1892. *Autobiographical Sketches and Personal Recollections*. Boston: The American Humane Education Society. Unless otherwise attributed, Angell's memoir is the source for the biographical information given here.
16. Sprague, William B. 1860. *Annals of the American Baptist Pulpit*. New York: Robert Carter & Brothers, p. 606.
17. Holmes, Oliver Wendell. 1860. 'The Professor's Story: Chapter I: The Brahmin Caste of New England'. *The Atlantic Monthly*: V, p. 93.

18. Angell, George Thorndike, and American Humane Education Society. 1892. *Autobiographical Sketches and Personal Recollections*. Boston: The American Humane Education Society, p. 2.
19. Angell, *Autobiographical Sketches*, p. 3.
20. Angell, *Autobiographical Sketches*, p. 4.
21. Angell, *Autobiographical Sketches*, p. 8.
22. Angell, *Autobiographical Sketches*, p. 8.
23. Angell, *Autobiographical Sketches*, p. 10.
24. Angell, *Autobiographical Sketches*, p. 13.
25. Angell, *Autobiographical Sketches*, p. 20.
26. Angell, *Autobiographical Sketches*, p. 21.
27. Angell, *Autobiographical Sketches*, p. 28.
28. Angell, *Autobiographical Sketches*, Appendix, p. 2.
29. Angell, *Autobiographical Sketches*, p. 94.
30. UWM Libaries. 2022. 'Uncle Tom's Cabin and the American Literary Canon · The Classic Text · Digital Exhibits – UWM Libraries Special Collections' (liblamp.uwm.edu/omeka/SPC2/exhibits/show/classictext/stowe/cabin).

Chapter 10: 'The Very Spot for Authorship' (1858–66)

1. Bayly, *Life and Letters of Mrs Sewell*, p. 164.
2. Bayly, *Life and Letters of Mrs Sewell*, p. 135.
3. Plaister, Andrew. 2014. 'Wick and Abson'. *Bath & Avon Family History Society Journal*: 157 (bafhs.org.uk/wick-and-abson/?v=79cba1185463).
4. Williams, Carolyn A. 2010. *The River Ran Red: A History of the Golden Valley Wick*. Radstock: Fosseway Press, p. 12.
5. Williams, *The River Ran Red*, pp. 8–9.
6. Plaister, 'Wick and Abson'.
7. Bayly, *Life and Letters of Mrs Sewell*, p. 165.
8. Bayly, *Life and Letters of Mrs Sewell*, p. 186.
9. Bayly, *Life and Letters of Mrs Sewell*, p. 174.
10. Sewell, Mary. 1886. *'Thy Poor Brother': Letters to a Friend on Helping the Poor …* 3rd ed. London: Jarrold & Sons, p. 145.
11. Bayly, *Life and Letters of Mrs Sewell*, p. 188.
12. Bayly, *Life and Letters of Mrs Sewell*, p. 171.
13. Bayly, *Life and Letters of Mrs Sewell*, p. 259.
14. Bayly, *Life and Letters of Mrs Sewell*, p. 186.
15. Bayly, *Life and Letters of Mrs Sewell*, p. 135.
16. Bayly, *Life and Letters of Mrs Sewell*, p. 153.
17. Trollope, Anthony. 4 February 1867. 'Mrs Sewell's The Rose of Cheriton: Review'. *Fortnightly Review*, p. 1867.
18. Arnold, Matthew, and R.H. Super (eds). 1962. *Lectures and Essays in Criticism*. 4th ed. Ann Arbor, MI: University of Michigan Press, p. 42.

19. Bayly, *Life and Letters of Mrs Sewell*, p. 177.
20. Bayly, *Life and Letters of Mrs Sewell*, p. 166.
21. Bayly, *Life and Letters of Mrs Sewell*, p. 167.
22. Chitty, *Anna Sewell*, p. 168.
23. Bayly, *Life and Letters of Mrs Sewell*, p. 190.
24. Bayly, *Life and Letters of Mrs Sewell*, p. 172.
25. Bayly, *Life and Letters of Mrs Sewell*, p. 257.

Chapter 11: 'You Have Been Doing Angels' Work' (1867–77)

1. Buxton-Norfolk. 2022. 'Buxton Norfolk History of Buxton' (www.buxton-norfolk.co.uk/h_houses.htm).
2. Children's Homes. 2022. 'Buxton Reformatory / Industrial / Approved School for Boys, Norwich, Norfolk' (www.childrenshomes.org.uk/BuxtonRfy/).
3. Chitty, *Anna Sewell*, p. 176.
4. Bayly, *Life and Letters of Mrs Sewell*, p. 206.
5. Dickes, William Frederick. 1905. *The Norwich School of Painting: Being a Full Account of the Norwich Exhibitions, the Lives of the Painters, the Lists of Their Respective Exhibits and Descriptions of the Pictures*. London, Jarrold & Sons.
6. Catton Park Trust. 2022. 'Catton Park History' (www.cattonpark.com/about/park-history.html).
7. Bayly, *Life and Letters of Mrs Sewell*, p. 216.
8. ACAD search result (venn.lib.cam.ac.uk/cgi-bin/search-2018.pl?sur=Sewell&suro=w&fir=Margaret+Annie&firo=c&cit=&cito=c&c=all&z=all&tex=&sye=&eye=&col=all&maxcount=50).
9. Sewell and Baker, 'Introduction' in *Black Beauty*.
10. Bayly, *Life and Letters of Mrs Sewell*, p. 270.
11. Bayly, *Life and Letters of Mrs Sewell*, p. 232.
12. Met Office. 2016. 'Eastern England: Climate'. (www.metoffice.gov.uk/binaries/content/assets/metofficegovuk/pdf/weather/learn-about/uk-past-events/regional-climates/eastern-england_-climate---met-office.pdf).
13. Bayly, *Life and Letters of Mrs Sewell*, p. 227.
14. Bayly, *Life and Letters of Mrs Sewell*, p. 217.
15. Bayly, *Life and Letters of Mrs Sewell*, p. 227.
16. Bayly, *Life and Letters of Mrs Sewell*, p. 236.
17. Bayly, *Life and Letters of Mrs Sewell*, p. 235.
18. Bayly, *Life and Letters of Mrs Sewell*, p. 237.
19. Bayly, *Life and Letters of Mrs Sewell*, p. 228.
20. Quoted in Bayly, *Life and Letters of Mrs Sewell*, p. 238.
21. Bayly, *Life and Letters of Mrs Sewell*, p. 272.
22. Wright, Maria. 1873. *The Happy Village and How It Became So*. London: The Book Society, p. 1.

23. Wright, *The Happy Village and How It Became So*, p. 12.
24. Bayly, *Life and Letters of Mrs Sewell*, p. 243.
25. Bayly, *Life and Letters of Mrs Sewell*, p. 272.
26. Bayly, *Life and Letters of Mrs Sewell*, p. 260.
27. Barabas, Steven. 1952. *So Great Salvation: The History and Message of the Keswick Convention*. Eugene, OR: Wipf & Stock, p. 23.
28. Bayly, *Life and Letters of Mrs Sewell*, p. 263.
29. Bayly, *Life and Letters of Mrs Sewell*, p. 257.
30. Bayly, *Life and Letters of Mrs Sewell*, p. 256.
31. Bayly, *Life and Letters of Mrs Sewell*, p. 256.
32. Chitty, *Anna Sewell*, p. 201.
33. Bayly, *Life and Letters of Mrs Sewell*, p. 271.
34. Bayly, *Life and Letters of Mrs Sewell*, p. 275.
35. Bayly, *Life and Letters of Mrs Sewell*, p. 274.
36. Bayly, *Life and Letters of Mrs Sewell*, p. 280.
37. Bayly, *Life and Letters of Mrs Sewell*, p. 281.
38. Bayly, *Life and Letters of Mrs Sewell*, p. 285.
39. Norfolk Historic Environment Service. 2022. 'Record Details – Norfolk Heritage Explorer' (www.heritage.norfolk.gov.uk/record-details?uid=MNF47010).
40. Bayly, *Life and Letters of Mrs Sewell*, p. 28.
41. Bayly, *Life and Letters of Mrs Sewell*, pp. 289–90.
42. Bayly, *Life and Letters of Mrs Sewell*, p. 293.
43. Wright, Maria. 1877. *Jennet Cragg: The Quakeress – A Story of the Plague*. 1st ed. London: Partridge & Company, p. 24.
44. 'Jarrold & Sons Scrap Book'. Norfolk Records Office. 'Review'. 1878. Norwich.
45. 21 March 2021. 'Emma Saunders Is Better Known to Posterity as "The Railwaymen's Friend"', *Bristol Times* (twitter.com/Bristol_Times/status/1373575360340713474).
46. Moss, *Valiant Crusade*, p. 95.
47. Moss, *Valiant Crusade*, p. 120.
48. Moss, *Valiant Crusade*, p. 96.
49. 'Jarrold & Sons Scrap Book'. 2022. Norwich. JD 3/3/226. Norfolk Records Office.

Chapter 12: 'At Last the Book Has Come to Me' (1884–85)

1. Angell, George Thorndike (ed.). 1872. 'The Little Black Dog Etc', *Our Dumb Animals* (babel.hathitrust.org/cgi/pt?id=hvd.hnqb2k&view=1up&seq=1).
2. Angell, 'The Little Black Dog Etc'.
3. Angell, *Autobiographical Sketches*, p. 40.
4. Angell, *Autobiographical Sketches*, p. 95.

5. Angell, *Autobiographical Sketches*, p. 96.

Epilogue

1. Fisher, Mark. 11 December 2016. 'Black Beauty Review: A Galloping Five Star Triumph'. *The Guardian* (www.theguardian.com/stage/2016/dec/11/black-beauty-traverse-theatre-edinburgh-review-anna-sewell).
2. Campbell-Johnston, Rachel. 1 December 2020. 'Black Beauty is Now a Lunge Line of Cliches'. *The Times*.

Bibliography

Archive Resources

Massachusetts Historical Society: Appleton 9.8.a, 1863, Jan; Appleton 9.8.B, 1865, Feb–Mar; Appleton 9.8.C., 1865, April–May; Appleton 9.9.A, 1865, July–Sept; Appleton 10.3.B, 1870, May–July; Appleton 10.3.C, 1870, Aug–Dec; Appleton 10.16, 1882; Appleton 11.1.A., Jan–Jun; Appleton 11.1.b, 1883, Aug–Dec; Appleton 11.3, 1885–86; Appleton 11.5, 1889–90; Appleton 11.6.a., 1891, Jan–May; Appleton 11.6.b, 1891, June–Dec; Appleton 11.8.a, 1893, Jan–May.

Massachusetts Society for the Prevention of Cruelty to Animals: Emily Appleton Research File; Series I, George Thorndike Angell, 1811–1992, Subseries B, Scrapbooks/Books, 1811–1914, 1992; Box 14: Angell Photo Album, Series III; Administrative and Historical Records, 1868–2019, Subseries A; Founding Documents and Record Books, 1868–1979, Box 1; Early Records Folder, Emily Appleton, Donations and Will, 1876–1905; Series III, Administrative and Historical Records, 1868–2019, Subseries B; American Humane ES and MSPCA Files, 1877–2019, Box 57; AHES, Subject, A–Z Folder, *Black Beauty*, Correspondence Related to the Book, 1889–1924.

Norfolk Records Office: Letters to Miss Sewell (MC 144/1–54); Jarrold & Sons Scrap Book and other documents (JLD 3/3/212; JLD 3/3/226; JLD 3/3/228; JLD ¾/94; JLD 4/11/54; JLD 4/12/2).

North Carolina State University: ASPCA Letter Books 1867 and 1868 (d.lib.ncsu.edu/collections/catalog/aspca_20210121_ 8902https://d.lib.ncsu.edu/collections/catalog/aspca_20200303_2917#?c=&m=&s=&cv=&xywh=387%2C-5447%2C6659%2C10893).

Sotheby's: 'Anna Sewell: Two Autograph Letters Signed, with Four Related Family Letters, 1832–63' (www.sothebys.com/en/buy/auction/2021/books-and-manuscripts-19th-and-20th-century-2/anna-sewell-two-autograph-letters-signed-with-four).

Novels, Short Fiction and Poetry

Andersen, Hans Christian. 1843. *New Fairy Tales: First Volume: First Collection*. Copenhagen: C.A. Retzel.

Austen, Jane. 1813. *Pride and Prejudice*. London: Military Library.

Austen, Jane. 1817. *Northanger Abbey*. London: John Murray.

Bond, Michael. 1958. *A Bear Called Paddington*. London: William Collins & Sons.

Brontë, Charlotte. 1847. *Jane Eyre*. London: Smith, Elder & Co.

Dickens, Charles. 1839. *Oliver Twist*. London: Richard Bentley.

Edgeworth, Maria. 1802. *Moral Tales for Young People*. London: Blackie.

Eliot, George. 1871–72. *Middlemarch*. London: William Blackwood & Sons.

Holmes, Oliver Wendell. 1860. 'The Professor's Story: Chapter I: The Brahmin Caste of New England'. *The Atlantic Monthly*: V.

Sewell, Anna. (1877) 1932. *Black Beauty*. London: The Readers Library.

Sewell, Mary. 1858. *Homely Ballads*. London: Smith, Elder & Co.

Sewell, Mary. 1859. *The Children of Summerbrook*. London: Jarrold & Sons.

Sewell, Mary. 1860. *Mother's Last Words. A Ballad for Boys*. 1st ed. London: Jarrold & Sons.

Sewell, Mary. 1861. *Our Father's Care*. London: Jarrold & Sons.

Sewell, Mary. 1861. *Patience Hart's First in Service*. London: Jarrold & Sons.

Sewell, Mary. 1867. *The Lost Child: A Ballad of English Life*. London: Jarrold & Sons.

Sewell, Mary. 1867. *The Rose of Cheriton*. London: Jarrold & Sons, S.W. Partridge.

Stowe, Harriet Beecher. 1852. *Uncle Tom's Cabin*. Cleveland: John P. Jewett & Company.

Wright, Maria. 1873. *The Happy Village and How It Became So*. London: The Book Society.

Wright, Maria. 1877. *Jennet Cragg: The Quakeress – A Story of the Plague*. 1st ed. London: Partridge & Company.

Non-Fiction Books and Articles

Almeroth-Williams, Thomas. 2020. *City of Beasts*. Manchester: Manchester University Press.

Angell, George Thorndike, and American Humane Education Society. 1892. *Autobiographical Sketches and Personal Recollections*. Boston: The American Humane Education Society.

Animal Legal & Historical Center. 1972. 'The History of the RSPCA' (animallaw.info/article/history-rspca).

Animal Welfare Research Network (awrn.co.uk).

Appleton, William. 1926. *Selections from the Diaries of William Appleton, 1786–1862*. Boston: privately printed.

Arnold, Matthew, and R.H. Super (eds). 1962. *Lectures and Essays in Criticism*. 4th ed. Ann Arbor, MI: University of Michigan Press.

Bagster, Samuel. 1834. *The Management of Bees. With a Description of the 'Ladies' Safety Hive'. With Forty Illustrative Wood Engravings*. London: Saunders & Otley.

Barabas, Steven. 1952. *So Great Salvation: The History and Message of the Keswick Convention*. Eugene, OR: Wipf & Stock.

Batchelor, John. 2014. *Tennyson*. London: Vintage Books.

Bayly, Elizabeth Boyd. 1888. *The Life and Letters of Mrs Sewell*. 2nd ed. London: James Nisbet & Co.

Bayly, Mary. 1859. *Ragged Homes and How to Mend Them*. Echo Library (2018).

Beers, Diane L. 2006. *For the Prevention of Cruelty: The History and Legacy of Animal Rights Activism in the United States*. Athens, OH: Swallow Press/Ohio University Press.

Berry, Sue. 2000. 'Pleasure Gardens in Georgian and Regency Seaside Resorts: Brighton, 1750–1840'. *Garden History*: 2:28, pp. 222–30.

Berry, Sue. 2011. 'Places of Worship in Georgian and Regency Brighton and Hove'. *The Georgian Group Journal*: XIX, pp. 157–72.

Boyce, Charlotte. 2012. 'Representing the "Hungry Forties" in Image and Verse: The Politics of Hunger in Early Victorian Illustrated Periodicals'. *Victorian Literature & Culture*: 40, pp. 421–49.

Brewer, E. Cobham. 1912. *A Dictionary of Phrase and Fable*. London: Cassell & Co.

Brighton Quakers. 2022. 'History of Brighton Meeting' (www.brightonquakers.co.uk/content/history-brighton-meeting).

Brighton Works (brightonlocoworks.co.uk).

Bristol Times. 21 March 2021. 'Emma Saunders Is Better Known to Posterity as "The Railwaymen's Friend"' (twitter.com/Bristol_Times/status/1373575360340713474).

Bruin, Mary. 2005. 'The Transcription and Notation of Elizabeth Fry's Journal 1780–1845'. Dissertation, Brunel University London.

Burke, Lois Margaret. 2019. 'Nineteenth-Century Girls and Authorship: Adolescent Writing, Appropriation, and Their Representation in Literature, *c.* 1860–1900'. Dissertation, Edinburgh Napier.

Butler, Marilyn. 1972. *Maria Edgeworth*. Oxford: Clarendon Press.

Buxton-Norfolk. 2022. 'Buxton Norfolk History of Buxton' (www.buxton-norfolk.co.uk/h_houses.htm).

Campbell-Johnston, Rachel. 1 December 2020. 'Black Beauty is Now a Lunge Line of Cliches'. *The Times*

Carlson, Ashley Lynn. 2011. 'Influence, Agency and the Women of England: Victorian Ideology and the Works of Sarah Stickney Ellis'. Dissertation, University of New Mexico.

Catton Park Trust. 2022. 'Catton Park History' (www.cattonpark.com/about/park-history.html).

Charles River Editors. 2017. *The Quakers: The History and Legacy of the Religious Society of Friends*. 2017. 1st ed. CreateSpace.

Charlesworth, Maria Louisa. 1854. *Visits to the Poor*. London: Seeleys.

Children's Homes. 2022. 'Buxton Reformatory / Industrial / Approved School for Boys, Norwich, Norfolk' (www.childrenshomes.org.uk/BuxtonRfy/).

Chitty, Susan. 1971. *Anna Sewell: The Woman Who Wrote Black Beauty*. 2nd ed. London: Hodder & Stoughton/Stroud: Tempus Publishing (2007).

Cicoria, Rachel. 2021. 'The Ability System and Decolonial Resistance: The Case of the Victorian Invalid', *Journal of World Philosophies*: 6:2, pp. 45–60.

Cobbett, William, and Margaret Cole. 1930. *Rural Rides*. Vol. 2. P. Davies.

Cockburn, J.S., and T.F.T. Baker. 1962. *A History of the County of Middlesex*. London: Oxford University Press for the Institute of Historical Research.

Croft, Christina. 2016. *Queen Victoria's Creatures: Royalty & Animals 1800–1918*. London: Hilliard & Croft.

Cronin, J. Keri. 2018. *Art for Animals: Visual Culture and Animal Advocacy, 1870–1914*. Harrisburg, PA: Penn State University Press.

Daniels, Peter. 2022. 'Quakers in Stoke Newington: the 19th and 20th Centuries', *Hackney History*: 14.

Dickens, Charles. 1861. *The Life and Adventures of Nicholas Nickleby*. New York, NY: W.A. Townsend & Company.

Dickes, William Frederick. 1905. *The Norwich School of Painting: Being a Full Account of the Norwich Exhibitions, the Lives of the Painters, the Lists of Their Respective Exhibits and Descriptions of the Pictures*. London, Norwich: Jarrold and Sons.

Dictionary of National Biography. 2022. 'Dictionary of National Biography, 1885–1900/Maitland, Charles (1815–1866)' (en.wikisource.org/wiki/Dictionary_of_National_Biography,_1885-1900/Maitland,_Charles_(1815-1866)).

Douglas, Averil. 2015. *While It Is Yet Day: A Biography of Elizabeth Fry*. Leominster: Orphans Publishing.

Edgeworth, Maria, and Richard Lovell Edgeworth. 1815. *Practical Education*. 2nd ed. Boston: By J. Fancis Lipitt, Providence (RI) and T.B. Wait & Sons.

Ellis, Linda. 2022. 'A Family Story' (www.afamilystory.co.uk/default.aspx).

Ellis, Sarah Stickney. 1839. *The Women of England*. 1st ed. London: Fisher, Son & Co.

Ellis, Sarah Stickney. 1842. *The Daughters of England*. London: Fisher, Son & Co.

England and Wales Census, 1871. 'Charlotte J. Sewell in Household of Philip E. Sewell, St Clement, Norfolk, England', *1871 England, Scotland and Wales Census*, Index and Images (www.findmypast.com). Citing PRO RG 10, Folio, p. 16, Norwich Registration District, Coslany Subdistrict, ED 18, Household 87, The National Archives, Kew, Surrey; FHL Microfilm 838,803.

Fairholme, Edward. 1924. *A Century of Work for Animals: The History of the RSPCA*. 2nd ed. London: John Murray.

Farrant, Ann. 2014. *Amelia Opie: The Quaker Celebrity*. 1st ed. Hindringham, Norfolk: JJG Publishing.

Fisher, Mark. 2016. 'Black Beauty Review: A Galloping Five Star Triumph'. *The Guardian* (www.theguardian.com/stage/2016/dec/11/black-beauty-traverse-theatre-edinburgh-review-anna-sewell).

Forrest, Susanna. 2022. 'A (Not So) Short History of Women Riding Astride' (susannaforrest.blog/2012/06/15/a-not-so-short-history-of-women-riding-astride/).

Fowle, Frances. 2000. 'Dignity and Impudence'. Tate, London (www.tate.org.uk/art/artworks/landseer-dignity-and-impudence-n00604).

Garrett, Jan. 2015. 'W.E. Channing, "Unitarian Christianity" (Abridged Version)' (people.wku.edu/jan.garrett/channsht.htm).

The Gentleman's Magazine. 1857. Vol. 203. Google Books (books.google.co.uk/books?id=KUFDAQAAMAAJ&pg=PA663&redir_esc=y#v=onepage&q&f=false).

Glendinning, Victoria. 1995. *A Suppressed Cry*. 1st ed. London: Virago.

Godfrey, B., et al. 2017. *Young Criminal Lives: Life Courses and Life Chances from 1850*. Oxford: Oxford University Press.

Harman, Claire. 2016. *Charlotte Brontë: A Life*. 2nd ed. London: Penguin.

Harrington, Peter. 2016. *Anna Sewell, Black Beauty, [1877]*. Peter Harrington Rare Books (youtu.be/qhvgD_aSGII).

Hawkins, Andrew. 2020. 'Friends Meeting House'. Norwich 360 (www.norwich360.com/friendsmeetinghouse.html).

Hearfield, Marion. 2009. 'Cowkeepers – Introduction' (www.johnhearfield.com/Cowkeeping/Cowkpr_Intro.htm).

Heyrick, Elizabeth. 1823. *Cursory Remarks on the Evil Tendency of Unrestrained Cruelty; Particularly That Practised in Smithfield Market*. London: Harvey & Darton.

Heyrick, Elizabeth Coltman. 1824. *Immediate, Not Gradual, Abolition*. 4th ed. London: Forgotten Books.

Heyrick Elizabeth, et al. 1827. *Album*. Birmingham: Ladies' Society for the Relief of Negro Slavery [historic title] *c.*1827, RCIN 1125994.

Heyrick, Elizabeth. 1828. *Apology for Ladies' Anti-Slavery Associations*. 2nd ed. London: J. Hatchard and Son.

Hibbert, Christopher. 2000. *Queen Victoria: A Personal History*. 2nd ed. London: HarperCollins.

Howsam, Leslie. 1998. *Kegan Paul: A Victorian Imprint*. Toronto: University of Toronto Press.

IMDb. 2022. 'IMDb: Ratings, Reviews, and Where to Watch the Best Movies & TV Shows' (www.imdb.com).

Isichei, Elizabeth Allo. 1970. *Victorian Quakers*. London: Oxford University Press.

Jarrold & Sons Ltd. 2022. 'History & Heritage – Jarrold & Sons Ltd' (www.jarrold.com/about-us/history-heritage/).

Kemble, Fanny. 1879. *Records of a Girlhood*. 2nd ed. Project Gutenberg.

King, Edward. 1858. *The Horse Book: Simple Rules for Managing a Horse*. 1st ed. London: RSPCA.

Lieber, Mark. 2018. 'Equine Therapy May Help Autism, PTSD and Pain: Why Isn't It Used More?' CNN, 10 July, sec. Health.

Lincolnshire Life. 2019. 'Bull Running in Stamford' (www.lincolnshirelife.co.uk/heritage/bull-running-in-stamford/).

'Lis Hartel Biography and Olympic Results'. 2012. Olympics at Sports-Football-Reference.com. USA Today Sports Media Group (web.archive.org/web/20120131132041/http://www.sports-reference.com/olympics/athletes/ha/lis-hartel-1.html).

Lloyd, Amy J. 2007. *Education, Literacy and the Reading Public*. Detroit, MI: British Library Newspapers.

Lloyd, Marie. (n.d.). 'Don't Dilly Dally on the Way' (monologues.co.uk/musichall/Songs-D/Dont-Dilly-Dally.htm).

Lloyd-Morgan, C. 1889. 'The Geology of the Wick Rocks Valley'. *Proceedings of the Bristol Naturalists Society*: VI, part II, p. 183.

Lynam, Shevawn. 1989. *Humanity Dick Martin 'King of Connemara' 1754–1834*. Dublin: The Lilliput Press.

Lytton, Judith Anne Dorothea Blunt. 1911. *Toy Dogs and Their Ancestors. Including the History and Management of Toy Spaniels, Pekingese, Japanese and Pomeranians. With … Illustrations [Including Portraits]*. New York: D. Appleton & Company.

Macdonald MD, Ashlee, and Gillian Soles MD. 2022. 'Home', Orthopaedic Trauma Association (OTA) (ota.org/).

McGuiggan, Amy. 'Christmas for the Horses', *Vita Brevis* (vitabrevis.americanancestors.org/2019/12/christmas-for-the-horses).

Martineau, Harriet. 1844. *Life in the Sickroom*. 2nd ed. London: Bradbury & Evans.

Marwick, William H. 1960. *Quaker Biographies*. London: Friends House Service Committee.

Mayhew, Henry, and William Tuckniss. 1861. *London Labour and the London Poor*. London: Griffin, Bohn and Co.

Met Office. 2016. Eastern England: Climate (www.metoffice.gov.uk/binaries/content/assets/metofficegovuk/pdf/weather/learn-about/uk-past-events/regional-climates/eastern-england_-climate---met-office.pdf).

Milligan, Edward H. 2007. *The Biographical Dictionary of British Quakers in Commerce and Industry 1775–1920*. York: William Sessions Ltd.

Mitsuda, Tatsuya. 2018. 'Incapacitated Horses, Traffic Policing and Spectator Morals in Late Victorian London', *The Hiyashi Review of Humanities*: 33, pp. 263–88.

Montessori, Maria, and Annette Haines. 2018. *The 1946 London Lectures*. Amsterdam: Montessori-Pierson Publishing Company.

Moss, Arthur W. 1961. *Valiant Crusade*. London: Cassell.

Murray, Frank. 2004. *Oxford Dictionary of National Biography*. Oxford: OUP.

Nash, Roderick Frazier. 1989. *The Rights of Nature: A History of Environmental Ethics*. Madison, WI: University of Wisconsin Press.

Nelson, Kylie. (n.d.). 'A Lawyer, a Diplomat, and a Socialite: Origin Stories and Gender Constructs in the Infancy of the MSPCA and ASPCA'. Dissertation, University of Massachusetts, Boston.

Newton, Lucy. 2022. 'Change and Continuity: The Development of Joint Stock Banking in the Early Nineteenth Century'. Dissertation, Centre for International Business History, University of Reading.

Norfolk Historic Environment Service. 2022. 'Record Details – Norfolk Heritage Explorer' (www.heritage.norfolk.gov.uk/record-details?uid=MNF47010).

Norfolk History Society. 1990. *Anna Sewell Country: Home of Black Beauty*. 1st ed. Norwich: Style Associations.

'Obituary. Henry Vignoles, 1827–1899'. 1899. *Minutes of the Proceedings of the Institution of Civil Engineers*: 137, pp. 435–37. Doi:10.1680/Imotp.1899.18999.

Olaizola, Juanjo. 2019. 'ABUAF – Ferrocarril Tudela De Navarra – Bilbao' (www.abuaf.com/bilbao/index.htm).

O'Kane, John. 2015. *Portillo's State Secrets*. BBC Two (www.bbc.co.uk/programmes/p02mw8j5).

Ormond, Richard, Joseph Rishel and Robin Hamlyn. 1981. *Sir Edwin Landseer*. London: Thames & Hudson.

Oswald, John. 1791. *The Cry of Nature: or, an Appeal to Mercy and to Justice on Behalf of the Persecuted Animals*. 2nd ed. London: British Library: Ecco Print Editions.

Peacock, Mabel. 1904. 'Notes on the Stamford Bull Running'. *Folklore*: 15:2, pp. 199–202.

Pearson, Susan J. (n.d.). 'The Inalienable Rights of the Beasts: Organized Animal Protection and the Language of Rights in America, 1865–1900'. Dissertation, Northwestern University.

Phelps, Norm. 2007. *The Longest Struggle: Animal Advocacy from Pythagoras to PETA*. New York: Lantern Books.

Philips, C.J., and C.F. Molento. 2020. 'Animal Welfare Centres: Are They Useful for the Improvement of Animal Welfare?' MDPI (www.mdpi.com/2076-2615/10/5/877).

Plaister, Andrew. 2014. 'Wick and Abson'. *Bath & Avon Family History Society Journal*: 157 (bafhs.org.uk/wick-and-abson/?v=79cba1185463).

Ricks, Christopher. 2006. 'Tennyson, Alfred, First Baron Tennyson'. *Oxford Dictionary of National Biography*. OUP (doi.org/10.1093/ref:odnb/27137).

Rose, June. 1980. *Elizabeth Fry: A Biography*. 2nd ed. London: Macmillan.

Roser, Max, and Esteban Ortiz-Ospina. 2022. 'Literacy'. *Our World in Data* (ourworldindata.org/literacy).

Ross, Elizabeth Kubler. 1969. *On Death And Dying*. 1st ed. New York: Macmillan.

The Rowntree Society. 2020. *Quakers in the 18th–19th Century*. The Rowntree Society, Clements Hall, Nunthorpe Road, York YO23 1BW (www.rowntreesociety.org.uk/history/rowntree-a-z/quakers-18th-19th-century/).

RSPCA. 2021. 'We Remember' RSPCA (www.rspca.org.uk/-/2019_03_08_international_womens_day).

Salt, Henry S. 1893. *Animals' Rights Considered in Relation to Social Progress*. 1st ed. London: George Bell & Sons.

Sewell, Anna, and Margaret Baker. 1935. 'Introduction' in *Black Beauty ... With Recollections of Anna Sewell by Margaret Sewell*. London: G.G. Harrap & Co.

Sewell, Mary. 1863. *An Appeal to Englishwomen. By the Author of 'Mother's Last Words'*. 1st ed. London: Jarrold & Sons.

Sewell, Mary. 1883. *Autobiography*. Norwich. Jarrold & Sons.

Sewell, Mary. 1883. *The Suffering Poor*. Norwich: Jarrold & Sons.

Sewell, Philip Edward. 1912. *Philip Edward Sewell. A Sketch. 14 January 1822–6 February 1906*. London: Jarrold & Sons.

Shaffner, T.P., and W. Owen. 1862. *The Illustrated Record of the International Exhibition of the Industrial Arts and Manufactures, and the Fine Arts ... 1862*. Google Books. (www.google.co.uk/books/edition/The_illustrated_record_of_the_Internatio/WycBAAAAQAAJ).

Shevelow, Kathryn. 2008. *For the Love of Animals: The Rise of the Animal Protection Movement*. 1st ed. New York: Henry Holt & Co.

Smith, R.B.J., and M.J. Brakspear. 1998. 'The Ochre Mine and Works at Wick, South Gloucestershire'. *BIAS Journal*: 31.

Smithies, Catherine. 1862. *A Mother's Lessons on Kindness to Animals*. London: Partridge & Co.

'Soap, Safety & Sail Dressing'. 2019. Raybel Charters (raybelcharters.com/soap-safety-sail-dressing/).

Sprague, William B. 1860. *Annals of the American Baptist Pulpit*. New York: Robert Carter & Brothers.

Starratt, Vincent. 1921. *Black Beauty / Anna Sewell [with a Memoir of the Author by Vincent Starrett]*. 3rd ed. London: J.M. Dent.

Stone, James. 2022 (Jamesstone.net/More-about-James-Stone/).

Tennyson, Alfred, and Cecil Y. Lang. 1981. *The Letters of Alfred Lord Tennyson, Vol. 2: 1851–1870*. Cambridge, MA: The Belknap Press of Harvard University Press.

Tennyson, Hallam. 2012. 'Derbyshire and Yorkshire Letters, 1862–1864', in *Alfred, Lord Tennyson: A Memoir* (Cambridge Library Collection – Literary Studies, pp. 487–96). Cambridge: Cambridge University Press. Doi:10.1017/CBO9781139237147.025. Cambridge.

Thomas, D.P. 2014. 'The Demise of Bloodletting'. Dissertation, Royal College of Physicians, Edinburgh.

Thornbury, Walter. 1878. 'The Metropolitan Meat Market', in *In Old and New London, Vol 2*. London.

Tidrick, Kathryn. 2007. *Gandhi: A Political and Spiritual Life*. London: I.B. Tauris.

Traïni, Christophe. 2016. *The Animal Rights Struggle*. Amsterdam: Amsterdam University Press.

Treasure, Tom. 2021. *Dr Samways Writes to the Editor: The Life and Times of an Exceptional Physician*. Cambridge: Cambridge Scholars Publishing.

Trollope, Anthony. 4 February1867. 'Mrs Sewell's The Rose of Cheriton: Review'. *Fortnightly Review*.

UK Parliament. 2022. 'Railways in Early Nineteenth Century Britain' (www.parliament.uk/about/living-heritage/transformingsociety/transportcomms/roadsrail/kent-case-study/introduction/railways-in-early-nineteenth-century-britain).

Ulrich, Melanie Renee. 2005. *Victoria's Feminist Legacy: How Nineteenth Century Women Imagined the Queen*. Dissertation, University of Texas at Austin.

UNESCO. 2022. 'The Great Spa Towns of Europe' (whc.unesco.org/en/list/1613).

UWM Libaries. 2022. 'Uncle Tom's Cabin and the American Literary Canon · The Classic Text · Digital Exhibits – UWM Libraries Special Collections' (liblamp.uwm.edu/omeka/SPC2/exhibits/show/classictext/stowe/cabin).

Valenze, Deborah. 1991. 'The Art of Women and the Business of Men: Women's Work and the Dairy Industry *c.* 1740–1840', *Past and Present*: 130:1, pp. 142–69. Doi:10.1093/past/130.1.142.

Vignoles, Olinthus John. 1889. *Life of Charles Blacker Vignoles*. London: Longmans.

Walker, Charles. 1969. *Thomas Brassey: Railway Builder*. London: Frederick Muller.

Weber, Caroline. 2005. *Queen of Fashion*. London: Picador Press.

White, M.P., et al. 2016. 'Improving Health Through Time Spent in Nature', Utah University (extension.usu.edu/healthwellness/physical/nature-as-medicine).

Williams, Carolyn A. 2010. *The River Ran Red: A History of the Golden Valley Wick*. Radstock: Fosseway Press.

Wilson, Cindy C., J.C. Fitzpatrick and J.M. Tebay. 2001. 'Essay' in *Companion Animals in Human Health*. Thousand Oaks, CA: Sage.

Winter, Alison. 1995. 'Harriet Martineu and the Reform of the Invalid in Victorian England', *The Historical Journal*: 3, pp. 597–616.

Wright, Anne. 1859. *The Observing Eye: Letters to Children on the Three Lowest Division of Animal Life*. London: S. Fisher & Sons.

Wright, E.H., and Anne. 1861. *A Brief Memorial of Mrs. Wright, Late of Buxton, Norfolk [Signed: E.H. With a Portrait.]*. London: Jarrold & Sons.

Index

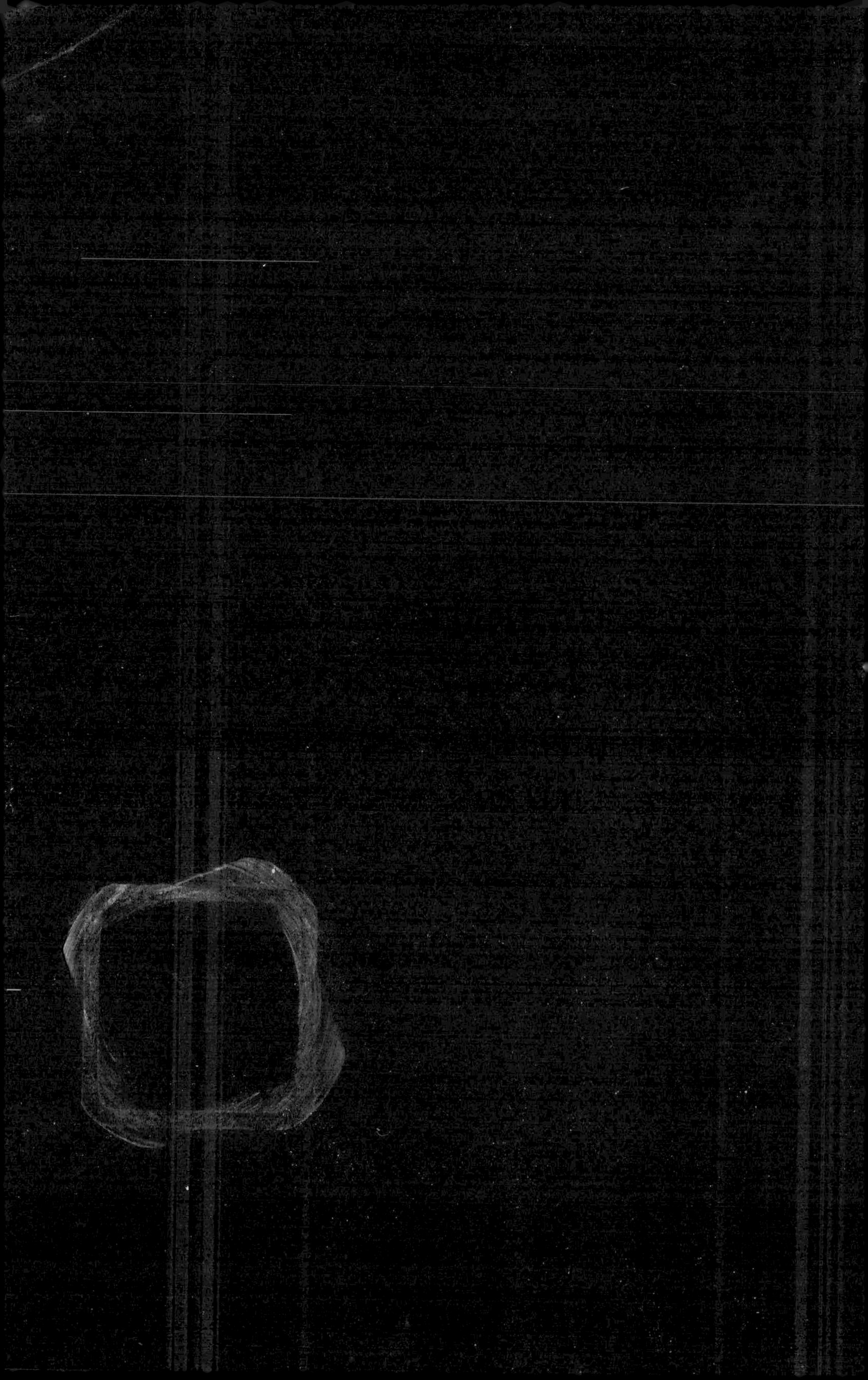